RO
CO

THE STATEWIDE GUIDE

D0802516

TEXT AND PHOTOGRAPHY BY

MICHAEL SEEBERG

 WESTCLIFFE PUBLISHERS
www.westcliffepublishers.com

International Standard Book Number: 1-56579-433-8

Text and photography copyright: Michael Seeberg, 2003. All rights reserved.

Editors: Heather Garbo and Elizabeth Train
Design and Production: Craig Keyzer and Carol Pando

Published by:
Westcliffe Publishers, Inc.
P.O. Box 1261
Englewood, CO 80150
www.westcliffepublishers.com

Printed in China by C & C Offset Printing Co., Ltd.

Library of Congress Cataloging-in-Publication Data:
Seeberg, Michael.
   Road biking Colorado : the statewide guide / text and photography by Michael Seeberg.
      p. cm.
   Includes index.
   ISBN 1-56579-433-8
   1. All terrain cycling--Colorado--Guidebooks. 2. Colorado--Guidebooks. I. Title.
   GV1045.5.C6S44 2002
   796.6'3'09788--dc21
                                                                    2002016769

For more information about other fine books and calendars from Westcliffe Publishers, please contact your local bookstore, call us at 1-800-523-3692, write for our free color catalog, or visit us on the Web at **www.westcliffepublishers.com**.

Please Note: Risk is always a factor in highway, backcountry, and high-mountain travel. Many of the activities described in this book can be dangerous, especially when weather is adverse or unpredictable, and when unforeseen events or conditions create a hazardous situation. The author has done his best to provide the reader with accurate information about mountain travel, as well as to point out some of its potential hazards. It is the responsibility of the users of this guide to learn the necessary skills for safe travel, and to exercise caution in potentially hazardous areas, especially on busy thoroughfares and near avalanche-prone terrain. The author and publisher disclaim any liability for injury or other damage caused by mountain travel or performing any other activity described in this book.

Cover Photo: *Splendid scenery along Wolfensberger Road, Route 31*
Previous Page: *Early fall on Red Mountain Pass, Route 97*
Opposite: *Late spring morning on Dallas Divide with Sneffels Range, Route 98*

ACKNOWLEDGMENTS

Many people came together to make this guide a reality. I am forever indebted to the following individuals and organizations for providing support, both technical and financial. Without their help, plus a large dose of cheerleading and friendship, I certainly would not have accomplished my dream.

Thanks to Mom, who taught me to dream in the first place; my sister, Brita, and her family, Michael and Fisher Darling, who opened their lives, their home, and their pocketbook; Aunt Joanne, who has always stood by me, even when I didn't deserve it; Don Seeberg, my brother, whose advice over the years and whose help with this guide have been incalculable, and only possible with the caring support of Pam and Andrew Seeberg as well as a bit of patience from baby Alden; my cousins and their significant others (Valerie Van Natter and Ken Wagley, Roxanne Carman and Gordon Speir, Rob Carman and Suzanne Legler, and Renee and Greg Spannuth), who have all been there for me throughout the years, especially while I was working on this guide. Also, special thanks to Rick and Calli Van Den Akker for their years of friendship and personal sponsorship.

Thanks to Scott Smith and Brett West at Imagesmith in Durango for letting me cut in line with my film; Andrew Councill for the photos; Armando, Megan, and

Lookout Mountain Road, Route 25

Frank for unconditional couch-surfing privileges; Fred Hutt, Ted MacBlane, and Ron Snow; Brock at Orange Peel Bicycle and Sean Madsen at Wheat Ridge Cyclery for route info, advice, and camaraderie; Kristine Jensen and the Gallery of Food for letting me be me; the wonderful people at the Steaming Bean in Durango and Epic Cafe in Tucson, who affectionately kept me caffeinated as I spent endless hours in their establishments writing text and sorting photos; Mort Freedman and Beverlee Lane for the use of their space to get our act together; Ann Girvin for her great typing; Mark Falconer, Joy Mockbee, Eric Sibley, and Ruth Grunerud for their valued opinions; Michael Aisner; Mary Malone for her enthusiastic thoughts and information; and to Brent for his research help.

To John Fielder and his staff at Westcliffe Publishers, especially Linda Doyle, Jenna Browning, Martha Gray, Elizabeth Train, Craig Keyzer, Carol Pando, Heather Garbo, and Misty Lees. John, your photography and the books your company publishes inspired me to pick up a camera and to get to know my home.

There are many others who have helped—some unknowingly. My apologies if I have not mentioned you here. Your help is appreciated.

Thanks also to my dogs, Ellie and Canyon. Ellie's company throughout my summer of research brought me great pleasure and kept the dialogue interesting. And Canyon, too old to travel, waited patiently for his adopted daughter and me to return before peacefully passing away. He was a loyal and loving companion for countless backcountry adventures and a real trouper!

Finally, let me not forget the pavement of Colorado, whose years of service made it all possible.

This guidebook is dedicated to all those who love good life, good fun, good people, and the incredible landscape all around us; to those who choose to take care of our natural world and to be mindful of their place in the surrounding environment; to those who visit or live in such a place and come to understand these issues; and to all those who own a road bike, or any bike, and love cycling in amazing locations on inspiring roads. I hope you will enjoy putting this guide to good use.

—Michael Seeberg

TABLE OF CONTENTS

Perfect fall conditions on the way up to Lizard Head Pass, Route 99

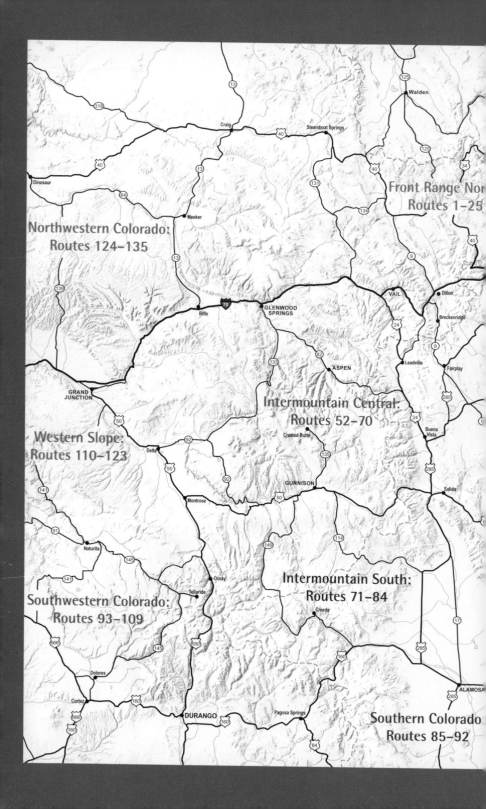

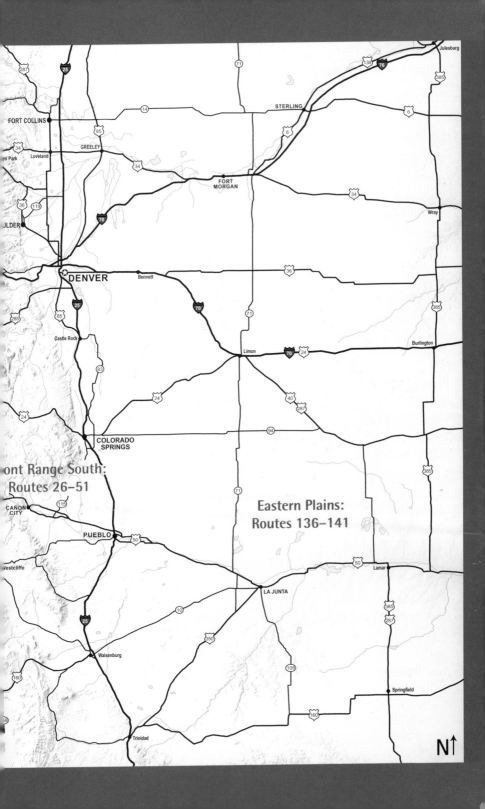

PREFACE

THE UNIVERSAL LOVE OF THE BICYCLE

Bicycles are everywhere—on all corners of the globe. There is a great deal of history and a sense of worldwide camaraderie in bicycling. Despite regional and cultural differences, one thing holds true worldwide: We all love our bikes.

Bicycles are reliable, inexpensive, and environmentally friendly forms of transportation. They're also popular for recreation and sport. Whether you ride a commuter bike, a road bike, a mountain bike, or a tricycle, and whether you bike to work, for exercise, or in competition, it's always fun. Love of this sport does not fade.

While not necessarily for commuters or tricyclists, this guide is most definitely a celebration of cycling. Humans didn't have to make roads over mountains, through narrow valleys, and across the open plains, but we did. Many of Colorado's roads are testaments to creativity and courage. I believe cycling these marvelous stretches of pavement is a celebration of nature, human ingenuity, and the connections between all things. I hope this guide will serve to heighten your enthusiasm for cycling and inspire you to ride the roads of Colorado for years to come.

THE COLORADO EXPERIENCE

Crystal clear rivers cascade down majestic mountainsides and flow through grand, forested valleys. A lush green carpet of trees, shrubs, and endless wildflowers covers everything in sight. Peaceful, sunny days and fresh, fragrant air create a feeling of rejuvenation and vitality that is hard to come by in this day and age.

Sound like utopia? Or maybe paradise? Utopia—no. But paradise? Most definitely! It's summertime in the Colorado Rockies.

Colorado's roads are absolutely spectacular. They also hold many thrilling unknowns for the cyclist. While riding this state's pavement can be pure joy, you must have an immense sense of physical as well as mental commitment in order to attempt some of these routes. On a bad day it can be very windy, the sky can be dark and foreboding, and conditions can be cold and wet. But on a good day the sky is deep blue, the views extend forever, and the warmth of the sun combines with the fresh air to create some of the best cycling conditions found anywhere. For me, these contrasts are among the things that make cycling in Colorado so intriguing and wonderful.

When I was growing up in southeast Denver, I lived a considerable distance from the mountains. Because I did not own a car, I rode my bike across the city to get to the Front Range. Although I loved riding in Denver, the mountains had the lure of unknown possibilities—ominous climbs up towering peaks on tiny, winding roads with very few guardrails!

Some of my first mountain rides are still vivid in my memory. There I was —cycling shorts, a cotton T-shirt, beat-up old sneakers, and what seemed like a hundred-pound bike—slogging my way up I-70 and over Berthoud Pass to Winter Park. Once, I hitched a ride through the Eisenhower Tunnel so I could ride to Breckenridge and meet my family for the weekend. Just before the tunnel, I saw a sign for Loveland Pass and the road heading abruptly up the mountain. That sight put the fear in me and opened me up to a different dimension in cycling.

Many things would come into play on a mountain pass that didn't affect me as a cyclist in the city. Suddenly there were logistics to consider. Weather and altitude would be major factors. Proper clothing would be essential. As I rode by the exit for Loveland Pass, I thought, "Someday, I'll get that one." That's when I realized that a mountain road is an amazing thing. It has a look and feel that draws me in. It's like a track to a sprinter, or a green course to a golfer. It's not just a road—it's an exciting adventure.

Those early rides spawned a tradition of traveling for hours to enjoy a particular piece of pavement somewhere across the state. One summer, a friend and I did a nine-day ride across Colorado's mountains with our girlfriends as driving support. It was the ultimate tour. We didn't have to carry anything, and every day we explored a new mountain route.

But if you don't race or tour, you might not do much riding far from home. Fortunately, Colorado offers many beautiful and challenging routes for cyclists that are within a few hours' drive of the state's major metropolitan areas. Get in your car and head to one of the many classic and convenient routes covered in this guide. Two routes that I try to get to every summer are Trail Ridge Road (Route 5, p. 35) and Mount Evans (Route 22, p. 65)—the epitome of the Colorado cycling experience.

Or you can venture a bit farther than your doorstep. All you need is a day or two, a tent or cheap motel, and a bike. Nowhere else in North America can you find as many routes, with as much diversity in altitude and terrain, as in Colorado. (In Appendix A, you will find a list of highly recommended routes to consider and dream about.)

At this point in my life, I find myself closer to cycling than ever. With up-to-the-minute reports on road races in Europe and television coverage that didn't exist in my racing days, I am continually amazed and inspired to hit the road! (I don't know about you, but I always ride harder during the Tour de France.) Riding these amazing routes every summer keeps a smile on my face all year long, and I'm humbly honored to have had the opportunity to record them. I took great pleasure in seeking out every nook and cranny, from the hills to the plains, yet I'm sure I missed some rides. I hope you will find this guide to your liking and, by all means, let me know if I skipped one of your favorite routes.

The Making of This Guide

I guess I've had this idea for six years or so. It didn't come to me like a lightning bolt or lightbulb above my head—it just sort of settled into my consciousness. Colorado has one of the richest cycling histories in the United States, and its roads are the epitome of quality cycling terrain. While there are many mountain-bike guides, I haven't come across any comprehensive road-cycling guides.

One day I decided to test my theory on how to go about writing such a guide. A friend and I packed up my truck, loaded our bikes, and grabbed the dog for a whirlwind trip across the state. From Durango to Estes Park and back, we summitted 13 passes, recorded route information, and shot photos. We did this in three days—like journalists who'd had too much espresso. It was an informative trip and a great time, to boot.

When I got home, I concluded that, with only summer weekends available, it would take several years to document Colorado's many roads. That seemed a bit overwhelming, so I shelved the idea. Occasionally, I would go back and develop the idea some more, and before I knew it, this little project emerged into a celebration of amazing landscapes and incredible roads.

My sister, Brita, and her husband, Michael, have always loved and supported the idea. Michael was a good sounding board, as he had completed graduate research for Bicycle Colorado, a nonprofit group working to promote bicycle use around Colorado. Brita and Michael proposed that I spend the winter with them in Tucson, living in their guest studio and working on the guide.

Thus, the stage was set. The plan: to spend the summer in Colorado—with my dog Ellie, my bike, a camera, and a tape recorder—documenting the classic road routes. However, when the time came to choose which routes were "in" and which routes were "out," it was very difficult. The question was then put to me: Could I cover them all? I stopped, and as I thought of the endless backroads meandering through the state, a rather large lump grew in my throat: "Uuuh...yeaah." A neat little guide featuring selections from a diverse landscape suddenly turned into a comprehensive documentation of just about every piece of pavement in the rural areas of Colorado. It was no longer about me or my book. It was about *the book*—the first and only one of its kind in the state. I thought, "I don't *have* to—I *get* to write this guide!" I felt honored and fortunate to be the one to do this project.

I spent a dream summer traipsing through the mountains, bathing in rivers (brrr!), and sleeping under the stars. Many friends and relatives across the state offered accommodations and provided emotional support when the project seemed overwhelming. If it hadn't been for the generosity of my sister, my brothers, my mom, my aunt, my cousins, my friends, and my dogs, this guide surely would not exist.

And if I wasn't a coffee junkie before, I surely am now! I took great pleasure in searching out good coffee, which is less of an art form in rural places than it used to be. In some areas, however, it still requires diligence! I wanted to include all of the bike shops I came across, but I also wished to avoid information that would become outdated. So I compromised by including some notable places where the services and people were exceptional.

Speaking of dream summers, my chocolate lab, Ellie, also had hers. She put up with a hectic regimen of sleeping outside in the woods every night and waking up to take a dip in the nearest mountain stream. To this day she will not forgive me...for finishing this guide, that is! I figure that Ellie has now dog-paddled in more rivers and lakes in Colorado than perhaps any other canine. As for me, I drove 20,000 miles, took many photographs, used up countless notepads, and came to know and understand my home state and myself more intimately than ever before.

For me, this guidebook is pure love. For you, I hope it can be many things. In the bigger picture, I hope to foster a more mindful approach to our open roads and scenic terrain. These places, like many others around the world, are precious. They are as vital a resource to humankind as any—and a finite one, as well.

Ride on! See you on the road.

—*Michael Seeberg*

INTRODUCTION

Many places in this country offer excellent cycling conditions, and Colorado is no exception. In fact, this state is a gem because it offers an incredible diversity of routes. But there are many considerations to ponder before you hit the road, particularly if you're not familiar with mountain conditions. The following text highlights some important things to keep in mind as you plan your rides.

RULES OF THE ROAD

Colorado's roads are generally cyclist-friendly. I have rarely had any problems with motorists. These days, however, the presence of more people, more cyclists, and more traffic make it more essential than ever to promote goodwill toward those on the road. I don't want to try to tell you how to ride your bike, but there are a few things that I should mention, especially for those from out of state or out of the country.

As a cyclist in Colorado, you have all the rights that autos do, which also means you must follow all of the same rules. Always ride in the same direction as traffic. Use your hand signals to communicate with drivers. Try to make eye contact with motorists to ensure communication. Always be courteous to others on the road. Always wear a helmet and stop at stoplights and signs. Of course, it's dangerous not to stop, so you probably do, but also consider the public reputation of cyclists. Those of you who don't like to obey traffic laws are giving fellow cyclists a bad rap. It's just not cool.

For a wealth of indispensable information on bicycling in this state, check out Bicycle Colorado at www.bicyclecolo.org, or call (303) 417-1544. The website features the *Colorado Bicycling Manual* (you can download or order it), which includes a recitation of all the Colorado statutes concerning rules of the road for bicycles, complete with commonsense descriptions of these laws. On the website you'll also find maps, contacts, and a newsletter that addresses current state and national biking issues.

LEAVE NO TRACE

In Colorado, as well as everywhere else, the environment is an issue. Wherever you find yourself on this beautiful planet, be mindful of the need to protect our natural environment by respecting the rules and regulations regarding open spaces, campgrounds, and the landscape in general. For guidelines on low-impact camping, contact Leave No Trace at (303) 332-4100 or www.lnt.org.

Mount Maestas towers over North La Veta Pass, Route 86

Plan Ahead

As an avid backcountry enthusiast, I am well aware of the importance of good planning. It can sometimes make or break a trip and, more important, failure to plan properly can be dangerous. Cycling is no exception. Many of the routes in this guide are at high altitudes, in rural areas (some quite remote), and services often are limited, at best.

Don't get caught unprepared. Being a bit overprepared for a ride is usually just right. Always know your entire route and any alternatives. Be knowledgeable of possible water and food stops. Check the weather as close to your departure time as possible. You can visit the National Weather Service website at www.nws.noaa.gov, or check the Colorado Department of Transportation website at www.dot.state.co.us.

Tell someone where you're going! Bring phone money, as cell phones aren't dependable on in the mountains or in many rural areas.

Cycling Safety

Cycling is a lot of fun. Having said this, however, I am mindful of how inherently dangerous it can be. A couple of 50-mph crashes I had as a young racer straightened me right up! You don't want to learn about safety the hard way.

Always pay attention to traffic. Always wear a helmet. Watch out for sand on the road; although it is used for winter snow removal, it can linger well into summer. Bring extra food, water, and clothing. Remember that your visibility to motorists is your best protection against accidents with them.

Medical Considerations in the Mountain Environment

Cycling in the Colorado mountains can take you to altitudes at which your body no longer feels at home. Adding strenuous activity to the mix doesn't help. Less oxygen combined with colder temperatures and thinner atmospheric protection from the sun can zap you fast!

Symptoms to be aware of include rapid breathing, dizziness, nausea, headache, general weakness, and loss of appetite. (Gee, that sounds like some bad days I've had on my bike!) While basic athletic exhaustion is nothing to ignore, these symptoms can indicate altitude sickness. So pay attention. Those who live at lower elevations must allow sufficient time to acclimate to the altitude.

With changing altitude and weather conditions likely during a mountain ride, hypothermia can become a very real issue for cyclists. Hypothermia is the decrease in normal body temperature. Without intervention, this progressive decline in the body's core temperature will lead to increased mental and physical difficulty and can even lead to death. Most people who die of hypothermia do

so at air temperatures in the low 60s. While this might seem relatively warm, when you add altitude, wind, sweat, exhaustion, and inadequate clothing to this mix, the situation can become dangerous. On several occasions in the mountains, the simple, quick task of fixing a flat tire has caused me to experience the initial symptoms of hypothermia—even on nice days. With the addition of the classic Colorado summer afternoon thunderstorm,

You can ride to the top of a fourteener on the exciting Mount Evans Road, Route 22

hypothermia can become a critical issue very quickly. Good advice as far as clothing: When in doubt, more is better.

There are many publications on mountain safety and medical conditions. Any outdoor sports store should have books covering these subjects, or try your local library.

WEATHER AND ROAD CONDITIONS

Colorado roads are generally fair, but they do take a lot of abuse from the changing seasons. They are often narrow, and shoulders can be inconsistent or nonexistent. Gravel and debris are always possibilities. While rural and mountain roads have inherent dangers, they usually have fewer hazards than urban pavement. Most of the time, you won't have to worry about things like open gutters, glass, traffic, pedestrians, and car doors, but you will need to watch for blind corners, potholes, cattle guards, gravel, and other debris. A cyclist's speed on many of these routes can reach more than 50 mph for several miles at a time. Take extra care to stay focused at high speeds.

Road shoulders are always an issue for cyclists in Colorado. I refer to the presence or absence of shoulders throughout the guide, but only in a general sense. Most shoulders, particularly on mountain roads, waver between being inconsistent and nonexistent. Just because a road starts out with a good shoulder doesn't mean you can expect it to last throughout your entire ride. (Don't expect to see many guardrails, either.) The references I make to shoulders on the roads are to *paved* shoulders only. I do not mention dirt shoulders, which are pretty common. You'll have space to pull over on most roads, whether they are paved or not.

Rumble strips—those grooves ground into the pavement to alert swerving motorists—are not too common in Colorado, but sightings are increasing. They can be very dangerous for cyclists, so watch out. As for cattle guards, the pavement at their edges can be damaged and there is a seam in the center that is capable of swallowing your front wheel. Try crossing them as perpendicularly as possible.

Roadwork seems to be a perpetual occurrence throughout both rural and urban areas. I would love to be able to warn you of roadwork on these routes, but you never know how long it will last or what road will be torn up next. It is up to you to contact the state patrol or county sheriff in the area to find out where roadwork exists.

Another big factor that directly affects road conditions, as well as logistics and safety, is the weather. Colorado's weather is notorious for being fickle and changing abruptly. A clear blue sky in the morning can turn to dark, cold walls of water and lightning by noon. This pattern of afternoon thunderstorms is

Sandstone walls tower over a first-rate road ride in Colorado National Monument, Route 115

particularly common during the summer throughout the mountains and plains, and floods and lightning can pose serious threats.

Remember, just because you're on a paved highway doesn't mean that there are services nearby! There are many places in these mountains where, if not for the help of a passing motorist, you would be in a serious predicament if you found yourself stranded and unprepared, miles from warm accommodations or a phone.

GEAR CONSIDERATIONS

I can't say enough about having adequate gear. Proper clothing can make or break the fun factor on a ride, and it can prevent you from getting hypothermia or overheating. Don't forget that cool temperatures on a bad-weather day can become dangerously cold when you're descending a pass. In the winter, I wear a wetsuit under my cycling clothes. It might sound funny, but if you can ride a pass on a February day and be comfortable, you'll have the last laugh come spring when others are just dusting off their bicycles!

You'll find a wide selection of cycling clothes available today. Just choose what works best for you. You should have a complete arsenal of gear if you intend to ride in the mountains. I pack all my cycling garments in my car, and when I get to the start of the ride, I base my clothing decisions on current weather and road conditions.

Coloradans know that the weather outside their front door can vary greatly from the conditions miles down the road. When you're riding from your door-step, it's always better to bring too much gear than too little. You can stuff a lot of things into the back of a jersey. Two jerseys double the pocket space. Always pack extra tubes, water, energy food, a pump or compressed air system, and other quick-fix-it tools.

OTHER HELPFUL RESOURCES: BOOKS, MAPS, AND CONTACTS

Along with this book, a good general guide such as *John Fielder's Best of Colorado* would be useful if you are planning multi-day tours, have non-biking companions accompanying you, or are from out of the state. Gil Folsom's *Colorado Campgrounds: The 100 Best and All the Rest* is a great guide to camping options.

There are a few maps that would be very helpful in planning your rides and as companions to the maps in this guide. DeLorme's *Colorado Atlas & Gazetteer* is excellent. The *Gazetteer* covers the entire state and is large-scale, providing up-to-date information, shaded topography, and detailed mapping of all backroads. Although it's a great all-around atlas, it doesn't distinguish very well between paved roads and unimproved roads. This atlas can be found in many sporting-goods stores, as well as bookstores and food markets of all kinds.

Latitude 40° makes state-of-the-art, highly detailed recreational maps. These maps are works of art, as far as I'm concerned, and are the most current maps of the Colorado mountains. Unlike the DeLorme atlas, Latitude 40° maps differentiate between dirt and paved surfaces. This is a very useful feature when creating your own routes or speculating on short pieces of pavement that are not included in this guide. Latitude 40° maps, however, cover only limited areas of the state—mostly the more popular mountain areas. These maps are also available where books, maps, and sporting goods are sold.

Latitude 40° maps will be helpful for many routes in this guide, but they don't cover the mountains in a seamless fashion. DeLorme's atlas is comprehensive and seamless, but it doesn't differentiate between dirt and paved roads. This leads to my third map recommendation, *Recreational Map of Colorado* from GTR Mapping. This simple road map of the state was the most useful for me when documenting the roads that appear in this book. It contains the whole state on one small map and shows all of the paved roads. It does not, however, label all roads.

The Colorado Department of Transportation's Bicycle/Pedestrian Program also publishes a useful resource, the *Colorado Bicycling Map*. This state map differentiates between paved and unpaved roads, indicates stretches of highway that are prohibited for bicyclists, identifies highways with good shoulders for riding, and provides other information essential to cyclists such as pass elevations and grades. However, it doesn't show all of Colorado's roads. Contact CDOT at (303) 757-9982 to obtain this map.

Bicycle Colorado (www.bicyclecolo.org) can provide you with all kinds of useful information for your travels, including events, road laws, maps, route information, and much more (see Appendix C). The State of Colorado's official website, www.state.co.us, can help you with services and events in individual towns, and offers links to chambers of commerce and tourism offices. The Colorado Department of Transportation also offers a helpful website for trip planning (www.cotrip.org), providing highway conditions, traveler information, and a link to the National Weather Service (303-494-4221). For road condition info by phone, call Colorado Road Conditions at (877) 315-7623.

Beyond this guide, local bike shops, sports stores, bike clubs, and even coffee shops and restaurants can also fill you in on area biking options. Most mountain towns are full of avid cyclists and adventurers; just ask around.

HOW TO USE THIS GUIDE

While organizing this guide, the main issue I faced was how to communicate large and complex amounts of information while minimizing confusion. One of the ways I handled this challenge was to break the routes down to their basic elements. Colorado has a lot of open road with many route options, as well as loops that riders in each community consider local favorites. With a few exceptions, I chose to present isolated stretches that function well on their own, rather than plot out any specific loop routes. Not only does this eliminate gaps and repeated documentation, it allows for more flexibility: You can choose to ride only one segment at a time, or link adjacent ones together to create your own route. If you want to connect different segments to make loops, start by looking at the maps that introduce each region.

The resulting collection of highway sections and backroads is very comprehensive. I know that I've certainly missed a few, but for the most part, this guide includes just about all of Colorado's paved roads outside of urban areas.

I chose not to give crosstown routes for any of the larger towns and cities in the state. I left these out for a reason. The metro areas of Colorado, especially along the Front Range, are constantly changing and growing, and I hesitated to get tangled up with all of the ways to get across town only to have that information become inaccurate. Countless bike shops along the Front Range, as well as cycling clubs, can answer your questions about riding in metro areas throughout the state. See Appendix C for information on cycling clubs and associations, including the nonprofit Bicycle Colorado, which can help you plot your urban routes.

ROUTE DESCRIPTIONS

I spent many memorable days venturing to places I'd never been in order to explore a particular piece of road—often knowing very little about what lay ahead! I didn't want to produce a guide that would completely rob you of your sense of adventure, so I've given enough information for you to know what you're getting into without compromising the element of surprise.

Each route description includes basics about services, terrain, and mileage, as well as some tidbits about the surrounding area. I've described each stretch of pavement from a designated starting point to an ending point, reflected in the route titles. Also included in the route headings are alternate road names, as many have two or three names or change as they cross county lines or forest boundaries. The sequence of information follows the stated direction of travel.

When describing available services, I am very general. When I say that a place has the "basics," I am referring to water and some sort of caloric intake, whether it be junk food or real food. In many rural areas, high-quality food stores can be hard to come by. When I mention that a town has full services, you can count on good coffee and a bike shop or two. I do mention a few specific shops, but I was leery of naming many. Businesses come and go, and you might not be able to count on such information in the long term.

Roadside accommodations in Colorado range from quaint motels and cozy B&Bs to world-class hotels and resorts. There are hundreds of campgrounds as well, and endless backcountry access roads for quiet, secluded camping. Activities along the way run the gamut. There's truly something for everyone in Colorado.

MAPS AND ELEVATION PROFILES

Most of the maps in this guide are regional snapshots designed to give you a broad overview of the routes and how they relate to one another. Each route is marked by the route number, with starting and ending points shown in red. If the starting or ending point is a town, it appears as a red circle; when it's outside a town, it appears as a red square. In certain cases, detail maps provide a closer view of particularly complex areas difficult to depict on the regional maps.

The elevation profiles in this guide were designed using topographical software. Some of the profiles consist of more than a thousand data points— each at an exact elevation (to the foot)—rendering an accurate accumulation of vertical gain and loss. Nevertheless, these profiles do compress a great deal of distance into a very small space, resulting in a visual exaggeration of the terrain. What this means for the cyclist is that the elevation profiles should only be used as a quick glimpse of what to expect, rather than an actual representation of every single up and down that you'll find on the ground. Route descriptions and maps should serve as your primary sources of information.

The total vertical gain and loss figures printed on each profile do *not* represent the difference in elevation between the route's low point and high point. Instead, these numbers combine all of the ups and downs encountered from start to finish, giving you a calculation of the work ahead. Note that if your cyclocomputer or altimeter gives you actual vertical gain, your results might differ from those in the text.

Because of the difficulty in depicting complex networks of off-highway routes, elevation profiles are absent for a few sections that focus on backroad areas. Instead, these sections feature supplementary maps with a closer view than the regional maps provide to better clue you into the topography and the road's twists and turns.

DIFFICULTY RATINGS

This guide rates each route as **Easy, Moderate, Difficult,** or **Very Difficult.**
These ratings are highly subjective and entirely relative to a cyclist's fitness and
experience. Furthermore, no two routes can be compared as equal, even if they
bear the same rating. The combination of road segments on some routes means
that the route's difficulty can vary greatly depending on the stretch of road
you're traveling.

These ratings are based on my own cycling ability. I do not consider myself
to be a fast rider, but I am fit and ride mountain roads often. If you're not
accustomed to a lot of hills or long climbs, if you come from a lower elevation,
or if you ride at a casual pace, then you might find my ratings to be a bit more
challenging. For example, if I give a ride a moderate rating, you might find that
route to be difficult for you. Conversely, if you are a strong rider, the ratings
might be more appropriate, or perhaps even a bit soft—it's your call. One way
to match the book's rating system to your abilities is to ride several easy routes
before committing to a more challenging one.

Wonderful high country scenery awaits on Red Mountain Pass, Route 97

Moderate routes require more effort than **Easy** ones, and might contain some harder sections. **Difficult** routes require sustained effort and generally more logistical preparation. **Very Difficult** routes require the most preparation and can be a big commitment without auto support. Again, your personal rating of each ride depends on your fitness level and cycling experience.

ACCURACY AND MILEAGE

Although we live in a world where we have massive amounts of information at our fingertips, accuracy remains an elusive thing. I think it's safe to say that no two vehicles could travel the same distance and register exactly 1 mile on each odometer. And I dare say that no two highway markers are exactly 1 mile apart, either. There are other issues that contribute to inaccuracy, as well. Road signs are sometimes inconsistent. For example, it's 5 miles from Poncha Springs to Salida—or is it 4? That depends on which direction you are coming from, according to the road signs! Maps vary as well when it comes to mileage calculations. While most odometers, road signs, and maps are considered to be "accurate," I must say there is a bit of gray area.

Most of the information in this guide is based on what I saw on the roads: signs and mile markers. When no mile markers were present, I used my truck odometer. For total distances, I used a combination of mileage signs and my odometer, both of which varied at times from the printed maps.

As you can see, calculating distances wasn't as straightforward as it might have seemed! When bits of information were at odds, I went to great lengths to arrive at an average. Having said that, an occasional inconsistency might arise between the road signs, your calculations, and this guidebook. But don't fret. This book still maintains the highest possible level of accuracy. No guidebook, however, can replace common sense and general awareness of your environment.

The Nokhu Crags loom above the road to Cameron Pass, Route 3

REGION 1

FRONT RANGE NORTH

In the foothills and peaks of the Front Range, between Denver and the Wyoming state line, you can find what is probably the highest concentration of quality cycling routes in the state. The diversity runs the gamut—from lowland flats and rollers to major mountain passes, you'll find a route that suits you.

There are countless bike shops in the cities of the northern Front Range, as well as services and accommodations that will cover all your other needs. In the far north, you'll find peace and quiet on country roads with lots of open spaces. Farther south, toward Boulder and Denver, you'll encounter excellent roads in all directions with lots of steep climbs. The well-established cycling community here is the hub of the Colorado road-biking scene.

Routes that stand out in this region are Trail Ridge Road (Route 5, p. 35), Peak to Peak Scenic and Historic Byway (Route 16, p. 51), and the mother of all Colorado rides, Mount Evans (Route 22, p. 65), where you can ride pavement to 14,000 feet.

ROUTES

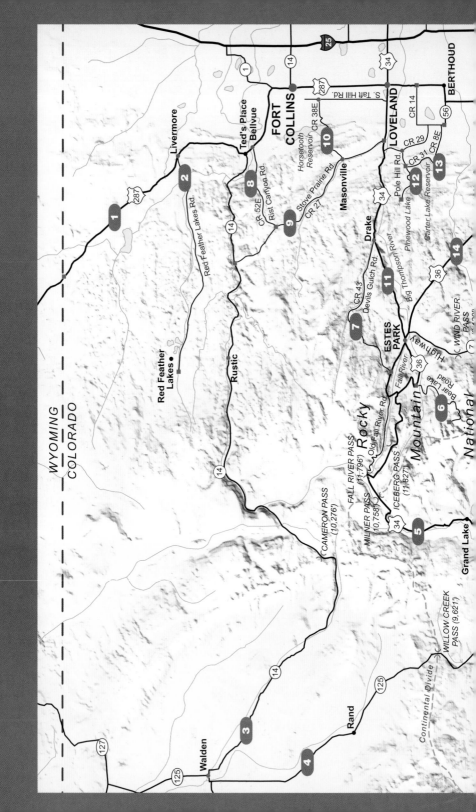

Route 1

US 287
FORT COLLINS TO WYOMING STATE LINE

38 Miles • Moderate

Leading north from Fort Collins, US 287 is a great road with an excellent shoulder (despite some rumble strips). There's usually not much traffic in this area, and it really feels like you're in the boonies. You'll find a lot of big rollers of moderate grade. It's 19 miles to The Forks—a general store where you'll find the basics and the junction with Red Feather Lakes Road (CR 74E —Route 2, p. 31). Continue heading north on US 287 for 14 miles to Virginia Dale—basic services if any. It's 5 miles more to the Wyoming state line.

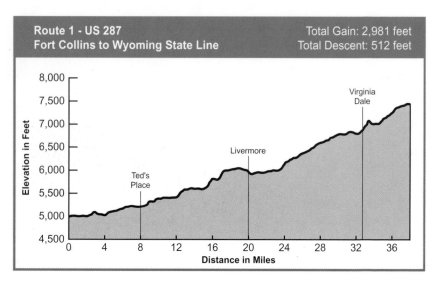

Route 1 - US 287
Fort Collins to Wyoming State Line
Total Gain: 2,981 feet
Total Descent: 512 feet

Route 2

RED FEATHER LAKES ROAD
CR 74E: THE FORKS (LIVERMORE) TO RED FEATHER LAKES

23 Miles • Moderate

Treat yourself to a tour through some beautiful country by taking Red Feather Lakes Road (CR 74E) from its junction with US 287 at The Forks general store, near the town of Livermore, to Red Feather Lakes. The road is great, with little or no shoulder and some substantial rollers, and you'll gradually ascend into the Laramie Mountains. There isn't much traffic, and the Medicine Bow Mountains loom large in the west. You'll see a general store just before the pavement disappears at the end of this ride.

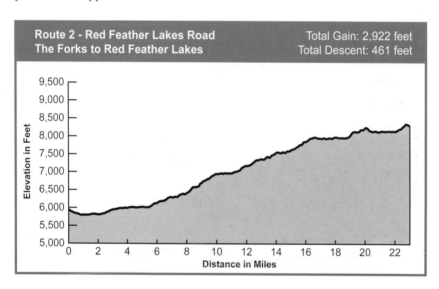

Route 2 - Red Feather Lakes Road
The Forks to Red Feather Lakes
Total Gain: 2,922 feet
Total Descent: 461 feet

CAMERON PASS
CO 14: WALDEN TO RUSTIC

60 Miles • Moderate

If you like being in the middle of nowhere, this one's for you. There's just nothing out there except for grand sweeping vistas and jagged peaks. Walden has very basic services and a Wyoming-like feel.

Cycle east out of Walden on CO 14. As you start out, the road is great, just straight and flat with little or no shoulder. Walden is at mile marker (MM) 35 on CO 14, and by MM 47 you're in the boonies. At MM 55, you'll find the Howlin' Coyote Restaurant and Lounge.

The base of the climb up Cameron Pass (10,276') is approximately 27 miles from Walden, and you'll see the Never Summer Range spread out before you like a barrier. The Nokhu Crags are particularly noticeable on your right just before you summit the pass. After a solid, moderate climb of about 4 miles on an excellent road with a great shoulder, you'll be at the top of Cameron Pass (MM 65). There's a restroom but no water.

The descent is fantastic and heads down along Joe Wright Creek through aspen groves into the town of Rustic. This town is, as the name implies, very rustic. The basics in Rustic are very basic. I do not recommend going any farther, as the valley closes in and the road becomes very narrow with blind curves and absolutely no space for cyclists. The traffic is also very heavy down below, where there's lots of fishing and campsites. For another great Walden route, check out Willow Creek Pass (Route 4, p. 33).

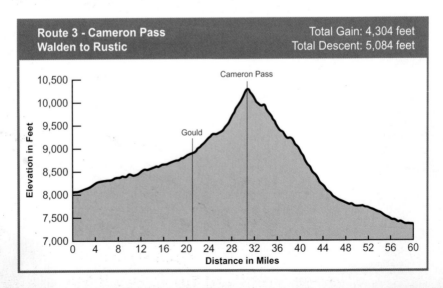

Route 4
WILLOW CREEK PASS
CO 125: US 40 TO WALDEN
54 Miles • Moderate

This route starts close to nowhere and ends up miles from anywhere. Tranquility is the word that comes to mind. Willow Creek Pass (9,621') is moderate and short as well as beautiful and deserted. Granby, near the route's start, is a fairly small town where you'll find the basics and then some.

Mile markers begin at the junction of CO 125 and US 40. As you start, you'll encounter mellow, uphill, rolling terrain heading toward the Continental Divide where Willow Creek Pass crosses the Rabbit Ears Range.

By MM 18, you'll find yourself deep in a beautiful, secluded valley along Willow Creek. The climb becomes more sustained, but it is still a moderate ride. At MM 22, you'll reach Willow Creek Pass. Just after the summit, you'll see a phenomenal view of the Never Summer Range to the east. You'll be heading down a fast, 2-mile descent. By MM 24, you'll be riding on moderate rollers that eventually flatten a bit.

Lush forests of the Rabbit Ears Range along CO 125

At MM 30, you'll abruptly come out of the trees into a magnificent, broad valley along the Illinois River. About a mile later is the town of Rand, home of the Rand Yacht Club. You can find water here, as well as a great sense of humor. I recommend turning back at this point unless you're planning on an extended-mileage day. If you do continue, the road flattens out, and it's another 21 miles from here to Walden where you can load up on the basics.

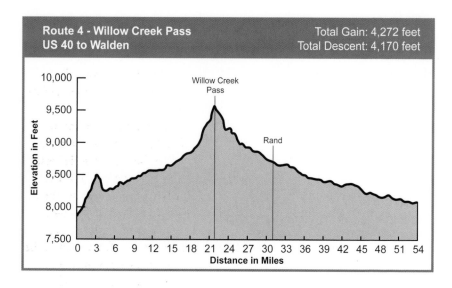

Route 4 - Willow Creek Pass
US 40 to Walden
Total Gain: 4,272 feet
Total Descent: 4,170 feet

Route 5

TRAIL RIDGE ROAD,
Rocky Mountain National Park
US 34: GRANBY TO ESTES PARK
FEE REQUIRED: $5/BIKE, $15/VEHICLE
CLOSED IN WINTER

63 Miles • Very Difficult

Quite possibly Colorado's ultimate ride, this route might even be described as infamous. In the whole state, only one other route— Mount Evans (Route 22, p. 65)—compares. While Mount Evans is a long, hard, high-altitude climb, Trail Ridge Road (12,183' at the high point) is longer, contains several large climbs, and is much more diverse.

You can begin this route in Granby (west side of Rocky Mountain National Park), Grand Lake (west side), or Estes Park (east side). While Estes Park is a wonderful town, and has much to offer in the way of activities, shops, and services, it can be significantly more crowded than either Granby or Grand Lake. Nothing against Estes Park, but if you go there *as a cyclist* on a summer weekend, you might find it frustrating. US 34 is bumper-to-bumper all day long. Grand Lake is busy too, but it's much smaller, more quaint, and on the other side of the mountains from most of the activity. While I do not suggest riding this route on a weekend, if you do, ride it from the west side of the park, and get an early start to beat the traffic.

One of Colorado's ultimate rides

Longs Peak rises above US 34 in Rocky Mountain National Park

If you're interested in a shorter ride that's just as rewarding, try starting in Grand Lake. Granby to Grand Lake is an excellent piece of road, but this adds 15 miles one way and 30 miles round trip to an already long, punishing ride.

Should you begin in Granby, the largest town in the area, you will find basic services and a little more. Just west of Granby on US 40 is the junction with US 34. Go right. It's 15 miles of excellent road with a large shoulder to Grand Lake. On the way you'll pass Lake Granby (MM 5), flanked by the Indian Peaks and the Continental Divide. It's an awesome sight. You'll be cycling over these mountains on your way to Estes Park. As you pass Shadow Mountain Reservoir at MM 12, the alpine terrain is absolutely gorgeous.

Grand Lake (MM 15) is small and very comfortable with a nice town park and many restaurants and shops. If you're heading into town, turn right. Otherwise, continue on US 34 toward the national park entrance.

After a short hill, you'll be on a gradual incline until you pass the park gate (a mile and a half away). At the gate (8,720'), you'll be charged $5 as a cyclist or $15 per car, and the passes are good for a week. The road is closed to vehicles in snow season, so call ahead first. From the gate forward, the mile markers disappear.

It is 8 miles from the park entrance to Timber Creek Campground. The slightly rolling terrain slowly gains altitude on an excellent road with no shoulder. As you ride through this section, look to your left. This beautiful valley might seem insignificant, but buried in the tall grass of the meadow is a small river (which, by most definitions, would be a creek). Here, in the Kawuneeche Valley, lie the headwaters of the mighty Colorado River—and they can be crossed with a few easy steps.

After Timber Creek Campground, the road begins a subtle rise toward Milner Pass, the base of the first major climb. Ten miles from the park entrance, the road narrows with consistent, moderate climbing. In another mile, the road steepens as you come to the first of five switchbacks. Through this section, the road is very steep and narrow—classic climbing here.

Fourteen miles from the park entrance, the grade backs off as you come around a broad, sweeping, left bend. You'll start to see where the road cuts through the peaks at Milner Pass. The summit of Milner Pass sits at 10,758 feet, and you'll find restrooms and a parking lot.

The descent from the pass is no descent at all. You may think you will have a big downhill, as you start speeding along, but this is not the case. The road changes into an uphill almost immediately as you start the climb to the Alpine Visitor Center and continue upward to Trail Ridge High Point. Soon you can see the road above, and it's a bit daunting, especially if you're hurting. The trees begin to dwindle in size as you approach treeline—approximately 11,500 feet, which might explain why you are wheezing.

About 21 miles into the park, the views get even better. The Never Summer Mountains loom to the left (west), and at the switchback (Medicine Bow Curve) you can peer into Wyoming and the northern ranges spread out below. Barely a mile from Medicine Bow Curve is the Alpine Visitor Center, where you'll find food, water, and a lot of people. The visitor center marks the summit of Fall River Pass (11,796'). From the Alpine Visitor Center, it's 17 miles to the junction of US 34 and US 36—and another 8 miles to the town of Estes Park.

"But the road is still climbing?" you wonder. "What a strange road. Passes that aren't really passes—what's up with that?"

A bit more than a mile later, you'll reach Trail Ridge High Point at 12,183 feet (unmarked). Yippee! Or, maybe not. What you realize now is that you've just summitted another climb with no descent. Who is the cruel bastard responsible for this? Now you are way above treeline, and the high elevation

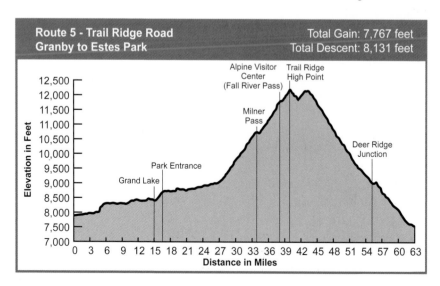

requires a different mentality. (See pages 16 and 19 for information on mountain conditions and gear for high-altitude cycling.)

Finally, after you ride through Trail Ridge High Point, you will be rewarded with several miles of moderate, rolling terrain including the summit of Iceberg Pass (unmarked on the road). You'll soon realize that the altitude and mileage combine for an overall effect of no breaks—just work and wheezing— but the views are awesome.

Then comes your grand prize—an actual descent! If you are hurting, this is the time to turn back, as the road begins to plummet into Estes Park, a descent of nearly 5,000 feet. If you have SAG support awaiting you in Estes Park, you'll be loving life here on one of Colorado's finest descents. But watch out for humans, cars, and animals.

If you're heading directly into Estes Park, you have two choices. Either go straight at the junction of US 36/US 34 (Deer Ridge Junction), which puts you on US 36 and gives you an 8-mile, downhill ride into town, or turn left and stay on US 34—a 9-mile trip.

If you plan to head back to Grand Lake or Granby, any time is a good time to turn around. But if you wish to suffer more first, wait until you reach Deer Ridge Junction before heading back for the 4,000-foot climb up to Trail Ridge High Point.

BONUS: Haven't suffered enough yet? Then turn left to stay on US 34 at Deer Ridge Junction. You'll head down into an incredibly pristine valley called Horseshoe Park. A very fast descent into the valley will bring you to the junction with Old Fall River Road, a smooth, hard-packed dirt, one-way road with 9 miles of climbing. If you're anything like I am, you'll be grinning from ear to ear. Turn left onto Old Fall River Road. When you get to Endovalley picnic grounds (barely a couple of miles) the road turns to dirt, one-way traffic begins, and no RVs are allowed. It's a moderate climb with steep switchbacks. The road will bring you back to the Alpine Visitor Center and the summit of Fall River Pass. The summit is directly behind the visitor center, where you'll meet back up with the pavement of US 34.

This out-and-back (including Old Fall River Road) is long and difficult. It's a ride you'll never forget.

Route 6

BEAR LAKE ROAD,
Rocky Mountain National Park
US 36 TO END OF ROAD
FEE REQUIRED: $5/BIKE, $15/VEHICLE

9 Miles • Easy

You'll find this road inside Rocky Mountain National Park, just past the Beaver Meadows Entrance off US 36. It's a great little road, but it's a bit narrow and can get a lot of traffic. The road itself is in fair shape, but with no shoulder.

Bear Lake Road gently winds its way through the valley below Longs Peak (14,255'). You'll climb gradually toward Bear Lake at first, but the last few miles of this 9-mile route become moderately steep, and you'll finish with a few sharp corners. Watch for traffic. This road dead-ends, and the way back is very fast when traffic is light. For more rides in the area, check out the Peak to Peak Scenic and Historic Byway (Routes 16 and 16A–C, pp. 51–56), and Trail Ridge Road (Route 5, p. 35).

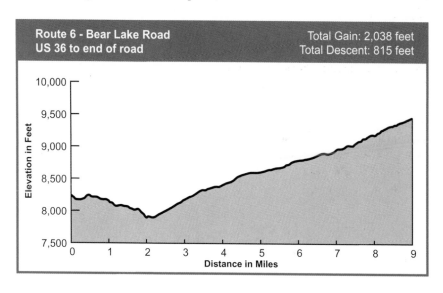

Route 6 - Bear Lake Road
US 36 to end of road
Total Gain: 2,038 feet
Total Descent: 815 feet

Route 7

DEVILS GULCH ROAD
CR 43: ESTES PARK TO DRAKE

Approximately 15 Miles • Moderate

This is an excellent ride north of Estes Park. Devils Gulch (CR 43) is a great road (with no shoulder) that leads into a beautiful, secluded valley. From Estes Park, head west on US 34. Shortly, you will see a right turn for Devils Gulch–Glen Haven. As you begin, you can't help but notice the massive granite cliffs that seem to surround you. You'll ride moderate, rolling terrain at the start and be treated to

A wide-open descent into Devils Gulch

staggering views. As you climb above the town, make sure to look back across the valley. You might want to get off your bike to take in the view, as this scene is one of incredible grandeur.

Approximately 5 miles into the ride, you'll head down into a very steep set of switchbacks. The curves are extremely tight and there is no room for error. After a half-mile or so of switchbacks, the road straightens out, backs off in grade, and starts winding through a narrow, canyonlike valley. There's more fast, winding road ahead.

I recommend turning back in the town of Drake, where CR 43 junctions with US 34, as US 34 can have a lot of traffic.

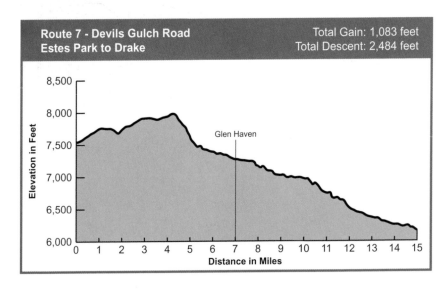

Route 7 - Devils Gulch Road
Estes Park to Drake

Total Gain: 1,083 feet
Total Descent: 2,484 feet

Route 8

RIST CANYON ROAD
CR 52E: BELLVUE TO STOVE PRAIRIE ROAD

Approximately 13 Miles • Moderate

A great, steep climb up into the hills west of Fort Collins starts here. You'll get some spectacular views of the Mummy Range as you look west from the top of the climb. I start the route in Bellvue, a crossroads just a few miles northwest of Fort Collins. CR 52E is in great shape but has no shoulder; however, there is very little traffic. You'll soon be climbing moderately as the road starts winding into the canyon.

From Bellvue, it's just over 12 miles to the top of the climb, and the curves get sharper and steeper as you go. Near the top, you'll ride 12-percent grades! After the summit, you'll get a nice fast descent of about a mile to the junction with Stove Prairie Road (CR 27—Route 9, p. 42). There are no services along this route, but Fort Collins has everything you'll need.

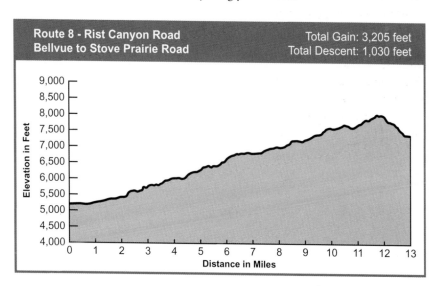

Route 8 - Rist Canyon Road
Bellvue to Stove Prairie Road

Total Gain: 3,205 feet
Total Descent: 1,030 feet

Route 9

STOVE PRAIRIE ROAD
CR 27: US 34 TO CO 14

25 Miles • Moderate

Here's another great ride! Easy and moderate hills roll through beautiful pastures as you cruise this quaint little valley tucked away in the foothills west of Loveland and Fort Collins. Stove Prairie Road (CR 27) is in good shape. There's little or no shoulder, but there's hardly any traffic.

You'll find CR 27 at a junction with US 34, about 5 miles west of Loveland. Head right (north) at this junction, and ride up a beautiful valley along Buckhorn Creek. You'll encounter a gentle roll, and it's about 5 miles to Masonville, where you can get basic supplies. Go left at the "T" intersection in order to stay on Stove Prairie Road. (A right turn here would take you to Fort Collins via Horsetooth Reservoir—Route 10, p. 44.) Continue on rolling, winding terrain from Masonville for about 15 miles to a three-way intersection with Rist Canyon Road (CR 52E), which is also a spectacular route to Fort Collins (Route 8, p. 41). Stay left in order to continue on Stove Prairie Road. The terrain is mostly downhill, and the road is more sharply curved as you continue for about 5 miles to where Stove Prairie Road junctions with CO 14 (Route 3, p. 32). CO 14 is narrow and has many blind curves; I do not recommend riding on it east of Rustic. You can turn around here and head back to US 34.

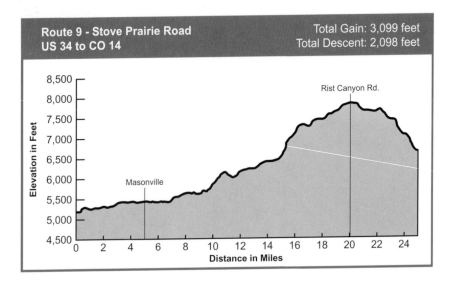

Route 9 - Stove Prairie Road
US 34 to CO 14
Total Gain: 3,099 feet
Total Descent: 2,098 feet

Gorgeous, secluded Stove Prairie Road

Route 10

HORSETOOTH RESERVOIR
CR 38E: SOUTH TAFT HILL ROAD TO STOVE PRAIRIE ROAD

10 Miles • Moderate

Here's a great route and an excellent connection to Stove Prairie Road (Route 9, p. 42). In Fort Collins, you can take care of all your needs and then some—it's a cool college town. To find the start of this route, head south from the west side of town on South Taft Hill Road and turn right (west) onto CR 38E. CR 38E is in great condition, but it has little or no shoulder. The road starts out flat, but you'll soon begin a solid little climb to the dam. To the west, you can see Horsetooth Mountain, which is appropriately named.

You'll find a small market at Horsetooth Reservoir. The road descends moderately for about a mile, and you'll see a sign that says "Masonville 4 Miles." The first mile is moderate with some rolling, and the final three descend into "town." Masonville sits in a beautiful valley, and it really only amounts to the junction with Stove Prairie Road and a corner store where you will find the basics.

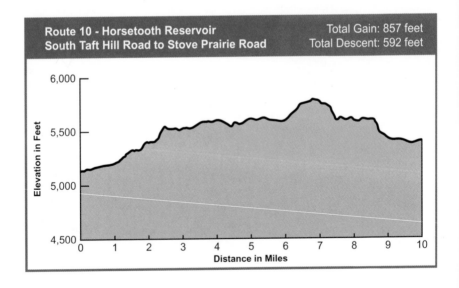

Route 10 - Horsetooth Reservoir
South Taft Hill Road to Stove Prairie Road

Total Gain: 857 feet
Total Descent: 592 feet

Route 11

BIG THOMPSON CANYON
US 34: LOVELAND TO ESTES PARK

30 Miles • Moderate

Loveland is a nice mellow town that can take care of most of your needs. US 34 is an excellent road that's in super shape and has a great shoulder. As you leave Loveland from the corner of US 34 (Eisenhower Boulevard) and Wilson Avenue, the road is flat and straight, and about 5 miles west of town you'll see a right turn (north) for CR 27 (Route 9, p. 42). About a mile farther up US 34, you'll see a sign for Carter Lake—a left turn (south)—where you can find a couple of excellent routes including Carter Lake (Route 13, p. 47) and Pole Hill Road (Route 12, p. 46). Continuing west on US 34, it's 11 miles in a beautiful setting along the Big Thompson River to Drake, where you'll find basic services and a junction with Devils Gulch Road (Route 7, p. 40). US 34 continues to roll and climb moderately. It's 13 miles from Drake to Estes Park, and you'll find services along the way. The climbing will mellow out as you head into town, and Estes will have everything you need.

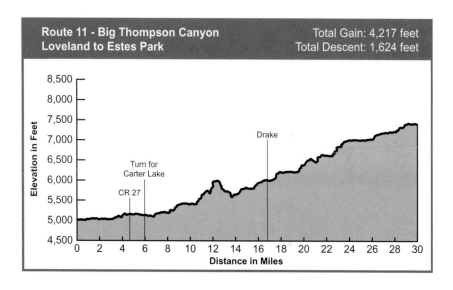

Route 12

POLE HILL ROAD
CR 18E: US 287 TO PINEWOOD RESERVOIR

14 Miles • Moderate

The road on Pole Hill offers splendid views

This is a fantastic climb up to Rattlesnake Park and a great addition to the ride along Carter Lake (Route 13, opposite). In Loveland, you can find most of what you need, but you will find no services on Pole Hill Road (CR 18E).

From US 287 (Lincoln Avenue in Loveland), head west on West 1st Street for nearly 7 miles to a "T" intersection with CR 29. (West 1st Street will turn into CR 20 just before this intersection.) Turn left (south) onto CR 29, and ride barely a half mile to a right turn (west) onto Pole Hill Road. The road will roll very gently, and in about 2 miles you'll see the left turn (south) for Carter Lake. Continue on Pole Hill Road; the terrain will change drastically. You'll ascend a steep hillside with lots of sharp curves and spectacular views. This climb is about 4 miles long. After you reach the top, you'll descend for a mile into Rattlesnake Park, where you will find more beauty, including Pinewood Reservoir, and the end of the pavement.

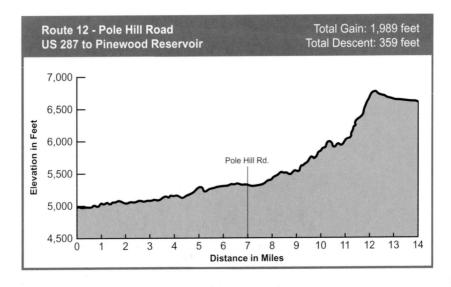

Route 12 - Pole Hill Road
US 287 to Pinewood Reservoir
Total Gain: 1,989 feet
Total Descent: 359 feet

Route 13

CARTER LAKE
CR 31/CR 8E: POLE HILL ROAD (CR 18E) TO CO 56

8.5 Miles • Moderate

Carter Lake is beautiful, as is the road along its eastern side. Pole Hill Road (Route 12, opposite) is the point of departure, and it's a great addition to this route. Go south from Pole Hill Road on CR 31. Soon you'll ride by the entrance to the reservoir (no fee is required for thru-traffic) and head up a steep hill for about 1.5 miles. At the top is a general store with the basics and a nice view of the lake. Follow the lake for about 3.5 miles on a good road,

Peaceful Carter Lake

with somewhat flat terrain and no shoulder. Watch for vehicles towing boats as you cross three dams by the lake. After the third dam, the road heads away from the lake and down a great little hill with some nice curves. Go left at the junction with CR 8E. The road will continue descending moderately for another 3.5 miles, with views out across the Eastern Plains and easy rollers along the way. You'll come to a "T" intersection with CR 23 and CO 56. You can turn right (south) on CO 56 and go 4 miles to Berthoud for basic supplies or go left (north) onto CR 23 and work your way back to Loveland, about 10 miles north.

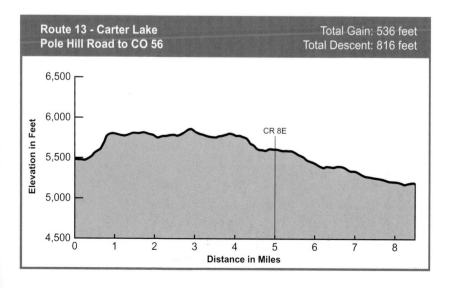

Route 13 - Carter Lake
Pole Hill Road to CO 56

Total Gain: 536 feet
Total Descent: 816 feet

CR 8E

Elevation in Feet

6,500

6,000

5,500

5,000

4,500

0   1   2   3   4   5   6   7   8

Distance in Miles

Route 14

US 36
BOULDER TO ESTES PARK

32 Miles • Moderate

Boulder is a fun town with all kinds of activities and services. It's home to a very large cycling community and many quality bike shops. As you ride through Boulder, look for 28th Street running north/south through town. This is US 36 (you'll see the signs). You can also take Broadway (CO 7) north and hook up with US 36 just outside of town, where this route description starts. Expect some big rollers as you head north on a great road with a great shoulder. The shoulder will become spotty as you get closer to Lyons, about 12 miles north. The views are fantastic, with mountains to the west and prairie to the east. In Lyons, you'll find the basics and a junction with CO 7 (Route 16C, p. 56).

Continuing on US 36, you'll start climbing moderately into the foothills below Estes Park. The road is great, but there is little or no shoulder, and there are lots of curves. This stretch of US 36 gets a great deal of traffic to and from Rocky Mountain National Park, so be alert. Moderate, rolling terrain with an uphill trend will take you from Lyons to Estes Park (about 20 miles), where you'll find all you need including access to some fantastic routes; check out Trail Ridge Road (Route 5, p. 35) and Devils Gulch Road (Route 7, p. 40). You can also access US 34 to Loveland (Route 11, p. 45) or the Peak to Peak Scenic and Historic Byway (Route 16, p. 51).

Weekend traffic on US 36 to Estes Park thins out on weekdays, rendering it an excellent route for cyclists

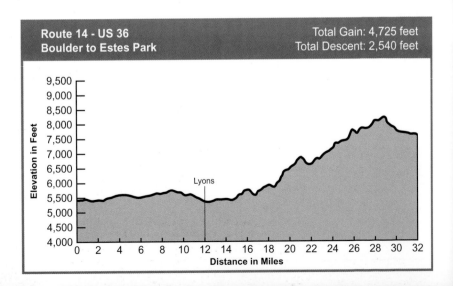

Route 14 - US 36
Boulder to Estes Park

Total Gain: 4,725 feet
Total Descent: 2,540 feet

Route 15

GOLDEN GATE CANYON ROAD
CO 46: GOLDEN TO CO 119

Approximately 19 Miles • Moderate

Even though it's not officially part of the Peak to Peak Scenic and Historic Byway (pp. 51–56), this route is the best way to access the byway from the south. Golden is a great little town, and it has managed to keep a quaint, local feeling among the metropolitan surroundings. You can care for all of your needs here, and Denver is just a few miles down the hill.

Head north out of Golden on CO 93, and look for signs for Golden Gate Canyon Road (CO 46/CR 70), just north of town. It will be a left turn, and you'll start a moderate climb right away. There isn't much of a shoulder (if any), but this is a well-known cycling route. You'll find some solid grades as you climb through the canyon, and then the terrain will mellow out and roll while continuing to gain altitude.

As you roll along, you'll come to the entrance to Golden Gate Canyon State Park. If you don't wish to ride into the park, continue on CO 46 past the park entrance. The road starts climbing again, and a rather solid, somewhat steep ascent of almost 4 miles will bring you to CO 119 (Route 16A, p. 53).

Alternately, to ride through Golden Gate Canyon State Park, turn right from CO 46 onto Road GC 1 (Mountain Base Road). This is an awesome climb through the park—not for the "ascent-challenged" crowd. The road is in great shape, but it's narrow with no shoulder. Road GC 1 starts with about 2 miles

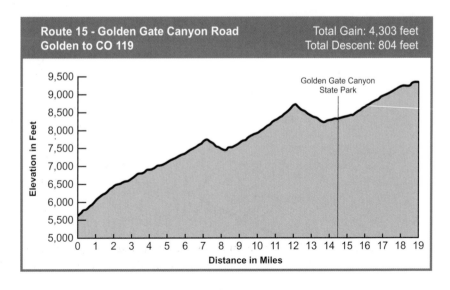

Route 15 - Golden Gate Canyon Road
Golden to CO 119
Total Gain: 4,303 feet
Total Descent: 804 feet

The Indian Peaks Wilderness as seen from CO 46

of moderate uphill rollers. Then the road changes in a big way. For about a mile, you will encounter sharp switchbacks and grades as high as 19 percent—ouch! After that, it mellows into a quick descent followed by moderate uphill rollers. Three miles from the park entrance, you'll come to a "T" intersection at Gap Road (CR 2). Go left for about a mile on excellent hard-packed dirt and hook up with pavement on CO 119 (about 4 miles north of 119's junction with CO 46).

Route 16

PEAK TO PEAK SCENIC & HISTORIC BYWAY
CO 119/CO 72/CO 7: BLACK HAWK TO ESTES PARK

60 Miles • Difficult

If you're in the Denver/Boulder area and want a route that keeps you up in the mountains all day, then the Peak to Peak Scenic and Historic Byway (more commonly known as simply the Peak to Peak Highway) is for you. This has got to be the ultimate Front Range route. The road is in excellent condition with a great shoulder nearly the whole way. The terrain is endlessly rolling, with some fairly large hills, but there's nothing too serious. The phenomenal landscape offers majestic views of the Front Range from the Indian Peaks Wilderness to Rocky Mountain National Park. You'll also get a spectacular glimpse of The Diamond (a 2,000-foot rock wall) on Longs Peak (14,255') as you approach the town of Estes Park.

Discerning the exact location of the Peak to Peak Highway can be a bit confusing, as this byway is actually a series of sections of state highways. When you're out on the road, there are two things that will help you to stay on course. First, there are road signs that read, "Peak to Peak Scenic Byway," with an arrow

View of the Front Range from the Peak to Peak Scenic and Historic Byway

pointing the way. Second, there are no state or U.S. highway junctions to the west of the Peak to Peak. Therefore, when you come to a highway junction, always stay to the west. For more detailed info, see the individual highways that make up the byway (Routes 16A–C, pp. 53–56).

The town of Black Hawk is at the southern end of the Peak to Peak Highway (CO 119) and provides the basics. Bicycles are not allowed on CO 119 south of town, so I suggest you either get a ride to the start, or ride or drive to the Peak to Peak Highway on any of the Peak to Peak roads or connections that are described in this section. For southern access, check out CO 46 (Route 15, p. 50).

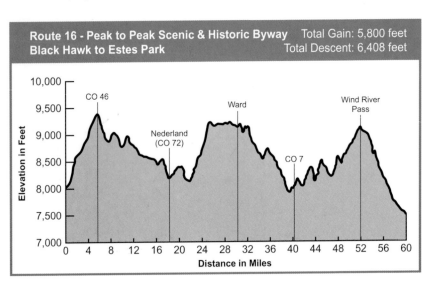

After almost 6 miles of moderate, sustained climbing from Black Hawk, CO 119 junctions with CO 46 and continues north through rolling, forested terrain. From this junction, it's about 13 miles to the town of Nederland.

In Nederland, stay left and get onto CO 72—the signs will show you the way. There's more rolling terrain on a great road with a wide shoulder, and it's about 12 miles to the town of Ward. (At Ward, there is a junction with Lefthand Canyon Drive—Route 17, p. 57—which comes out in the Boulder area.) As you continue through Ward on CO 72, it's 10 miles to the next junction, with more rollers along the way.

When CO 72 ends, you'll reach a "T" intersection. This is CO 7 (Route 16c, p. 56), and once again you'll want to stay to the left to get to Estes Park. On CO 7, the shoulder comes and goes. It's about 19.5 miles to Estes Park and the byway's end, with more rollers and incredible views of the Rocky Mountains. You'll ride by Lily Lake and Wind River Pass (9,130'), then enjoy an excellent descent for the last few miles into town. You'll find all you need in Estes Park, along with lots of shops and restaurants.

For more detailed info on all Peak to Peak segments, refer to the Peak to Peak routes listed in this section (Routes 16A–C, through p. 56).

Route 16A
CO 119
BLACK HAWK TO BOULDER
Approximately 32 Miles • Moderate

Black Hawk/Central City (two bordering towns) is a peculiar area unless you enjoy gambling, as there are countless casinos. However, this is the start of a beautiful ride through the northern foothills west of Denver and Boulder.

Head north out of Black Hawk on CO 119. You might notice something unique—the mile markers are posted in half-mile increments (go figure). The road climbs and rolls for almost 6 miles to its junction with CO 46 (Golden Gate Canyon Road, Route 15, p. 50). By MM 12.5, the road is excellent with a great shoulder. From this point, CO 119 continues with rollers of all sizes as you make your way to Rollinsville. After 1.5 miles of fast descent with some sharp corners, you'll be in Rollinsville (MM 19), where you can find the basics.

At MM 23, CO 119 intersects CO 72, which is one of many roads that lead into the Denver/Boulder area. (For more on CO 72, see Route 16B, p. 54.) Continuing on CO 119 (here combined with CO 72) toward Nederland, it's just rollers, rollers, and more rollers. As you ride through the pine forests and aspen groves, you'll see amazing views of the Front Range peaks. Just after MM 24, you'll come to Nederland, where you can find all of the basics and then some.

CO 119 between Nederland and Boulder is questionable for cycling. This section of the road is cramped and gets a great deal of traffic. Many people feel it is better to ride downhill (Nederland to Boulder) on this road rather than uphill (Boulder to Nederland), because it's easier to deal with traffic when you are going fast. And it's a fast 16 miles into Boulder, where CO 119 becomes Canyon Boulevard. Watch for rumble strips.

NOTE: If you want to ride up out of Boulder, and you don't mind some dirt, you can avoid traffic by taking CR 122 (Sugarloaf Road). Take CO 119 just a few miles up Boulder Canyon and go right (north) at CR 122. This superb road climbs steeply up into the hills north of Nederland, where it eventually turns to dirt a few miles or so before it junctions with CO 72.

Route 16B

WONDERVU
CO 72: SOUTH FOOTHILLS HIGHWAY (CO 93) TO CO 7

43 Miles • Moderate

Here's another great ride into the northern foothills. To get to the starting point, follow the South Foothills Highway (CO 93), which runs north/south at the base of the foothills between Boulder and Golden. The junction with CO 72 is roughly in the middle of this stretch (about 8 miles from either Boulder or Golden).

From its junction with CO 93, take CO 72 up into Coal Creek Canyon. At first, the ride is mellow on a slightly beat-up road with no shoulder. As you head west, you'll start into some moderate uphill rollers and find some basic services along the way. About 11 miles up, after some solid climbing, you'll come to Wondervu, where you'll find basics and incredible views of the Front Range peaks. Then some excellent descending on this relentlessly winding road awaits you. About 4 miles later, you'll go through Pinecliffe—watch out for the sketchy railroad crossing. After some mellow, rolling terrain (and about 19 miles from the start), you'll find the junction of CO 72 and CO 119 (Route 16A, p. 53), where they combine and head right (north). Now you're on the Peak to Peak Highway. It's about 2.5 miles to Nederland, where you'll

Rolling, forested terrain abounds in these foothills

find your basics and a bit more, including a great bike/coffee shop that's made up of several old train cars. You can't miss it. From Nederland, it's 21.5 miles to the junction of CO 72 and CO 7. There are tons of rollers of all sizes, surrounded by astounding beauty back in these hills, and you will find basic services along the way. To the right, CO 7 (Route 16c, below) takes you to Lyons; to the left, it leads to Estes Park.

Route 16c

WIND RIVER PASS
CO 7: LYONS TO ESTES PARK

33 Miles • Moderate

You will find basic services in Lyons. If you don't find what you need, the bigger cities of Boulder and Longmont are both nearby. Head southwest out of Lyons on CO 7 at its junction with US 36. The road winds alongside South St. Vrain Creek as you head up into the foothills and Roosevelt National Forest, and later it gets really nice, with an excellent shoulder. The climbing starts right away and is moderate and sustained all the way to the Peak to Peak junction at CO 72 (MM 19, about 14 miles) where CO 7 becomes part of the Peak to Peak Highway.

Continue heading straight on CO 7 for 19 more miles to the northern end of the Peak to Peak Highway in Estes Park. Along the way, the road rolls and winds moderately through pine and aspen forests with an astounding view of Longs Peak (14,255') from the eastern edge of Rocky Mountain National Park. The Diamond on Longs Peak's east face is a 2,000-foot rock wall, and it's a world-renowned rock-climbing mecca.

At Wind River Pass (9,130') and Lily Lake, you'll be just outside of Estes Park, and a nice fast descent will bring you into town, where you can find restaurants, lodging and supplies.

Route 17

LEFTHAND CANYON DRIVE/ LEE HILL DRIVE
CR 94/CR 106: US 36 TO WARD

Approximately 15 Miles • Moderate

The 14-mile stretch of US 36 between Lyons and Boulder links up with the Peak to Peak Highway via Lefthand Canyon Drive. There are two ways to get onto this section of the byway from US 36.

First, you can head west on Lefthand Canyon Drive (CR 94), which is 6 miles or so south of Lyons on US 36 (about MM 22). This is an excellent, quaint road with light traffic, no shoulder,

Lefthand Canyon Drive hugs Lefthand Creek

and a moderate, winding climb into the hills. A few miles up the road, and you'll spot a right turn to Jamestown. (This is a great, steep road that eventually turns to dirt, but keep left to stay on Lefthand Canyon Drive.) Here, Lefthand

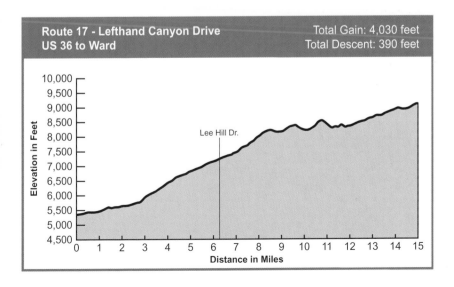

Canyon Drive becomes CR 81, and it changes yet again, to CR 106, before it reaches Ward. The last mile or so is extremely steep—a great challenge. The road winds through Ward (limited services), hooking up with CO 72 and the Peak to Peak Highway.

The second way to ride is to take Lee Hill Drive (CR 106) from Boulder to Lefthand Canyon Drive and, eventually, to CO 72. Take CO 7 (North Broadway) north from Boulder. Just as you are leaving town, you'll see a left turn for Lee Hill Drive—take it. Almost 2 miles later, you'll have to turn left to stay on Lee Hill Drive (there is also a left at CR 106A, but don't take that). The *next* left is CR 106—this is the road you want—just watch the road signs. Eventually, this road hooks up with Lefthand Canyon Drive and takes you up to Ward.

Regardless of the route you use to access Lefthand Canyon Drive, it is approximately 15 miles to Ward.

Route 18

FLAGSTAFF MOUNTAIN ROAD
CR 77: BOULDER TO END OF PAVEMENT

9 Miles • Difficult

This climb is as classic as it gets, and it's no place for whiners. In Boulder, the start of this ride, you'll find plenty of bike shops and services.

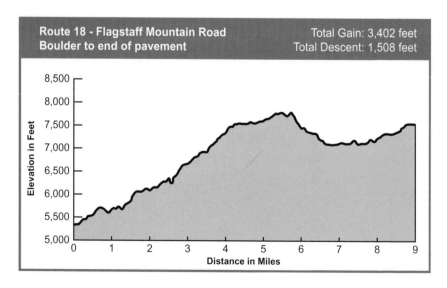

Route 18 - Flagstaff Mountain Road
Boulder to end of pavement
Total Gain: 3,402 feet
Total Descent: 1,508 feet

Baseline Road, on the south end of town, runs east/west. Take it west on a moderate climb out of town. You'll find excellent pavement with no shoulder and a fair amount of traffic, as this is a popular access to the mountains. Then the road will curve to the right, and everything will change. You'll climb for about 5 miles on grades that are upwards of 15 percent—absolutely brutal and demoralizing. There will be a few breaks along the way, and on the back side you'll find some large, very steep rollers before the pavement ends, about 9 miles from town. If you're in Boulder, this ride is a must. *Good luck!*

Flagstaff Mountain overlooks the city of Boulder

Route 19

BERTHOUD PASS
US 40: I-70 TO WINTER PARK

28 Miles • Difficult

Technically, this ride starts at the junction of US 40 and I-70 (Exit 232), between Idaho Springs and Georgetown. But if you're driving to the start of the ride, I suggest you continue for 2 miles up US 40 and park in Empire. This town is very small, but it has your basics, including espresso, and it even boasts a Dairy King malt shop! From Empire (MM 256), it's 26 miles to Winter Park.

The road begins very moderately with a gentle climb. By MM 251, you'll reach moderate rollers with an uphill tendency. At MM 249, you'll reach the town of Berthoud Falls, which has a small general store, and that's about it. The shoulder comes and goes throughout this stretch, but the road is good.

When I documented this route, Berthoud Pass (11,315') was being widened and the construction was a mess. By publication, however, the construction will probably be done, and US 40 will be superb with lots of room.

After Berthoud Falls, the climbing begins in earnest. You will face solid moderate climbing with five tight switchbacks as you ride into the Vasquez Mountains toward the Continental Divide. At MM 246, the grade levels off considerably and continues to back off all the way to the summit. By MM 244, you can see the rest of the road to the summit of Berthoud Pass, which sits at MM 243. You'll find a restaurant and a parking lot here. I've heard that

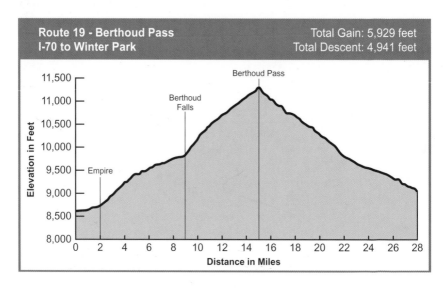

Route 19 - Berthoud Pass
I-70 to Winter Park

Total Gain: 5,929 feet
Total Descent: 4,941 feet

*T*his route is unique in my memory because it was my first mountain pass ride. I was 17 and had been cycling for maybe a year. I was also a distance runner at my high school, and felt I was ready to attempt a long climb at high altitude. I had worked all summer the year before at Dairy Queen to get my first quality bike. It was a Schwinn Super le Tour, and I thought it was perfect—what did I know?

I had my mom drop me off on the west side of Denver up against the foothills, and my 150-ton bicycle and I started off on my first real solo endeavor. I wish you could have seen me. For clothes I had a cotton T-shirt and a pair of old-style, wool cycling shorts. For shoes—oh man!—I used my retired running flats (minimal and lightweight) with duct tape around the ball of my foot so that the pedals (rattrap style) wouldn't dig into the bottom of my feet. Helmet? They didn't make them yet! Just kidding, but I wasn't about to wear one of those ridiculous mushroomlike helmets.

On the back of my bike was a rack, where I strapped some street shoes and a pair of shorts. If the weather had turned bad, I would have been up a creek without a paddle. Oh, wait. I seem to remember a light windbreaker—toasty!

Riding on I-70 is nuts, but necessary to reach some routes in Colorado. If you stay far right, there is a large shoulder and it's not so bad. Just watch for glass, pieces of truck tire, and God-knows-what-else! From Denver, it's about 40 miles to the junction with US 40 (Berthoud Pass Road), and virtually all of it is uphill. I was literally cycling from the edge of the prairie up into the Rocky Mountains.

Fred Hutt descends the north side of Berthoud Pass on wide-open curves

I slogged along with absolutely no technique to speak of. And my shoes? Most of my efforts must have evaporated into thin air, as the soles were about as rigid as over-cooked spaghetti. I was, nevertheless, completely thrilled and would not be stopped.

Needless to say, the ride up the pass nearly crushed me. I had never climbed hills like this before and had no sense of rhythm. But I made it. The feeling in my heart as I flew down into Winter Park was one of absolute infatuation for a sport I was only beginning to understand and appreciate. I pulled into my friend's place to spend the night in town. I would ride home the next day, a task I thought would be easy as it was mostly downhill into Denver. Little did I know...

In hindsight, that ride was the beginning of a lifetime of pass-bagging and the first memory of what, some 20 years later, has grown into a passion.

---

the Berthoud Ski Area (on the pass) is closing permanently, so I don't know what services will be up there in the future. For now, you can get H_2O and a snack if you wish. If you want a view of the road below, go over to the north edge of the parking lot and look down toward Winter Park and beyond.

The road descends quickly with some sharp corners on its way to Winter Park. It's very fast and sustained on the upper sections. There are two corners, then a long, fast, winding section followed by two more big turns. Then it straightens out as you fly into Winter Park.

Winter Park is a small ski-resort town. Here, you'll find your needs well tended. Definitely check out the coffee at Rocky Mountain Roastery, or head to Fraser (5 miles north of Winter Park on US 40) for its sister shop, Totally Wired Cyclery. Fraser also has a big grocery store and other amenities if you can't find what you want in Winter Park.

FRASER RIVER VALLEY
US 40: WINTER PARK TO GRANBY

20 Miles • Easy

More of a connection than an actual route, this section of US 40 is busy but has a good shoulder. It's a 20-mile stretch with a lot of services along the way, including the Totally Wired Cyclery in Fraser, where you can take care of all of your cycling and caffeine needs. The terrain is mostly flat and straight with tremendous views throughout the valley. You can satisfy most of your other needs in Granby, as it's the biggest town in the region.

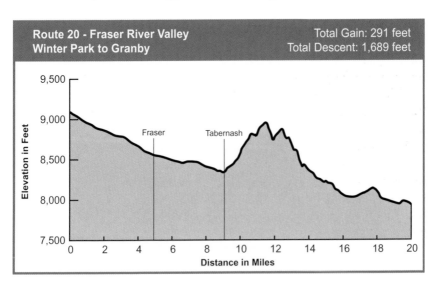

Route 20 - Fraser River Valley
Winter Park to Granby

Total Gain: 291 feet
Total Descent: 1,689 feet

Route 21

GUANELLA PASS
FR 381/FR 118: GEORGETOWN TO GRANT

24 Miles • Difficult

This has got to be the roughest road in this guide, but it is a route that I recommend highly. Road improvements are under discussion, but as of this printing, the south side of Guanella Pass (11,669') is mostly dirt, and it can be in poor shape at times. The north side is mostly paved but is generally narrow and riddled with craters. The dirt summit is above the trees, and has 360-degree views, including Mount Bierstadt and the Mount Evans Wilderness to the east. This pass is gritty, backroad, mountain riding at its best.

I suggest riding from Georgetown up the north (paved) side. If you really like dirt, you can head down toward Grant and turn back whenever you want to. I highly recommend two spare tubes or even a spare folding tire stuffed in your jersey for this route. You have to really pay attention and pick your line well ahead to avoid the inherent road damage that persists on this stretch.

Head south out of Georgetown on Rose Street. The climb starts abruptly, with some fairly steep climbing through several switchbacks before it straightens out a bit and backs off in grade. Soon, however, there are more switchbacks as you head toward Green Lake, Clear Lake, and then, the largest, Lower Cabin Creek Reservoir. The road in this area is totally hacked up and narrow. About 6 miles up from Georgetown, the pavement ends (after the power plant). The dirt is in fairly good condition, and the road gently winds along at a moderate grade.

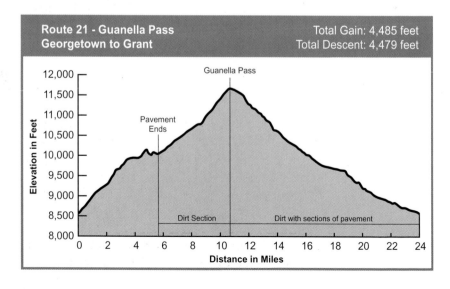

Route 21 - Guanella Pass
Georgetown to Grant

Total Gain: 4,485 feet
Total Descent: 4,479 feet

After 3 miles, the road starts getting steeper and its condition deteriorates. From here it's rough going, and I only recommend it if you love dirt and are prepared to fix a flat or two. It's a total of 5 miles of dirt from where the pavement ends to the summit of Guanella Pass, where you'll find parking, but no services. The views are spectacular. The descent toward Grant is hairball—a very poor dirt road with a few sections of pavement along the way. It's a total of 24 miles from Georgetown to Grant, and the round-trip is a testament to brutal cycling conditions. Grant has the basics but not much more.

A stretch of dirt road on scenic Guanella Pass

MOUNT EVANS
CO 103/CO 5: IDAHO SPRINGS TO MOUNT EVANS SUMMIT
FEE REQUIRED: $3/BIKE, $10/VEHICLE

28 Miles • Very Difficult

Mount Evans (14,264') speaks volumes for itself. There is not a more classic and challenging ride in all of Colorado. Many aspects of riding the Mount Evans Highway make it very different from other roads in the state. While you can find numerous long climbs to other high passes, none compare (except perhaps Trail Ridge Road—see Route 5, p. 35). Mount Evans is a bona fide, mountaintop finish with spectacular views that reach far across Colorado, including a bird's-eye view of Denver.

As someone who's ridden it many times, I'll give you a summary. There's pavement at 14,000 feet—I'll say it again—there's pavement at 14,000 feet. This ride also involves 7,000 feet of vertical gain and 28 miles of uninterrupted climbing. This is a heinous route. Never have I suffered so much on a ride. If you crack on Mount Evans, it can get ugly. If you push through a bonk on Mount Evans, you will spend the rest of the climb fending off a barrage of nausea, shivers, and an overwhelming feeling of suffocation. Now that you're excited, let's get started.

It is essential to take the time to acclimate to the elevation before starting this climb. If you do not acclimate, this climb *will crush you*. (It's definitely not the best choice as a first route for novices or flatlanders.) Pushing yourself on this peak without being acclimated can be dangerous, as you might be dealing with altitude sickness combined with heat and/or freezing temperatures. Remember that you are climbing one of Colorado's fourteeners, and basic mountaineering sense *must* prevail.

Although this is a route you must commit to, when bad weather moves in (thunder, lightning, wind, rain, hail, snow), you must be prepared to bail and head back down, no matter how close you are to the summit. High on Mount Evans, you are far above treeline and extremely exposed to all elements, especially lightning. Hypothermia is also a big concern. You can find more information on these issues under Medical Considerations in the Mountain Environment, Weather and Road Conditions, and Gear Considerations on pages 16–19. Read up before you attempt Mount Evans. Having read all this, don't be scared away. This route will be an experience you won't forget.

Rarefied air makes for difficult climbing on the upper reaches of Mount Evans

*I*f you really want to suffer, there is a race up Mount Evans every summer named for Bob Cook, one of Colorado's cycling pioneers. Cook was the country's finest hill climber when he died of cancer in 1981 at age 23. He not only held the record for Mount Evans (and was the six-time, consecutive winner of the race), but he was also aspiring to race in Europe when he was diagnosed. The race was dubbed the Bob Cook Memorial Mt. Evans Hillclimb in his honor.

You can inquire about this race at USA Cycling in Colorado Springs (see Appendix C, p. 301). Most people ride this road in 3–5 hours (all climbing, ouch!), while a fit rider will go under 3 hours. For those sick individuals called elite racers, the course record is about 1 hour and 48 minutes—mind-boggling!

Situated at the base of Mount Evans on I-70 is the town of Idaho Springs —the traditional starting point for this route. (There is an optional approach to Mount Evans from Bergen Park via Squaw Pass—see Route 23, p. 70.) Idaho Springs has various restaurants, gas stations, and stores to meet all of your basic needs. Head out of Idaho Springs on CO 103 via a bridge over I-70, just west of the main business district. You can't miss it. As you leave town, the road is in excellent shape, but has little or no shoulder. It's a low-pitch incline, and it winds gently. Just past MM 6, about 6.5 miles in, you'll come to a hard left. This is the start of the climb.

Around MM 7, you can look ahead to the ridges above and see the road as it threads its way along the mountainside. But that road up there is far from the summit. If you're not intimidated yet, just wait. At MM 9, look ahead and

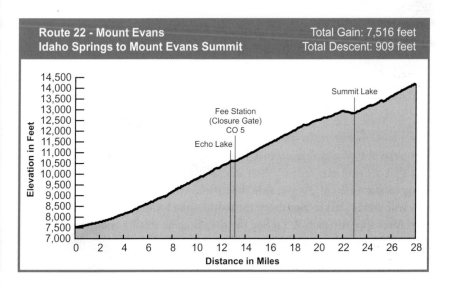

Route 22 - Mount Evans
Idaho Springs to Mount Evans Summit
Total Gain: 7,516 feet
Total Descent: 909 feet

to the right. Beyond the ridge, the road heads up to a group of peaks. That is your summit—and at MM 9, you have a long way to go.

At MM 13, you'll reach the Echo Lake Resort. There's camping, food, and lodging here as well as other services. It's a tremendous setting. Now you can really see the mountain you'll be climbing. Just past Echo Lake is your junction with CO 5. (If you continue going straight here you'll be on CO 103, which leads over Squaw Pass and into the town of Bergen Park.) Turn right onto CO 5 and take out your wallet; there's a fee of $3 per bike. (You can also pay with plastic.) If you forget your cash, begging at the gate usually doesn't help—I know this for a fact! Having purchased your ticket (which, incidentally, makes a nice vacation souvenir if you're a flatlander), you have gained entry into one of the world's great road rides.

Beyond Echo Lake, the road closes after Labor Day weekend and reopens, weather permitting, in the spring around the first or second week of June. In the fall, when it is closed, you can ride past the gate, but be aware that you'll be on your own and there will be *no* vehicular assistance. There are never services at the top. In the spring, you can ride up to snow-line, which progresses higher and higher up the road as the spring thaw takes over. This route is pretty cool when the

The road provides a fantastic descent as it winds its way down from the summit of Mount Evans

road is closed because you have it all to yourself except for the occasional cyclist, bighorn sheep, mountain goat, and such. Just go around the gate—it's legal. But first, read any posted signs so that you're not totally clueless.

Past the gate, the mile markers start over again, and the road immediately starts to feel different. As you ride the first few turns through the pine forests, you will slowly start to rise above the world—the feeling of enormity is incredible. After approximately 2.5 miles, the trees become smaller and the view opens up. CO 5 looms above, chiseled out of the mountainside. If you're feeling poorly, you will now feel instantly worse. You'll think, "That *must* be the summit."

But you are wrong, *so* wrong. You are only at MM 2.5. The summit is not until MM 14.

Another mile or so, and you're above the trees at approximately 11,500 feet. Here you'll be treated to an amazing bird's-eye view of Echo Lake down below, and to Squaw Pass Road as it ascends from CO 5. From this point on, the ride takes on a new identity. It's remote and exposed, and can look like a moonscape at times, except, that is, for the lush green carpet of tundra and wildflowers.

Next comes a couple of miles of relatively straight ramp on a very exposed northwest side of the ridge. Just before MM 5, you'll be treated to yet another stunning vista. The climb continues to be moderate. As you come around a right bend in the road at MM 6, reality will set in. Look waaaay across the valley; you'll see the road as it cuts into the mountain and disappears out of sight. "Surely that's the top," you'll think. But if you look above the road, to the peak's summit, you will see a white observatory dome that marks the top. The hardest part of the ride lies ahead—8 miles and about 2,000 vertical feet of gain.

By MM 7, you'll be awestruck. If you don't respect this mountain yet, you will soon, for it will draw out your deepest mental reserves. If you've misjudged and ridden too fast to this point, you will soon begin to suffer. If you feel good here, then get ready for the ride of your life. A good day on Mount Evans is the ultimate fitness gauge. Don't make the mistake of saving anything for the downhill on this one. This ascent is worthy of your best efforts. As long as you are not seeing double, you can steer your bike, and you can use your brakes, you'll make it down. If you have anything left at the top, then you've squandered a unique opportunity to push yourself to new levels.

Okay, I lied a bit. At MM 8 you actually get a break for about a mile as you descend moderately to Summit Lake, directly below the summit. Watch for ground swells on the road as you pass the lake. These amount to very nasty, natural speed bumps.

From here on out, you really must focus. It's 5 miles to the top. There are 15 major switchbacks ahead, and you are at 13,000 feet with over 1,000 vertical feet remaining. There is *no* air. If you think you can climb, here's where you'll prove it. The switchbacks are steep through the corners, and if you are feeling badly, they can stop you in your tracks.

At MM 11, you're on the southern slopes and the final headwall of your climb. If you feel good, you can really fly. If you're hurting here, it's all mental. Be patient, don't blow it. I've seen people get off their bikes within a mile of the summit, and it's not a pretty sight. But if this isn't hard enough for you, try turning your big chain ring for the last mile.

You round the last corner. At MM 14, a short sprint to the parking lot will have you gasping like never before. You've done it! This is the highest piece of pavement in North America, and, to my knowledge, one of the highest on the planet! There is a small parking lot and a restroom at the top, but no H_2O. There is, however, plenty of view. You can see halfway across the state, and there's nothing above you except the Mount Evans summit—a mere pile of rubble. You can hike to it if you wish, but you're already above 14,000 feet.

If it's cold on top, don't dally, as the descent is very long and will be even colder. Just point your bike downhill. This will be one of the most fantastic descents you'll ever do. Just remember to watch for beautiful animals and distracted humans on the road! I try to ride this one every summer, and over the years nothing has compared. My emotions have run the gamut on this route, and it has enriched my life immensely.

Route 23

SQUAW PASS
CO 103: BERGEN PARK TO ECHO LAKE

18 Miles • Difficult

Bergen Park is an excellent alternative to Idaho Springs as the starting point for the Mount Evans ride. This option only adds about 4 miles to the route, but it's noticeably harder because the terrain is steeper, with a couple of good-size rollers that can break up your rhythm on the climb. However, you might prefer these rollers to the continuous uphill start on the Idaho Springs side. Bergen Park is on CO 74 (Route 24, p. 72), just south of I-70, and can supply all of your basic needs. On the west side of Bergen Park, you'll find the intersection (stoplight) of CO 74, CR 65, and CO 103 (Squaw Pass Road). Head west on CO 103, and you'll be on your way.

CO 103 is a fun road. As you head out of Bergen Park, you'll start climbing through almost 9 miles of consistent, moderate grades with some rather steep, winding sections to Squaw Pass (9,807'). This road is pretty narrow at times with no shoulder and some rough spots. There can be a fair amount of traffic (mostly residential), but it's still better than the traffic coming out of Idaho Springs—the way most people drive Mount Evans. After Squaw Pass, you'll notice that the road is still climbing. This is because it's not a true pass—CO 103 actually traverses along a ridgeline and rolls a bit before descending to Echo Lake. As you ride west of Squaw Pass, the shoulder will improve, and you'll climb for

CO 103 over Squaw Pass makes a more challenging approach to the Mount Evans summit

about 6 more miles to CO 103's high point at just over 11,100 feet. About a mile from the high point, you'll hit Juniper Pass (approximately 10,900 feet and unmarked), and about 2 miles of fast descent will bring you into Echo Lake, where you'll find basic supplies and a left turn (south) onto the Mount Evans Highway (CO 5). From here, follow the description for Route 22, p. 65.

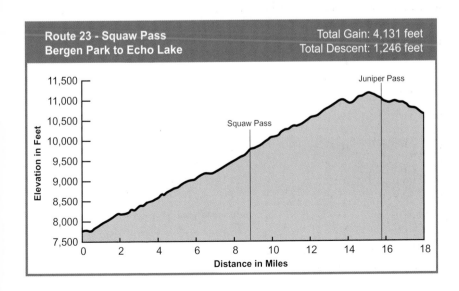

Route 24

BEAR CREEK ROAD
CO 74: MORRISON TO EL RANCHO

Approximately 18 Miles • Moderate

Bear Creek Road (CO 74) can connect you with several routes, including
Mount Evans (Route 22, p. 65), Parmalee Gulch Road/Myers Gulch Road
(Route 26A, p. 78), and CO 73 (Route 26B, p. 80). The road is in excellent
shape with a clean, wide shoulder and plenty of room. However, you won't see
a shoulder until after Evergreen. From Morrison (basic services) to Evergreen is
11 miles of blind curves, with no shoulder and plenty of traffic, especially during
commuting hours. You'll climb moderately as you start into the foothills. You
can find basic services in Evergreen, and it's 5 miles of open road to Bergen Park,
which also has the basics. Two more miles will put you at I-70's El Rancho exit.
From El Rancho, you won't have many options except one great route up the
back of Lookout Mountain (Route 25, p. 73). Just get on I-70 East for 2 miles
to Exit 254 (Genesee Park) and turn right (east) onto US 40. In about a mile,
you'll see a left (north) turn onto Lookout Mountain Road (CR 68), where you'll
find excellent climbing and an insane descent into Golden. You can also take
US 40 east into Denver.

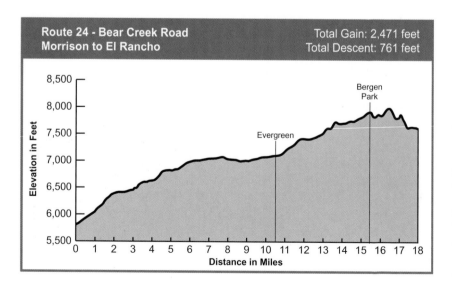

Route 24 - Bear Creek Road
Morrison to El Rancho

Total Gain: 2,471 feet
Total Descent: 761 feet

Route 25

LOOKOUT MOUNTAIN ROAD
CR 68: GOLDEN TO US 40

Approximately 7.5 Miles • Difficult

This is a nasty climb! If you love climbing as much as I do, you'll be drooling on this one. You'll encounter about 4.5 miles of climbing with some insanely steep grades and extremely tight curves along the way. Luckily, it's too steep for traffic to go very fast (the scenery makes this a popular place to drive), and on the descent no car will be able to keep up with you! This is also a popular route for cyclists, and you will always find a few comrades suffering along with you.

The climb starts at the intersection of West 6th Avenue (US 6) and Lookout Mountain Road (CR 68), in the southwest corner of Golden. If you're riding from the middle of town, you'll be climbing to this intersection. As you continue to head up (or down!), the views of Denver are astounding, and you can see the prairie to the east. At the top, you'll find Buffalo Bill's grave and many tourists, as well as basic supplies.

Continue through and down the south side, a moderate descent of about 3 miles to US 40, where a left turn (east) will take you into Denver. Or, if you head back the way you came, it feels like you're skydiving into Golden, as the town is right below you.

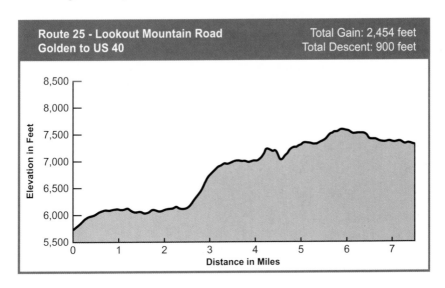

Route 25 - Lookout Mountain Road
Golden to US 40

Total Gain: 2,454 feet
Total Descent: 900 feet

REGION 2

FRONT RANGE SOUTH

The southern foothills, stretching from south of Denver down to Walsenburg, possess a subtle magnificence unparalleled in Colorado. Although you won't find many pass rides in this region, exceptional flats and huge rollers make for challenging rides. Routes in the southern Front Range amount to long days with constant tempo changes.

The cities in this region are full of amenities and will meet all of your cycling needs. Routes of note include South Deckers Road (Route 34, p. 92), The Gold Belt Tour Scenic and Historic Byway (Route 36, p. 94), and Greenhorn Highway (Route 49, p. 111). You can also visit USA Cycling (see Appendix C) at the U.S. Olympic Training Center in Colorado Springs.

ROUTES

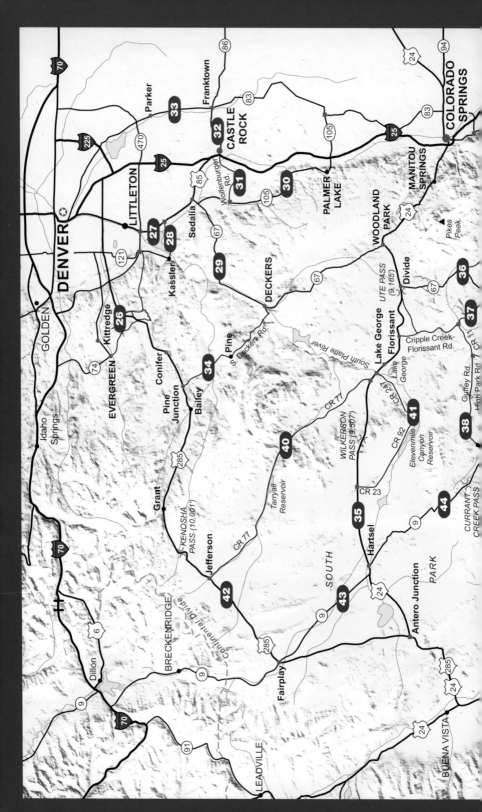

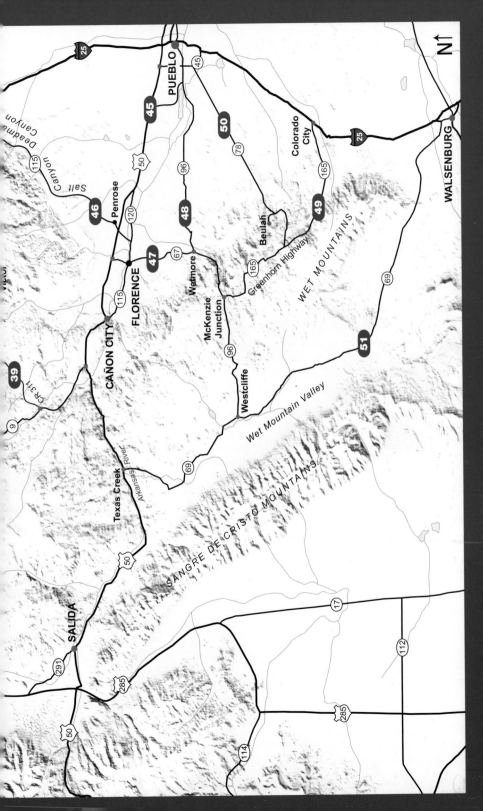

Routes 26A–H

CONIFER AND EVERGREEN BACKROADS

Some excellent routes wind their way through the hills around Conifer and Evergreen. You'll find rollers of all shapes and sizes, including some very steep sections here and there, and some climbs of several miles. These roads are generally in great shape, but many are narrow and have no shoulder. There are many homes in hidden driveways, and blind curves, so beware. Traffic can be a problem during commuting hours; it's best to ride these routes at off-peak times. Note that CR 73 is often locally referred to as "Highway 73."

Following, I will give brief descriptions of some of the area's best roads. Linking several of these routes together can make for a punishing day of huge, roller-coaster rides.

Route 26A

PARMALEE GULCH ROAD/ MYERS GULCH ROAD
US 285 TO KITTREDGE

Approximately 5 Miles • Moderate

This is an excellent road that winds, climbs, rolls, and then descends as it makes its way to Kittredge. The pavement is in excellent shape, but there is no shoulder as you ride through forested, rolling mountains. At its southern end, you will find Parmalee Gulch Road's junction with US 285, just west of Denver. If you're coming from Denver, look for the Indian Hills sign on the right, just before the exit for Tiny Town. The road climbs moderately as you head north. You can get basic supplies at a general store in Indian Hills. As the road approaches Kittredge, its name changes to Myers Gulch Road. At just over 5 miles, including a short descent, you'll be in Kittredge, which also has the basics.

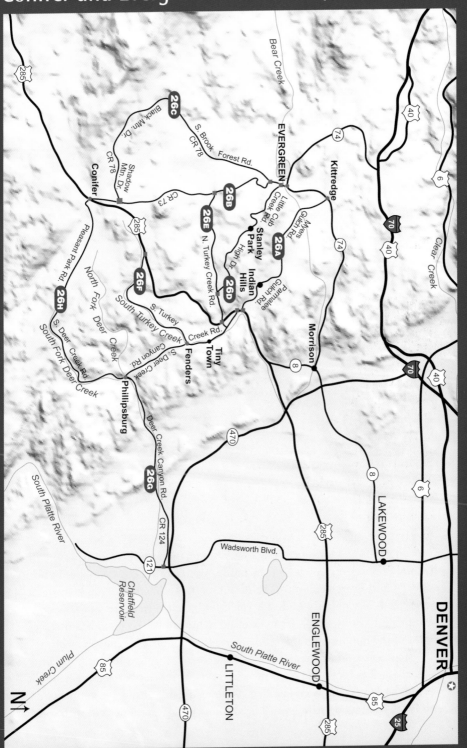

Route 26B

THE EVERGREEN EXPRESSWAY
CR 73: CONIFER TO EVERGREEN

Approximately 9 Miles • Moderate

Here is an excellent route from Conifer to Evergreen. Head northwest out of Conifer, which has basic services. You should see a sign for CR 73 near the intersection for Pleasant Park Road (Route 26H, p. 84). At this printing, there is a lot of road work in Conifer, and it's hard to tell where access points will be for the side roads when construction is complete. Be prepared to look for signs. CR 73 is a great road but has little or no shoulder, and it's a major area thru-route, so traffic can be bad on weekends and during rush hour. Shadow Mountain Drive (Route 26C, below) is a great alternate route between Evergreen and Conifer during traffic-heavy times.

CR 73 will climb and roll gently northward from Conifer with awesome views. A bit over 5 miles and you'll be at a junction with North Turkey Creek Road (Route 26E, p. 82). Continue on CR 73 for about 4 miles with a moderate descent into Evergreen, which has the basics.

Route 26C

SHADOW MOUNTAIN DRIVE/
SOUTH BROOK FOREST ROAD
CR 78: CR 73 TO CR 73

12 Miles • Moderate

Up in the hills just east of the Mount Evans Wilderness is a beautiful, top-quality route. It's a great way to get from Conifer to Evergreen, as CR 73 (Route 26B, above) can get lots of traffic. You can find basic supplies in both Conifer and Evergreen, but there are no services along the route. Just over a mile north of Conifer on CR 73, you'll find a left turn (west) onto Shadow Mountain Drive (CR 78). It's in excellent shape but has no shoulder. However, most of the motorists on this road are locals, and traffic is generally light.

The terrain starts out with a mellow incline through this peaceful area, and about 3 miles up the road, the grade gets fairly steep for about a half mile before backing off into some rollers. (The road name changes in this section to Black Mountain Drive.) You'll head into a fast, steepish descent with some sharp curves for about 2.5 miles. A small roller will interrupt this descent, and the road name will change again—now it's South Brook Forest Road. After this roller, the descent continues steeply for about a mile and mellows for the next 4 miles until the junction with CR 73, just south of Evergreen.

Route 26D
HIGH DRIVE/LITTLE CUB CREEK ROAD
NORTH TURKEY CREEK ROAD TO CR 73
9 Miles • Moderate

This road is in excellent shape. It has no shoulder, but traffic is very light. The start of the route is just over a mile west of North Turkey Creek Road's junction with US 285. There are no services on High Drive/Little Cub Creek Road, but at the northern end of the route you'll be very close to Evergreen, where you can find basic supplies.

From North Turkey Creek Road (Route 26E, p. 82), High Drive starts climbing moderately, but soon come some very steep sections climbing towards Stanley Park. Several short descents along the way will be welcome relief—no pun intended. After 4 miles, you'll ride through some small rollers and the road name will change to Stanley Park Road. A few more miles of rolling terrain, and you'll start a steep descent with very sharp curves toward the valley floor. You'll bottom out about 7.5 miles from the start of the route, and the road name will change to Little Cub Creek Road. Continue for 1.5 miles, with a gentle downhill trend, to the junction of CR 73 just south of Evergreen.

View of Mount Evans from High Drive

Route 26E

NORTH TURKEY CREEK ROAD
US 285 TO CR 73

Approximately 7 Miles • Moderate

What an awesome road! Secluded and quiet, it runs east/west through the foothills from US 285 to CR 73. The east end of the route junctions with US 285 just west of Denver, a mile and a half or so south of the Indian Hills turnoff. If you're coming from Denver, it will be a right (west) turn onto North Turkey Creek Road (CR 64), where you'll start climbing moderately as you wind your way into the hills just east of Mount Evans. It's gorgeous back here, and the road climbs and rolls before a short descent to its junction with CR 73 (Route 26B, p. 80), about 4 miles south of Evergreen. There are no supplies until the end of this route, where there is a gas station/food store at the junction with CR 73, and Evergreen has full services.

Route 26F

SOUTH TURKEY CREEK ROAD
US 285 TO US 285

Approximately 8 Miles • Moderate

South Turkey Creek Road (CR 122) splits off of US 285 and meanders its way along South Turkey Creek, heads south, and then turns west as it climbs back to US 285. There are a few excellent connecting routes in this vicinity—see Parmalee Gulch (Route 26A, p. 78), North Turkey Creek Road (Route 26E, above), and Deer Creek Canyon Road (Route 26G, opposite). There are no services on this road, but you can find basic supplies in the area.

If you're coming up US 285 from Denver, you'll see a sign for South Turkey Creek Road and Tiny Town. Go left (southeast). South Turkey Creek Road is in great shape but has no shoulder, traffic is fairly light but can pick up during commuting hours, and the terrain is relatively flat with lots of curves and a 5-mile climb at the end.

About 1.5 miles into the ride, you'll see a turn for North Turkey Creek Road on your right (west), and another 1.5 miles or so will bring you to a junction with South Deer Creek Canyon Road. As you continue past South Deer Creek Canyon Road, South Turkey Creek Road will start climbing moderately with some rolling terrain to US 285, 5 miles away.

Route 26G

DEER CREEK CANYON ROAD
CO 121 to South Turkey Creek Road

Approximately 10 Miles • Moderate

This is a great road that hooks up with other area routes; see Pleasant Park Road (Route 26H, p. 84) and South Turkey Creek Road (Route 26F, opposite). There are no services at the start of this route but there are plenty to the north, as Denver is nearby. CO 121 is Wadsworth Boulevard as it runs north/south through Denver, and it junctions with C-470 at the southwest corner of Denver. Less than a half mile south of this junction on CO 121, you'll find a right turn (west) onto Deer Creek Canyon Road (CR 124). This is a popular cycling route; many people park at the corner of CO 121 and Deer Creek Canyon Road. The road is in great shape, but it has no shoulder, and traffic can be heavy during commuting hours and on weekends.

The route starts out with some gentle rolling terrain as it winds through open pasture on the way to the foothills. About 2 miles down the road, you will come to an intersection with South Owens Street. Here you'll head left (southwest) to stay on Deer Creek Canyon Road, and you'll start riding into the foothills. It's a gentle incline, and the road will have a lot of sharp curves from here on out. You'll pass a "T" intersection with South Deer Creek Road (Route 26H, p. 84) at Phillipsburg (no services) in about 4.5 miles. Turn right here to begin a section of moderate climbing for 3 miles before a half-mile descent brings you to the junction with South Turkey Creek Road at Fenders. There are no services in this area, so be prepared.

Route 26H

PLEASANT PARK ROAD/ SOUTH DEER CREEK ROAD
CR 88: CONIFER TO DEER CREEK CANYON ROAD

Approximately 11 Miles • Moderate

If you head southwest of Denver on US 285, you'll come to the town of Conifer, where you can find basic supplies. As of this printing, Pleasant Park Road is a left turn (east) at the stoplight in the middle of town. However, road construction might alter the access to this route, so look for signs or ask around. When you access Pleasant Park Road, you'll start climbing somewhat steeply for about a mile, then enjoy a nice descent. Soon you'll head into some easy rollers, and about 3.5 miles out you'll start into an incredible descent along the South Fork of Deer Creek. It's big with lots of sharp curves on an excellent road with no shoulder for 5 miles or so; the valley will seem bottomless. About 8.5 miles from Conifer, the descent mellows out, but you should still prepare for some very fast riding and cornering. (I had the pleasure of experiencing this route in the reverse direction—at the end of a 40-mile ride. My buddy Ron didn't give out much information, so I never knew what was coming next. The hills were demoralizing, and I think he enjoyed seeing me suffer.)

Note that about 9 miles from Conifer, you'll come to three nasty speed bumps while cornering. Watch out! This road changes to South Deer Creek Road along the way, and about 10.5 miles out you'll come to a "T" intersection with Deer Creek Canyon Road at Phillipsburg.

A "bomber" descent into Deer Creek Canyon

Route 27

US 85
C-470 TO CASTLE ROCK

Approximately 16 Miles • Easy

There is a lot of great cycling south of Denver, but not a lot of access without riding through the mess of traffic in the Denver metro area. One way to get south of town is via US 85 (Santa Fe Drive), which heads southeast to Castle Rock. It's a good flat road, but it has little or no shoulder, and the traffic can be terrible. About 4 miles south of US 85's junction with C-470, you'll see an exit for Titan Road, which accesses a nice route around Chatfield Reservoir (Route 28, p. 86). About 5 miles later, you'll ride past Sedalia, where you can get basic supplies and find junctions with both CO 67 (Route 29, p. 87) and CO 105 (Route 30, p. 88). From Sedalia it's about 7 more miles to Castle Rock, where you'll be able to take care of most of your needs.

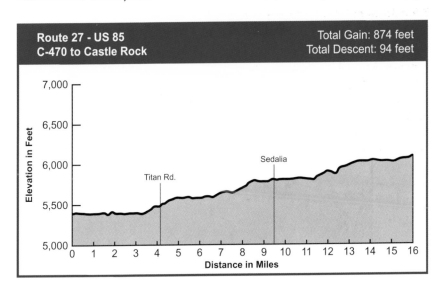

Route 27 - US 85
C-470 to Castle Rock

Total Gain: 874 feet
Total Descent: 94 feet

Route 28

CHATFIELD RESERVOIR
DEER CREEK CANYON ROAD TO US 85

10 Miles • Easy

The roads around Chatfield Reservoir provide an alternative to US 85. CO 121 (Wadsworth Boulevard) runs north/south through west metro Denver. While Wadsworth is a busy street in Denver, it changes drastically once you are south of C-470. CO 121 continues south as it crosses C-470; shortly thereafter you'll see a junction with Deer Creek Canyon Road, CR 124 (Route 26H, p. 84), a good place to park and start your ride. Heading south on CO 121, it's about 4 miles of big, easy rollers to get to Kassler, where you'll take a left turn (east) onto Waterton Road—a nice little two-lane road with no shoulder. Waterton Road casually rolls along and comes to a "T" intersection with Rampart Road. Go left (north), and soon the road name will change to Titan Road. Titan Road will make a 90-degree bend to the right (east) and head toward US 85 (Route 27, p. 85), a few more miles down the road.

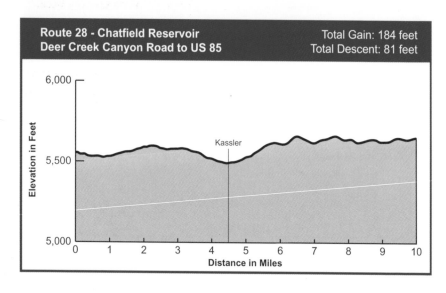

Route 28 - Chatfield Reservoir
Deer Creek Canyon Road to US 85

Total Gain: 184 feet
Total Descent: 81 feet

Route 29

JARRE CANYON ROAD
CO 67: SEDALIA TO DECKERS

Approximately 27 Miles • Moderate (Difficult with dirt section)

Sedalia is a very small town at the base of the foothills with basic supplies and a quaint feel. CO 67 is a beautiful, winding road surrounded by rolling, forested mountains—a gorgeous route to Deckers (if you don't mind some dirt). As you leave Sedalia, the pavement is great but the shoulder disappears. After about 4 miles of easy uphill rollers, you'll start climbing up a consistent, somewhat steep hill for about 6 more miles; as you near the town of Sprucewood, you'll hit some rollers and about 3 miles of fast descent—a great climb on the way back.

CO 67 takes you from the busy Denver area to rolling mountains and lush meadows

About 13 miles from Sedalia, the pavement ends at Sprucewood, where you can get some food and drink. Turn right (west) onto FR 515 at Sprucewood. About 3 miles of dirt descending to the South Platte River will provide some insanely steep grades (close to 20 percent) and spit you out onto pavement at South Platte River Road. A right turn, and the pavement will end. Go left, and it's 10 miles of somewhat flat, partially paved, road that winds along the river and through a beautiful valley to Deckers, where you'll find basic supplies.

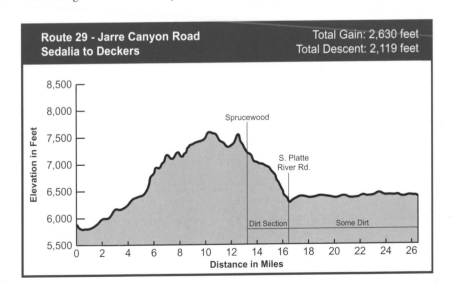

**Route 29 - Jarre Canyon Road
Sedalia to Deckers**

Total Gain: 2,630 feet
Total Descent: 2,119 feet

Route 30

PERRY PARK ROAD
CO 105: CO 83 TO SEDALIA

Approximately 32 Miles • Moderate

If you're heading from Colorado Springs to the Denver area and prefer not to ride on CO 83 (Route 33, p. 91) the entire way, you can take Perry Park Road, an alternate route that heads west and north from CO 83. You will find more services on this route, as well as a more mountainlike setting and a lot less traffic. From CO 83's junction with CO 105, about 12 miles north of Colorado Springs, head west on CO 105. The mountains loom large in the distance, and it's 5 miles and a few moderate rollers to I-25 and Monument, where you will find basic services.

From Monument, head right (north) through Palmer Lake and into the foothills. It's 3 miles to Palmer Lake, and nearly 25 more to Sedalia and the ride's end. The road is in great shape, but it has no shoulder. Just north of Palmer Lake, you'll need to take an abrupt left in order to stay on CO 105—just look for the sign. Lots of easy-to-moderate rolling terrain will greet you as you skirt the foothills, where beautiful scenery and light traffic make this an excellent route. Just after MM 32, you'll come to the junction with Jarre Canyon Road (Route 29, p. 87). Turn right and ride on to Sedalia, about a quarter of a mile away, where you'll find basic services.

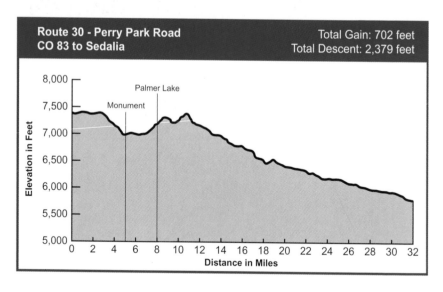

Route 31

WOLFENSBERGER ROAD
PERRY PARK ROAD (CO 105) TO CASTLE ROCK

6 Miles • Moderate

Just over 4 miles south of Sedalia on Perry Park Road, you'll find a junction with Wolfensberger Road. It's an excellent stretch of pavement with no shoulder that winds and moderately rolls its way east to Castle Rock, just over 6 miles away. The shoulder varies from skinny to nonexistent, but traffic is light and the views are amazing. This is a great way to get to Castle Rock from the south Denver metro area, as it avoids the traffic on US 85 (Route 27, p. 85).

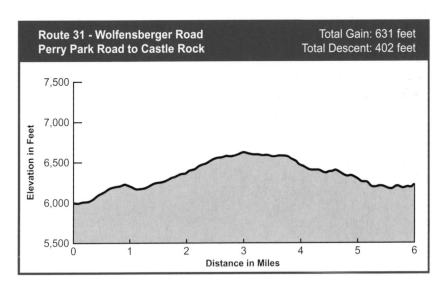

Route 31 - Wolfensberger Road
Perry Park Road to Castle Rock
Total Gain: 631 feet
Total Descent: 402 feet

Route 32

FRANKTOWN ROAD
CO 86: CASTLE ROCK TO FRANKTOWN

7 Miles • Moderate

Franktown Road (CO 86) is an excellent route on a great road, however, there is no shoulder, and traffic can be heavy at times. In Castle Rock, you'll find most of your needs taken care of. Check out Crowfoot Valley Coffee Co. for some of the best coffee in these parts. Franktown Road heads east out of Castle Rock and immediately starts climbing rather briskly for a couple of miles. It then descends quickly for a few miles before leveling out and heading into Franktown, where you can find basic supplies and a junction with CO 83 (Route 33, p. 91). The views are exceptional at the top of the climb—just watch the traffic.

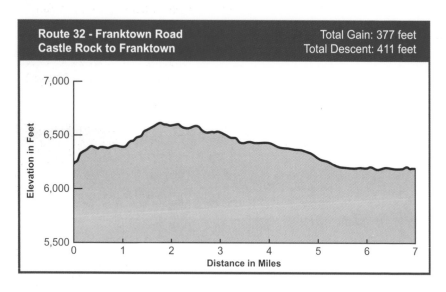

Route 32 - Franktown Road
Castle Rock to Franktown

Total Gain: 377 feet
Total Descent: 411 feet

Route 33

I-25 BYPASS
CO 83: COLORADO SPRINGS TO PARKER

Approximately 45 Miles • Moderate

This is a beautiful route and an excellent way to get between Colorado Springs and the Denver area. The Springs will have everything you need. You'll find lots of traffic as you head north out of town on Academy Boulevard (CO 83), but don't panic. It will quickly thin out as you leave town. There are a few intersections to get through, and you must make a right turn at Interquest Avenue in order to stay on CO 83. Just follow the signs. The wide shoulder will soon disappear, but the road, which changes from four lanes to two, is great. As you ride through the countryside, you'll enjoy lots of rolling hills, green pastures, and pine forests. The views of the Front Range are outstanding, but services are nonexistent until Franktown, which has the basics. Parker, 9 miles farther, should be able to meet most of your needs. North of Parker, CO 83 gets busy as you approach Denver, especially during commuting hours. If you must head into south Denver, I suggest heading west (left) out of Parker on Lincoln Avenue (which turns into South University Boulevard near Denver), where you'll find a bit less traffic.

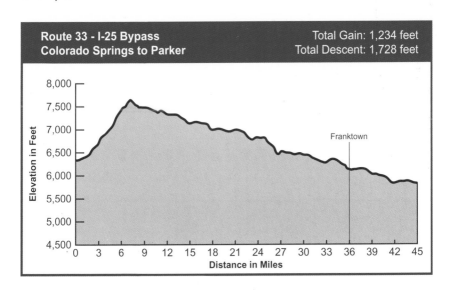

Route 34

SOUTH DECKERS ROAD
CR 126/CO 67: Pine Junction to Woodland Park

Approximately 46 Miles • Difficult

Pine Junction sits halfway between Conifer and Bailey on US 285. You'll find gas, food, bathrooms, and other basics here. Take Pine Valley Road (CR 126) for a 6-mile descent from Pine Junction to the town of Pine. The shoulder varies and can leave little room for cyclists at times. You'll want to stay on CR 126 in Pine, but the name changes to South Deckers Road. Soon you'll pass through the town of Buffalo Creek, after which you'll encounter huge, rolling terrain with climbs as long as 5 miles. You'll find the basics in Deckers, where the road turns into CO 67. The road flattens out as you continue south, but not for long. You'll soon launch into several very large rollers, and you'll be treated to spectacular views of Pikes Peak (14,110') as you continue into Woodland Park.

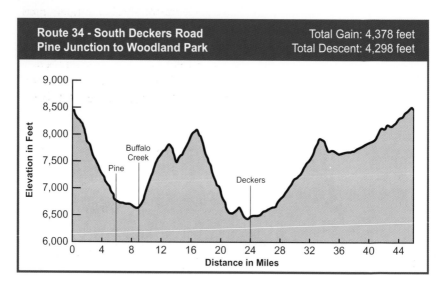

UTE PASS–WILKERSON PASS COMBO
US 24: COLORADO SPRINGS TO ANTERO JUNCTION/US 285

76 Miles • Moderate

Colorado Springs is a beautiful city at the foot of Pikes Peak (14,110'). The Springs has a healthy cycling community and can cover all of your other needs as well. It is home to the U.S. Olympic Training Center, and I highly recommend a tour of the facilities, especially USA Cycling.

Take US 24 west out of town for a moderate, 18-mile incline to Woodland Park. You'll find plenty of services along the way, as well as in Woodland Park itself. While traffic can be heavy, there is usually a good shoulder.

Although the stretch of road between Woodland Park and Antero Junction contains two passes (Ute and Wilkerson), you shouldn't be intimidated. This section of the route is moderate, with relatively small hills and nice flats. There is nothing moderate about the views, however. I think you'll agree that the massive valley known as South Park is the embodiment of subtle magnificence.

From Woodland Park, Florissant is another 15 miles of moderate terrain over Ute Pass (9,165'). About 31 more miles of easy terrain via Wilkerson Pass (9,507') will bring you to Hartsel, where you'll also find the basics. It's about 12 miles from Hartsel to Antero Junction (no services) and US 285. For routes that continue from this junction check out US 285 (Route 42, p. 102) and Trout Creek Pass (Route 84, p. 180).

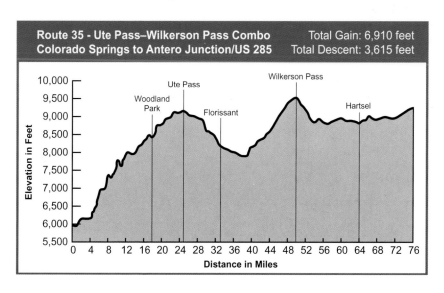

Route 35 - Ute Pass–Wilkerson Pass Combo
Colorado Springs to Antero Junction/US 285
Total Gain: 6,910 feet
Total Descent: 3,615 feet

Route 36

GOLD BELT TOUR SCENIC & HISTORIC BYWAY
CO 67: DIVIDE TO VICTOR

24 Miles • Moderate

If you are in the area, don't miss this ride; it is nothing but quality! If you're interested in Colorado's gold-mining history, you'll have an added bonus on this ride. Not only are there many small, abandoned mines dotting the hillsides, you'll also ride right through the Portland Mine on your climb to Victor.

On US 24 between Woodland Park and Florissant, you'll find the town of Divide (basic services) and the junction with CO 67. The route starts with some large, gradual, rolling terrain on a great road with little or no shoulder. The views of Pikes Peak (14,110') are amazing. Soon you'll launch into several hardy climbs—monster rollers of up to a few miles each. About 13 miles into this route, you'll find a crossroads called Gillette. You can go left or right, as this out-and-back ride has a nice loop alternative on its southern end.

Turning right and staying on CO 67 takes you on a more challenging route to Cripple Creek, about 5 miles away. After several miles of climbing up from Gillette, you'll be treated to an incredible descent into Cripple Creek. As you fly into town, you can't help but notice all of the tailing piles from old abandoned mines—a real scene from Colorado history. You'll find your basic needs well cared for, as this can be a busy town because of the casinos. That's

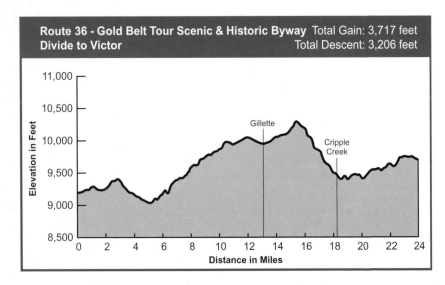

right—there's gambling in Cripple Creek. Try not to lose your shirt as you ride through town, and look for signs pointing the way to Victor.

In order to stay on CO 67, about halfway through Cripple Creek you'll turn left (south) where a sign reads, "Victor 6 miles." It's 6 miles of climbing up a steep, narrow, winding road. The rest of this ride just gets better and better. Amazing views of the Colorado interior abound as you head up the road to the Portland Mine and Victor.

To take the alternate loop back to Gillette (about 7 miles), once you're in Victor, follow the pavement through town until you come to a fork. Go left, staying on the pavement, and you'll see the road above. Now you'll be on Lazy S Ranch Road (CR 81), and another 1.5 miles or so will take you through the Goldfield settlement and to the top of the climb. A fun descent leads down to Gillette and back over the huge rollers to Divide and US 24. Refer to Cripple Creek–Florissant Road (Route 37, p. 96) for another way into Cripple Creek.

The Gold Belt Byway combines Colorado's scenic vistas with mining history

Route 37

CRIPPLE CREEK–FLORISSANT ROAD
CR 1: FLORISSANT TO CRIPPLE CREEK

Approximately 18 Miles • Moderate

This ride starts in Florissant, where you'll find basic supplies and the junction of US 24 and Cripple Creek–Florissant Road (CR 1). The route heads south and winds its way along CR 1 through beautiful, moderate, rolling terrain with steeper and longer climbs as you head southeast up to Cripple Creek. Incredible views abound and as you approach Cripple Creek, where CR 1 will change to West Carr Avenue. Shortly, you'll take a right (south) onto B Street and then a quick left (east) onto Bennett Avenue, which leads into the heart of town. For an awesome loop, add this route to CO 67: Divide to Victor (Route 36, p. 94).

Lower Twin Rock Road, another way to get to Cripple Creek

Lower Twin Rock Road (CR 42), just west of Ute Pass and the town of Divide, heads south from US 24 and is an alternate way to get onto Cripple Creek–Florissant Road. It's a wonderful rolling piece of pavement that winds its way along for nearly 6 easy miles, ending at a "T" intersection with Cripple Creek–Florissant Road. Turn left (south) at this intersection to get to Cripple Creek.

Route 37 - Cripple Creek–Florissant Road Florissant to Cripple Creek	Total Gain: 2,317 feet Total Descent: 905 feet

Elevation in Feet

CR 42 (Lower Twin Rock Rd.)

CR 11 (South Rd.)

10,000 — 9,500 — 9,000 — 8,500 — 8,000

0 1 2 3 4 5 6 7 8 9 10 11 12 13 14 15 16 17

Distance in Miles

Route 38

GUFFEY ROAD
CR 112/CR 59: CR 11 TO CO 9

Approximately 16 Miles • Easy

Back in the hills just west of Cripple Creek you'll find some absolutely stunning countryside full of gentle rolling hills that afford endless views of Colorado's interior. At its northern end, Guffey Road junctions with High Park Road, CR 11 (Route 39, p. 99). From there, Guffey Road heads southwest to the town of Guffey, changing along the way from CR 112 to CR 59. There is virtually no traffic (nor is there a shoulder), and the road's surface is pretty chewed up—lots of character! As you continue, Guffey Road becomes more and more hilly but stays pretty mellow except for the last couple miles, where you'll find a nice moderate descent to CO 9 (a nice little climb in the other direction).

Guffey Road offers a view of Pikes Peak as you ride northeast.

A mile or so before you reach CO 9, you'll ride through Guffey, where you can get very basic items at a small general store that doubles as a bar and restaurant and has an impressive collection of beer-tap handles. I went in for a jug of water and the next thing I knew, I was on the patio with a beer in my hand and no idea how I had gotten there—I swear! Guffey is very small and quiet, and it's easy to forget what day it is when visiting this little hideaway.

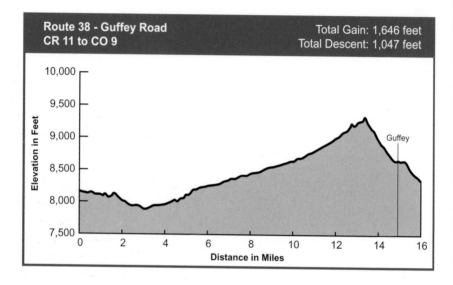

Route 39

SOUTH ROAD/HIGH PARK ROAD
CR 11/CR 311: CRIPPLE CREEK–FLORISSANT ROAD TO CO 9

Approximately 22 Miles • Moderate

This is an incredible stretch of road hidden in the hills southwest of Cripple Creek. It offers lots of nice, moderate rollers and incredible views of the area mountains, as well as distant views of Pikes Peak (14,110') to the east.

To access High Park Road's northern end, you'll have to use South Road, a stretch of dirt that's pretty rough. (This road might get paved in the future so don't be confused if you get there and it's smooth.) South Road shares the same County Road number as High Park Road (CR 11), and it's included in the mileage for this route.

High Park Road winds through hills

From its junction with Cripple Creek–Florissant Road (CR 1), South Road rolls along very gently for about 4 miles and brings you to a "T" intersection, where you'll turn left (southeast) onto High Park Road and the start of the pavement. (A right turn at this intersection will put you on Guffey Road—Route 38, p. 97.) High Park Road, which changes to CR 311 along the way, will begin to wind and moderately roll along as you head into this beautiful countryside dotted with piñon, juniper, and green pastures. The pavement is in good shape, with no shoulder to speak of, but very little traffic. You won't find any services, and you will have to watch for cattle guards on your way to the junction with CO 9.

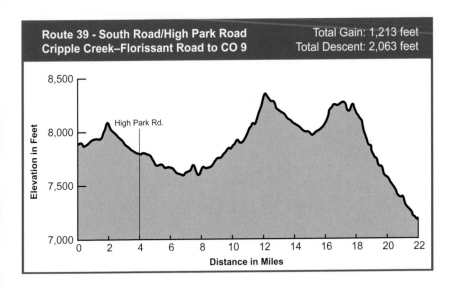

Route 39 - South Road/High Park Road
Cripple Creek–Florissant Road to CO 9

Total Gain: 1,213 feet
Total Descent: 2,063 feet

High Park Rd.

Elevation in Feet

Distance in Miles

Route 40

TARRYALL RESERVOIR
CR 77: US 24 to Jefferson

42 Miles • Moderate

Welcome to classic backcountry pavement! From US 24 just west of Lake George to its end at US 285 in Jefferson, CR 77 is packed with moderate, rolling terrain, and winds its way past some of Colorado's premier rock-climbing sites (the South Platte area). You will negotiate one of the most chunked-up roads I've ever seen—watch for craters! It's about 25 miles to Tarryall Reservoir and 42 miles to CR 77's junction with CO 285.

South Park and the Mosquito Range from CR 77

Here you will be treated to beautiful views of the Continental Divide and the Mosquito Range as you roll into the expansive South Park area. (There are basic services in Jefferson, but nothing along the route.)

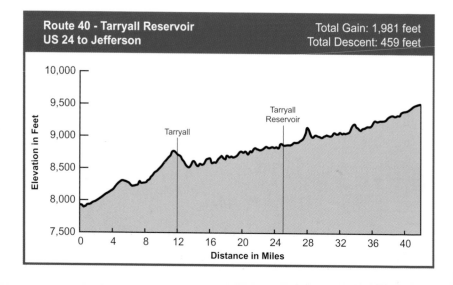

Route 41

ELEVENMILE CANYON RESERVOIR
FR 247/CR 92/CR 23: LAKE GEORGE TO US 24

Approximately 21 Miles • Moderate

Stunning views of Elevenmile Canyon Reservoir against the mountains make this a gorgeous setting for a ride. Lake George is located on US 24, just under 40 miles west of Colorado Springs. You can find the basics here, as well as many other route options.

Head west from Lake George on US 24. In less than a mile, just north of the lake, turn left for Eleven Mile State Recreation Area. On most maps this is FR 247, but what I saw on the road was CR 90! Anyway, go left (west). The road is narrow, and has no shoulder, and the edges are chewed up in places. There isn't much traffic, but summer weekends bring lots of trucks hauling boats. After about 4 miles, turn left to stay on FR 247 (which turns into CR 92) and follow the pavement. As you head toward the reservoir and into the Puma Hills, the road starts to wind, roll, and climb.

There's a nice descent to the reservoir, which is about 10 miles from the town of Lake George. You'll find a visitor center, food, water, and restrooms.

As you ride by the reservoir, you'll leave the hills behind and the road will become flat and straight. You'll be cruisin' through flats with sweeping views. About 18 miles from Lake George, you'll see a "T" intersection with CR 23. (By now CR 92 has become CR 59.) Go right on CR 23, and about 3 miles later you will pass a buffalo ranch on your way to US 24 (Route 35, p. 93) in Glentivar. From here, Lake George is 15 miles or so to the east (right).

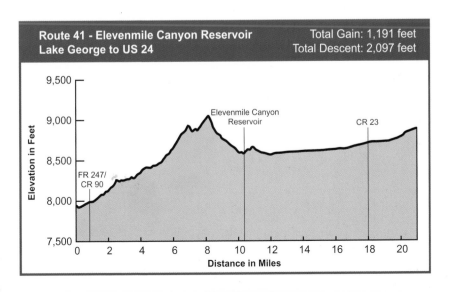

Route 41 - Elevenmile Canyon Reservoir
Lake George to US 24

Total Gain: 1,191 feet
Total Descent: 2,097 feet

Route 42

KENOSHA PASS
US 285: Conifer to Antero Junction

Approximately 73 Miles • Moderate

Southwest of Denver, traffic on US 285 can be very busy for the first 30 miles or so, particularly during commuting hours and on Sunday afternoons. Roadwork in recent years has helped considerably, but it seems endless. I don't recommend riding US 285 between Denver and Conifer (roughly 14 miles) because of traffic, however, there are some fantastic roads in this area that junction with US 285 and wind their way through the beautiful, rolling, forested foothills. Refer to Conifer and Evergreen Backroads (Routes 26A-H, pp. 78–84).

West of Conifer, US 285 continues undulating its way up into the mountains and affords some great views of the Mount Evans/Mount Bierstadt massif to the north (right) as you make your way toward Bailey (14 miles from Conifer). Shoulders on this route vary from good to nonexistent. As is true with Conifer, Bailey will take care of your basic needs. From here, it's 11 miles to Grant (no services), which is the southern terminus of the road up Guanella Pass (Route 21, p. 64). After Grant, you'll start making your way up Kenosha Pass. It is a

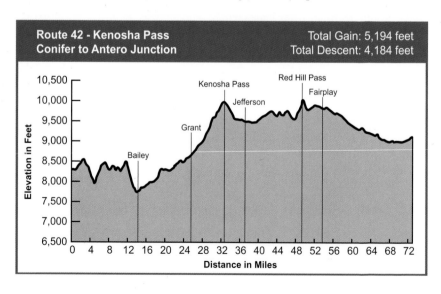

Route 42 - Kenosha Pass
Conifer to Antero Junction

Total Gain: 5,194 feet
Total Descent: 4,184 feet

moderate climb of a bit over 7 miles that contains several steep sections. The shoulder improves on this pass, but beware of rumble strips.

Kenosha Pass sits at 10,001 feet, and after a sweet, 4-mile descent into Jefferson (basic services), you'll head across a very wide and especially beautiful valley called South Park. The road here is relatively flat and straight. There are some gradual, sweeping rollers as you make your way to the base of a rather large one called Red Hill Pass (9,993'). From Jefferson up over Red Hill Pass and down into Fairplay is another 16 moderate miles with outstanding vistas of the Hartsel Valley and the Mosquito Range. You'll find the basics in Fairplay.

Another 21 miles of moderate rollers, and you'll arrive at Antero Junction, where US 285 meets US 24. To continue on US 285, refer to Route 84 (p. 181); for US 24, see Route 35 (p. 93).

Front Range cyclists head home after a weekend of "destination cycling"

Route 43

SOUTH PARK HIGHWAY
CO 9: FAIRPLAY TO HARTSEL

18 Miles • Easy

The immense valley of South Park is very peaceful. The countryside is ever so slightly tilted here and there, but for the most part it's flat. The views of distant peaks are phenomenal, and the sky goes on forever! You'll find the basics in the very friendly little town of Fairplay. From Fairplay, go right (south) on US 285 to its junction with CO 9 a mile away. Turn left onto CO 9 at the junction. This is a relatively flat ride—one might even say leisurely. The tranquility you'll feel while riding this stretch of highway is rarely found elsewhere. On the other hand, if you feel like mashin' big gears, you can do some serious speed work and spin development in this valley. It is a total of 18 miles to Hartsel, where you'll find the basics. CO 9 is a good road with a small shoulder.

When I last came through Fairplay, the town was absolutely packed. People— and burros—were everywhere. Folks were partying and cars were parked anywhere they could be squeezed—front yards, back alleys, and along the highway. Did I mention there were burros? It was the oddest thing.

Then I saw a banner strung over Main Street: "World Championship Pack-Burro Race." I was mystified and pleasantly surprised as I caught glimpses of a sport I had no idea existed.

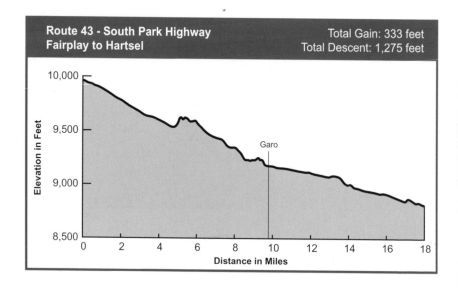

Route 44

CURRANT CREEK PASS
CO 9: HARTSEL TO US 50

47 Miles • Moderate

The tranquil valley of South Park

A beautiful stretch of road (with little or no shoulder), rolling hills, and distant peaks characterize this wide-open valley. Hartsel has fuel, a small mercantile store, and a liquor store.

Head south on CO 9. The road is gentle as you ride into some very majestic countryside. After some moderate rollers and amazing views, you'll start into a 3-mile climb, at the top of which is MM 36 and the unmarked summit of Currant Creek Pass (9,479'). The road continues on through MM 32, treating you to staggering vistas of Thirtynine Mile Mountain. The aspen groves are incredible as you head farther south, and the rollers get a bit larger, though they're still relatively moderate. About 25 miles from your starting point, you will see CR 59, the turnoff for Guffey (Route 38, p. 97), where you can meet your basic needs. As you continue on CO 9 and get closer to US 50, the vegetation becomes a bit scrublike. The terrain rolls along gently, and the views remain astounding. There are no services at the junction with US 50, but Parkdale is nearby and Cañon City, a large, full-service town, is 10 miles east on US 50 (Route 45, p. 106).

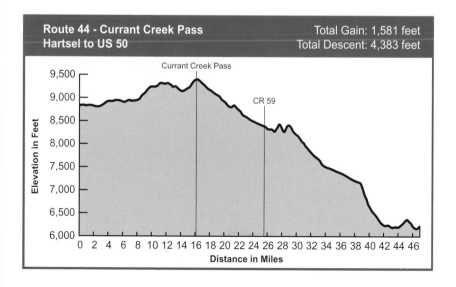

Route 44 - Currant Creek Pass
Hartsel to US 50

Total Gain: 1,581 feet
Total Descent: 4,383 feet

Route 45

ARKANSAS RIVER CANYON
US 50: SALIDA TO PUEBLO

90 Miles • Moderate

The stretch of US 50 between Salida and Pueblo is in excellent condition. It's a fairly flat, winding road with an occasional easy-to-moderate roller. The shoulder ranges from 8 feet wide to nonexistent, and there are a few sections of canyon that leave little room for cyclists. This highway can also be busy, with fast traffic, so be careful. You can access several high-quality rides from US 50; for an overview, see the map on p. 77.

Salida is a great town and an excellent hub for many outdoor activities. From here, US 50 follows the Arkansas River for most of the 56 miles to Cañon City, which also has full services, but there's nothing much in between except for the CO 69 junction at Texas Creek. From Cañon City to the western edge of Pueblo (US 50's junction with CO 45) is about 34 miles of easy terrain.

Parts of US 50 boast a nice, wide shoulder

The road is wide, has a huge shoulder, and gradually descends into town, which makes for some fast cycling. You'll find a couple of places for supplies along the way, and in Pueblo you'll find all you need.

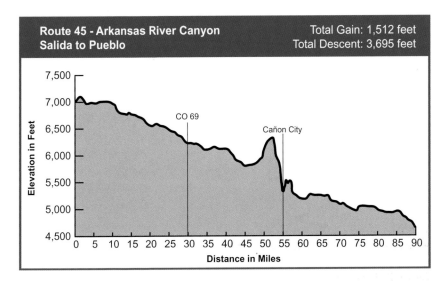

Route 45 - Arkansas River Canyon
Salida to Pueblo

Total Gain: 1,512 feet
Total Descent: 3,695 feet

CO 69

Cañon City

Elevation in Feet

Distance in Miles

Route 46

SALT CANYON/DEADMAN CANYON
CO 115: CAÑON CITY TO COLORADO SPRINGS

46 Miles • Moderate

This route heads through some incredible countryside on a road that is in great condition and has moderate traffic. Cañon City should have most of the supplies you'll need, and 9th Street, which runs north/south through town, is CO 115—the road you want. From Cañon City, CO 115 heads southeast for 9 miles on easy terrain to Florence, where you can find basic supplies and a junction with CO 67 (Route 47, opposite). Just east of Florence, CO 115 turns to the northeast and takes you across US 50 (Route 45, p. 106) to Penrose, 5 easy miles away, where you'll also find the basics.

As you head northeast out of Penrose, you'll pass MM 16 and enter rolling, forested mountains with prairie to the east. The rollers are moderate to large, and the shoulder is excellent. At about MM 22, you'll be riding through Salt Canyon. Watch for rumble strips as you pedal through this wide-open landscape of meadows, mountains, pine forests, and cottonwoods. As you approach Colorado Springs, you'll ride through Deadman Canyon—an excellent descent out of the mountains and into town.

The Springs has everything you need. It's home to the U.S. Olympic Training Center, where you can visit USA Cycling if you wish. There is a healthy cycling community in this town, so ask around at local bike shops for metro routes.

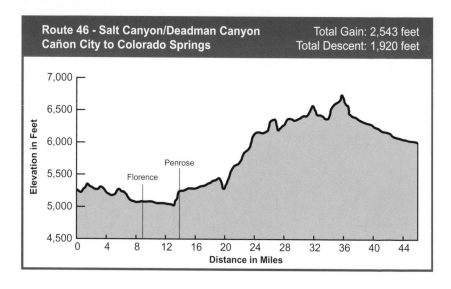

Route 47

FLORENCE TRAVERSE
CO 67: US 50 TO WETMORE

Approximately 14 Miles • Easy

Cruising over easy terrain just east of the Wet Mountains, this great little route accesses some excellent cycling to the south. About 6 miles east of Cañon City on US 50, you'll find a right turn (south) onto CO 67. This route is fairly flat and mostly straight. From US 50, it's 3.5 miles to Florence, a small town where you can find basic supplies. Just over 11 more miles of easy terrain leads to Wetmore, where you'll find a small general store and a junction with CO 96 (Route 48, p. 110).

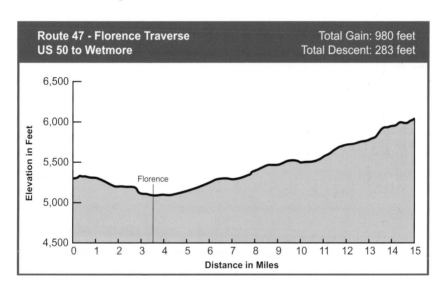

Route 48

FRONTIER PATHWAYS SCENIC BYWAY
CO 96: PUEBLO TO WESTCLIFFE

52 Miles • Moderate

Pueblo is a full-service town where all of your needs can be met. Head west out of Pueblo on CO 96. A gradual incline will take you out of town and past Pueblo Reservoir State Park on the right. (For a side trip, there is a cool little road that cuts through this park for about 12 miles and leads to US 50 to the north. It'll cost you a few bucks.) Continue on CO 96 and enjoy a straight road with a few gradual bends. As you head farther west, the mountain views are incredible, and the terrain will start rolling—this is an official scenic byway!

Once you enter the mountains, the landscape changes drastically to big hills and winding roads through lush forest. You won't find much shoulder here, but traffic should be light. It's 27 miles from Pueblo to Wetmore, with a tough but short climb just before you reach town. Wetmore is quaint and you can find munchies at its small general store.

Head west out of town on CO 96 as the road starts to wind its way up into the Wet Mountains. It's nearly 10 miles of moderate incline to CO 165 (Route 49, opposite) at McKenzie Junction. From here, CO 96 continues for nearly 17 miles, winding with a moderate climb to Hardscrabble Pass on its way to Westcliffe. The climbing fades into moderate, sweeping rollers once the Sangre de Cristo Range comes into view. Massive peaks fill the horizon as you gradually descend into Westcliffe—a neat little town with all of the basics.

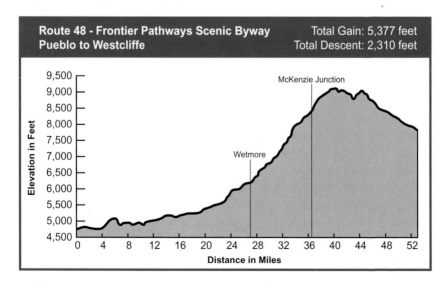

Route 48 - Frontier Pathways Scenic Byway
Pueblo to Westcliffe
Total Gain: 5,377 feet
Total Descent: 2,310 feet

The Sangre de Cristo Range emerges on the horizon as you descend into Westcliffe

Route 49

GREENHORN HIGHWAY
CO 165: CO 96 TO COLORADO CITY

Approximately 34 Miles • Moderate

You will find nothing but quality here. This piece of road is tremendous—rolling terrain with an alpine backdrop. As you head south from McKenzie Junction, CO 165 skirts along the eastern side of the Wet Mountains. The road starts with some very large rollers as you head up into the beautiful aspen- and pine-forested countryside. This road is cozy with no shoulder.

Just as you start to settle in, you'll pass MM 7, which brings you to the first of two sets of switchbacks. All of a sudden, this ride has a whole different feel to it! Another mile and you come to Bigelow Divide (9,350'), which is followed by a most excellent 2-mile descent. But it's not over yet. As you continue along the Greenhorn Highway, you will encounter more rollers. It doesn't get more peaceful than Lake Isabel (at the town of San Isabel, about MM 18), and there are more rewards to come as you ride over the endless rollers.

Switchbacks snake their way to Bigelow Divide

It seems like you could look into Kansas if you simply climbed one of the trees on the side of the road. (MM 20 is a good example—wow!) It's pretty cool to look from the mountains across the sweeping prairie as you roll your way through the Huckleberry Hills toward Rye, about 10 miles southeast of San Isabel. Once you have gone through the Huckleberry Hills, the rollers will mellow out and you will soon be in the little town of Rye. Rye has very limited services, but Colorado City, just a few miles east, has basic supplies.

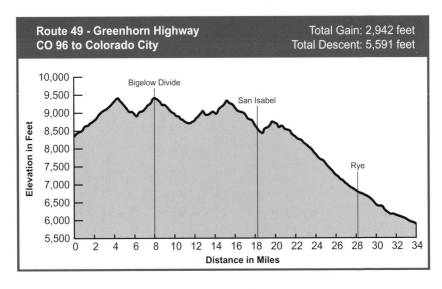

Route 50

NORTHERN AVENUE
CO 78: Pueblo to Beulah

Approximately 22 Miles • Moderate

This fantastic route into the foothills heads southwest from Pueblo, where you can take care of all your needs. CO 78 is in great shape with an excellent shoulder. This route is fairly straight and rolling, but you'll gain some altitude. The terrain gets more hilly as you approach the mountains, and you will encounter some rumble strips. At MM 14, CO 78 heads into the forest—beautiful, secluded,

The town of Beulah hides in a peaceful valley

and hardly any traffic. A nice short descent will bring you to a fork in the road. Turn right onto Grand Avenue and continue for almost 2 miles to Beulah—a magnificent spot with basic services. A left at the fork will take you through the forest for 3 more miles to the start of a 9-mile climb on good-quality dirt that leads to CO 165 (Route 49, p. 111).

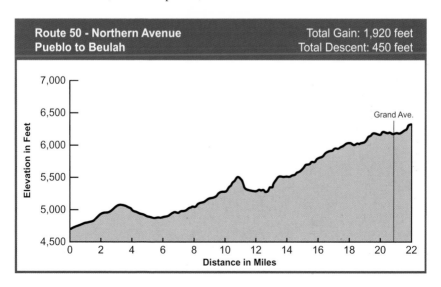

Route 50 - Northern Avenue
Pueblo to Beulah

Total Gain: 1,920 feet
Total Descent: 450 feet

Grand Ave.

Elevation in Feet

Distance in Miles

Route 51

WET MOUNTAIN VALLEY
CO 69: TEXAS CREEK TO WALSENBURG

Approximately 84 Miles • Moderate

A fairly straight, moderately rolling highway, CO 69 is top quality, and the view of the Wet Mountains and the Sangre de Cristos is tremendous. Moderate rollers rule the day as you head south from Texas Creek and CO 69's junction with US 50. There are no services in Texas Creek, but 24 miles south in Westcliffe you'll find basics including restaurants, coffee, and gas. Westcliffe and neighboring Silver Cliff are two very small towns with a nice, quaint, friendly feel—and locations to die for.

The Wet Mountain Valley offers unobstructed views of the Sangre de Cristo Mountains, and an incredibly peaceful feeling. From Westcliffe, it is about 33 miles to Gardner (no services) and 27 more miles from there to Walsenburg, where you'll be able to meet all of your basic needs and a little more.

Wet Mountain Valley

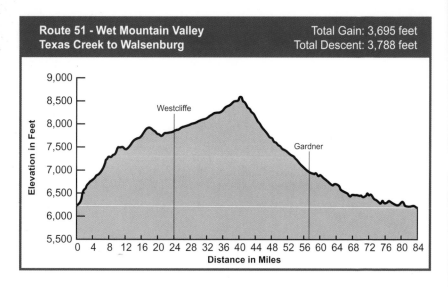

Route 51 - Wet Mountain Valley
Texas Creek to Walsenburg

Total Gain: 3,695 feet
Total Descent: 3,788 feet

REGION 3

INTERMOUNTAIN CENTRAL

The central mountains are the heart of the Colorado Rockies. You'll find many of the state's most notable ski towns here—places like Breckenridge, Keystone, Vail, Aspen, and Snowmass. There are other great towns in this area as well, and your needs will be easily met.

The routes described in this region consist of many high-mountain passes and the roads that connect them.

Loveland Pass, Route 54

There are some flats to be had, but you will have to look a little harder for them than you would in the rest of the state. Towering peaks are everywhere, and the routes that ascend them are usually long climbs at altitudes exceeding 10,000 or even 12,000 feet. Notable routes in this region include Loveland Pass (Route 54, p. 122), Frying Pan Road (Route 65, p. 138), the spectacular climb to the Maroon Bells (Route 67D, p. 145), and the glorious views from Independence Pass (Route 68, p. 148).

ROUTES

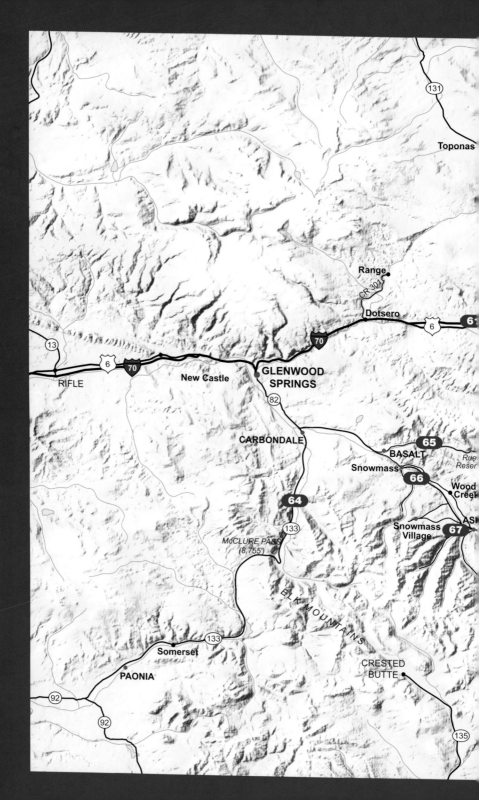

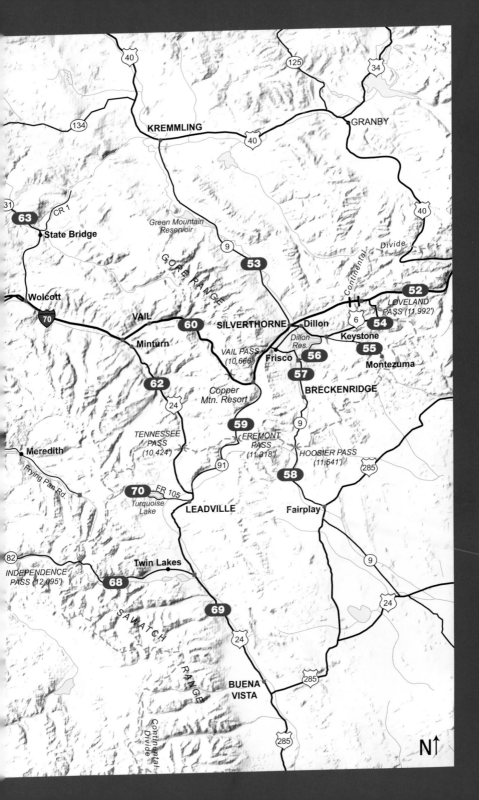

Route 52

I-70 CORRIDOR
IDAHO SPRINGS TO EISENHOWER TUNNEL

Approximately 24 Miles • Moderate

Many great routes junction with I-70, the main east/west artery through Colorado, and most of the time you can access these routes without riding on the interstate. Sometimes, however, you'll have no choice. It can be sketchy, but the shoulders are good—just watch out for debris. Also, many sections of I-70 are off-limits to cyclists, and when this is the case there is usually a frontage road or a bike path. For more information on sections of the interstate that are off-limits to cyclists, and on areas with paths, consult the Colorado Bicycling Map (see Appendix E, p. 303).

Idaho Springs has plenty of services including a bike shop. This town is also the starting point for a spectacular route up Mount Evans (Route 22, p. 65). Head west through Idaho Springs, and ride south under I-70 at Exit 239. The frontage road will weave back and forth under I-70 for about 12 miles to Georgetown, and you'll see the exit for US 40 and Berthoud Pass (Route 19, p. 60) along the way.

Get on I-70 in Georgetown (Exit 228) and ride west for about 2 miles to Silver Plume (Exit 226). Take the frontage road for about 5 miles to Exit 221, and get back on I-70 for another 5 miles or so, which will bring you to Exit 216. You must exit the interstate at this point, as you are not permitted to ride through the Eisenhower Tunnel. To continue west on a bicycle, you can ride over Loveland Pass on US 6 (Route 54, p. 122) to Dillon.

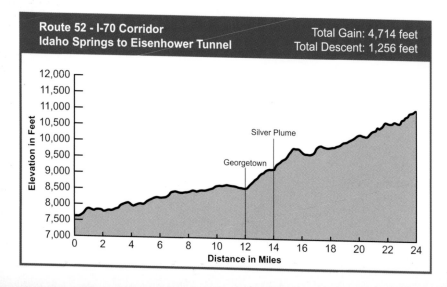

Route 53

BLUE RIVER VALLEY
CO 9: KREMMLING TO SILVERTHORNE

38 Miles • Moderate

In Kremmling you can find the basics and even espresso. The junction for CO 9 South is in the middle of town. You'll see the sign. Following CO 9, MM 137 is just south of town. At MM 126, Green Mountain Reservoir comes into view, and the Eagles Nest Wilderness and the jagged ridges of the Gore Range contribute to the spectacular scene. The terrain consists mostly of rolling, sage-covered hills, and the road is in great shape with a varying shoulder.

At MM 119, the road winds its way along Green Mountain Reservoir. The terrain continues to moderately roll, and it's about 19 miles from the reservoir to Silverthorne. Though I would not say that this route has any real climbing, Silverthorne is about 1,400 feet higher in elevation than Kremmling, and the rollers get noticeably larger along the way. In Silverthorne, Dillon, and Frisco, you will be able to meet all your needs and then some, as this area is a community hub.

The Gore Range and Green Mountain Reservoir make an awe-inspiring setting for this route.

BONUS: I didn't ride it, but there is a paved road around Green Mountain Reservoir. I'm sure it would be an excellent and very beautiful addition to the ride. Check it out and let me know.

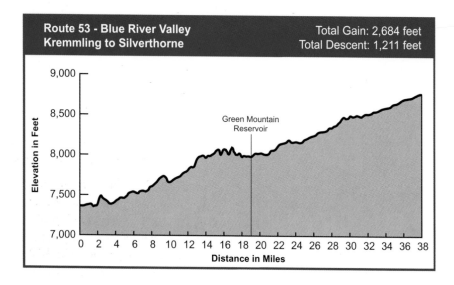

Route 53 - Blue River Valley Kremmling to Silverthorne — Total Gain: 2,684 feet — Total Descent: 1,211 feet

Route 54

LOVELAND PASS
US 6: Dillon to I-70

19 Miles • Difficult

This ride is an absolute classic! Surrounded by high peaks with a summit at nearly 12,000 feet, Loveland Pass (11,990') is a true mountain pass and one of Colorado's highest.

I prefer to start the route in Dillon (MM 210). US 6 runs through town and turns southeast as it heads to Keystone over mellow, gently climbing terrain. The road is excellent, with a great shoulder. You'll have tremendous views of Dillon Reservoir and the marina, and you'll pass Swan Mountain Road to the west (Route 56, p. 125), which leads to Breckenridge. US 6 starts to climb once it hits Keystone, and by MM 217, just after the turnoff for Montezuma Road (Route 55, p. 124), the pass starts in earnest.

Once you reach the Arapahoe Basin Ski Area (MM 221), the road is still good but has little or no shoulder. As you approach treeline, the altitude starts playing a bigger role—that is, you'll have less oxygen to breathe. At MM 224, you'll cruise through steep switchbacks surrounded by the Front Range peaks, and the

High peaks surround you on the challenging ride over Loveland Pass

pass will be in sight. There is a pullout at the top (MM 225), but there are no facilities—nothing but view here as you peer across the summits toward Vasquez Peak Wilderness and the mountains traversed by Berthoud Pass (Route 19, p. 60).

From Loveland Pass, you can see I-70 in the valley below. It's a staggering drop, and you're going to do it in 4 miles. The descent to the junction with I-70 is awesome! Fast! Sharp corners! Need I say more? The road does not waste any time getting to the interstate. If you're coming up this way, be ready to work hard. There is little or no shoulder here. US 6 junctions with I-70 (Route 52, p. 120) at Exit 216.

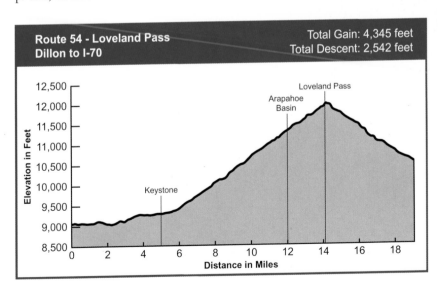

Route 55

MONTEZUMA ROAD
FR 5: KEYSTONE TO MONTEZUMA

5 Miles • Easy

Montezuma Road is a sweet little climb tucked away in the woods east of Keystone. At the east end of Keystone, US 6 bends left and starts up Loveland Pass. Take the exit for FR 5 (Montezuma Road) here. (You can also reach FR 5 by turning onto Gondola Road at Keystone and weaving your way through the resort area. This is a nicer ride than US 6.)

It's 5 miles to the town of Montezuma. This is my kind of road—narrow and a bit beaten-up, although plans to repave it are in the works. Go see for yourself! FR 5 winds along the Snake River, gently gaining altitude. The last mile or so is a fairly steep climb. This is an excellent road for added mileage or moderate interval training.

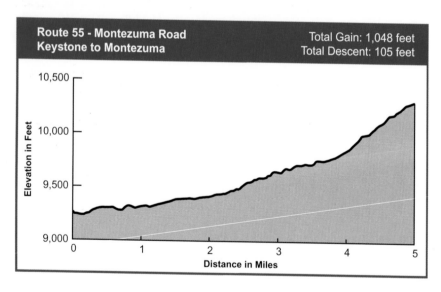

Route 56

SWAN MOUNTAIN ROAD
DILLON TO CO 9

9 Miles • Moderate

This is an excellent road that winds along the east side of Dillon Reservoir. If you're planning to ride between Dillon and Breckenridge, I highly recommend this route.

From Dillon, take US 6 east toward Keystone. Look for a right turn (at a stoplight) onto Swan Mountain Road; this is your route. You'll cross a beautiful little inlet on Dillon Reservoir, and you'll start climbing at MM 4. The views

A beautiful corridor between Dillon and Breckenridge, Swan Mountain Road skirts Dillon Reservoir

are spectacular! The climb undulates a bit, and then steepens with little or no shoulder as you head into the trees. At about MM 2, you'll see a sign for Sapphire Point Overlook where the climb tops out. The descent is very fast with some fairly tight curves. Watch for traffic. Views of the reservoir open up again as you come out of the trees on your way down. You can hook up with CO 9 (Route 57, p. 126) at the bottom of the descent or ride back the way you came.

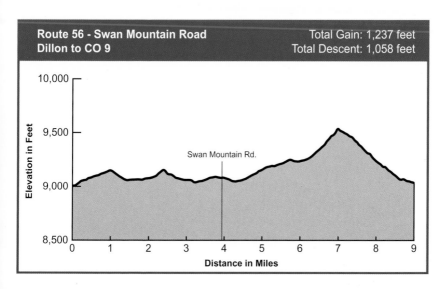

| Route 56 - Swan Mountain Road Dillon to CO 9 | Total Gain: 1,237 feet Total Descent: 1,058 feet |

Route 57

DILLON RESERVOIR
CO 9: DILLON TO BRECKENRIDGE

Approximately 16 Miles • Easy

The area between Dillon and Frisco can be very busy. However, you will love this spectacular ride around Dillon Reservoir—a huge mountain lake surrounded by peaks.

US 6 is the main drag through Dillon, and CO 9 junctions with it just west of town. You'll see the junction as you ride out of Dillon; just head toward the dam (Dam Road). You cannot, however, ride your bicycle across the dam on Dam Road. You *must* use the bike path that follows the road for this mile-long stretch. After the dam, you can hop back on CO 9.

Cyclists use a bike path to cross Dillon Dam

From here, CO 9 cruises along the shores of Dillon Reservoir into Frisco, where you can get most of the things you'll need. It is about 6 miles from Dillon to Frisco, and then it's 10 more miles to Breckenridge on a flat, wide road with a good shoulder but lots of traffic. For more on Breckenridge, see Hoosier Pass (Route 58, p. 128).

NOTE: There is an excellent bike-path system in this area that connects the towns of Keystone, Dillon, Frisco, Breckenridge, and Vail. If you are interested in the paths, pick up a free local activities guide. Just ask around in any of these communities, or try the nearest sporting goods store.

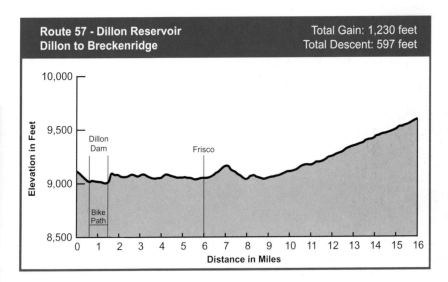

Route 58

HOOSIER PASS
CO 9: BRECKENRIDGE TO FAIRPLAY

22 Miles • Difficult

Breckenridge is a mountain-resort mecca. As with many resorts in the region, this large town has world-class skiing and a host of summer activities for all interests. "Breck" is by far the largest and most diverse town in Summit County, with a pleasant, Euro-resort feel. Watch your pocketbook, however, as it may feel a bit lighter after your stay.

Main Street in Breckenridge is CO 9; this is the road you want. Head south out of town (MM 86) on good pavement with a wide shoulder. (This shoulder will disappear at the base of the climb.)

Hoosier Pass is a great ride. There are a few somewhat steep sections, but the climb is only about 4 miles long, and the views are fantastic. The Tenmile and Mosquito Ranges accompany you from the west as you cruise through a beautiful alpine valley south of town. You'll pass the town of Blue River (no services) and Goose Pasture Tarn. Here the crowds of Breck are but a memory.

If you look ahead as you pass MM 82, you'll see where Hoosier Pass cuts through the hills. A sign at MM 81 reads, "Hoosier Pass Summit 4 Miles." The work begins at MM 80 with the first switchback—a steep little sucker. Up, up, up you go. The climb is a bit steep here and there, but by MM 76 you'll be on top.

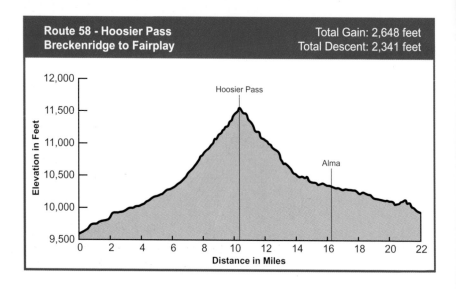

Route 58 - Hoosier Pass
Breckenridge to Fairplay
Total Gain: 2,648 feet
Total Descent: 2,341 feet

Tremendous views of the Mosquito Range and Montgomery Reservoir abound at the Hoosier Pass summit (11,541'). As you cross the Continental Divide, you'll catch sweeping views south into Fairplay. The descent is on a very fast, straight, wide-open road that will put a smile on your face if you're anything like I am. MM 73 is

Hoosier Pass is one of Colorado's highest pass-ride summits

at the bottom, and mellow, rolling terrain will lead you in a few miles into Alma. Alma is tiny but boasts a natural food market and espresso shop.

It's 6 more miles to Fairplay and the junction with US 285, where you'll find the basics and forever-views into the valley known as South Park.

For more on routes in the Fairplay area, see the Front Range South section.

Route 59

FREMONT PASS
CO 91: LEADVILLE TO COPPER MOUNTAIN

22 Miles • Moderate

There are a number of passes in this guide that I've called "unique," and a number that I've dubbed "excellent." Well, this ride is both unique *and* excellent. The massive Climax Mine makes Fremont Pass especially unusual. The mine is a huge operation that is eating away at the surrounding peaks, and the immensity of the facility is mind-boggling. North of Leadville just outside of town, you'll come to a fork in the highway. A left takes you to Vail over Tennessee Pass on US 24 (Route 62, p. 133), and a right takes you down to Copper Mountain on CO 91, the road for this route.

CO 91 is an excellent road with a large shoulder. It's busier than US 24 to Vail, but there's plenty of room. As you head out of Leadville, the road is wide open, fairly straight, and downhill. Not for long, though. By MM 6, you'll be

working your way up into the mountains on moderate uphill grades. Just before MM 8, a sign reads, "Fremont Pass Summit 4 miles." Around MM 9, the road levels out for just a bit. You will see the first big curve and your climb ahead at MM 10. The Climax Mine looms ominously in the background. At MM 11, you'll be near the top of Fremont Pass (11,318'). There are no services here.

As you begin your descent, you'll start into some large, rolling terrain with bizarre views of the Climax Mine's giant tailing ponds. The water runoff from the mining process was separated from the tailings into these massive ponds, and what's left looks like grand-

The Fremont Pass ride takes you by the massive Climax Mine

scale, psychedelic sand paintings.

After the tailing ponds, the descent becomes more sustained and fast with plenty of shoulder. At MM 21, you'll see the junction with I-70 just down the valley. To your left is Copper Mountain, which has great skiing and summer facilities. You'll find a service station on your right.

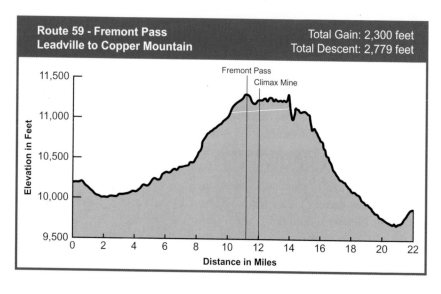

Route 60

VAIL PASS
VAIL PASS BIKEWAY: COPPER MOUNTAIN TO VAIL

20 Miles • Moderate

Vail Pass is a solid climb on a great road. Unfortunately, bicycles are not allowed on I-70 from Copper Mountain to Vail. However, an excellent bike path services this stretch and connects with paths between Keystone, Dillon, Frisco, and Breckenridge. (Inquire locally for a map of this bike-path system or contact the Summit County Chamber of Commerce at 800-530-3099 or www.summitchamber.org.)

Park at Copper Mountain Resort and follow the bikeway as it gains almost 1,000 feet in 6 miles. Expect some steep grades and switchbacks on this path. There is a rest area at the top of the pass, and the 14-mile descent into Vail is absolutely spectacular.

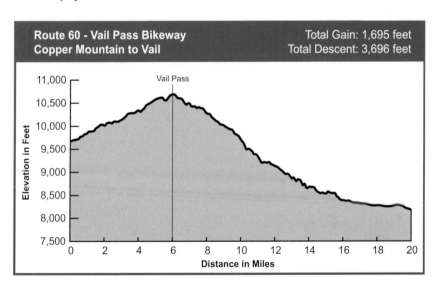

Route 60 - Vail Pass Bikeway
Copper Mountain to Vail

Total Gain: 1,695 feet
Total Descent: 3,696 feet

Route 61

EAGLE RIVER VALLEY
I-70/US 6: Vail to Glenwood Springs

61 Miles • Moderate

Of the I-70 routes covered in this guide, this one is probably the best for cycling because of the excellent frontage on US 6 (alongside I-70). From Vail, you can ride 3 miles on US 6 to West Vail and get back on I-70 at Exit 173. After a couple of miles of fast road with a huge shoulder, you'll reach Exit 171. Here you can get on US 24 and go south over Tennessee Pass (Route 62, p. 133), or you can head west on US 6—a very nice road and I-70's predecessor as the state's main east-west mountain route.

If it feels like you're leaving the mountains, you're correct. The landscape begins to change from an alpine environment to arid upland desert as you lose altitude and head west toward Grand Junction. It's 16 miles of moderate rollers to Wolcott on US 6 or I-70, whichever you choose. I prefer US 6—less road room, but also far less traffic. At Wolcott, you'll find the junction with CO 131 to Toponas (Route 63, p. 135). From here, ride 10 miles along the Eagle River through Red Canyon—not a canyon per se, but gorgeous nonetheless—on your way to the town of Eagle. Eagle has basic services, and it's about 7 miles from here to Gypsum (Exit 140).

It's another 7 miles or so on I-70/US 6 (they merge) to Dotsero. Exit 133 here takes you right (north) onto Colorado River Road (CR 301), a great side

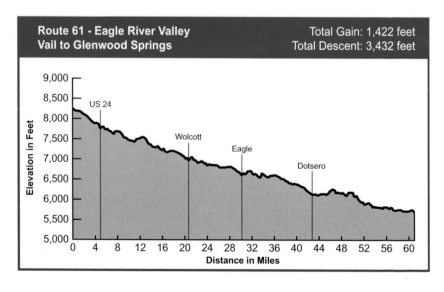

route. Anytime you go along the Colorado River, you're in for a beautiful ride. The road winds its way along the river for about 13 miles to the town of Range (no services), where the pavement ends.

Beyond Dotsero, I-70/US 6 heads through Glenwood Canyon. This canyon is staggeringly beautiful! It's very narrow and surrounded by rock walls several hundred feet high. Bikes are not allowed in Glenwood Canyon—you'd be crazy to attempt it anyway, as there is no room for a bike on this road. Fortunately, a nice bike path will take you from Dotsero to Glenwood Springs, and it is a spectacular, 17-mile ride over easy grade.

The drive is amazing as well. I-70 is divided and stacked on top of itself in places—truly an engineering marvel. I remember when I was a kid and this stretch of road was under construction—what a mess! Now it's a joy to travel.

Route 62

TENNESSEE PASS
US 24: I-70 TO LEADVILLE

32 Miles • Difficult

Here's another classic Colorado ride! The junction with US 24 and I-70/US 6 is at Exit 171 off I-70. (You'll see MM 143.) The town of Minturn is about 2 miles down the road. Minturn is very small and very cool. It seems to be out of the reach of Vail's tourist culture. The Cougar Ridge Cafe is a great little espresso shop/restaurant where you'll find some mighty friendly folks.

From Minturn, it's 30 miles of good road, with little or no shoulder, to Leadville. But before you can reach the pass and continue to Leadville, you'll have another hill to climb. As you head south out of Minturn, at about MM 148 a road sign will read

"Going the extra mile" to read a mile marker sign

"Battle Mountain Summit 4 miles." (You won't actually summit the 11,507-foot Battle Mountain.) After you cross the Eagle River, the climb becomes moderately steep and fairly sustained to the road's first high point.

A fast, 2-mile descent takes you to the base of the south side of Battle Mountain. It's 21 miles to Leadville from here with more climbing ahead. You'll cross a beautiful bridge as you pass the turnoff to Red Cliff (basic services).

At MM 161, you will experience moderate, consistent climbing and pass a sign that reads, "Tennessee Pass 5 Miles." On your left, you'll pass Camp Hale, a training facility designed to train the Army's 10th Mountain Division for winter battle in the Alps during World War II. The summit of Tennessee Pass (10,424') is at MM 166. You will also see a memorial to the 10th Mountain Division here.

It's not much of a descent into Leadville, as the elevation of Leadville is 10,159 feet (making it the highest incorporated town in the United States). However, you'll find nice, moderate downhill road with some small rollers along the way. Leadville offers your basics and two decent coffeehouses. Surrounded by high peaks that line the horizon, including Mount Elbert (14,433'), the state's highest peak, Leadville feels like it's miles from anywhere. Other routes out of Leadville include Fremont Pass (Route 59, p. 129), Independence Pass (Route 68, p. 148), and US 24: Leadville to Buena Vista (Route 69, p. 151), as well as a great loop around Turquoise Lake (Route 70, p. 152).

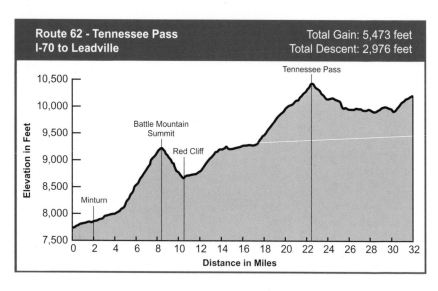

STATE BRIDGE
CO 131: WOLCOTT TO TOPONAS

34 Miles • Moderate

Tucked away in a beautiful valley with incredible views south across the Eagle Valley to the northern peaks of the Sawatch Range and Red Table Mountain, this is a tremendous piece of road. There's not a lot of room, though, and traffic can be fast during commuting hours. However, if you ride it during low-traffic hours (weekdays and midday), and especially during the off-season (spring and fall), you might have this road to yourself.

The route begins in Wolcott at CO 131's junction with I-70 and US 6. Nine miles of sustained climbing greet you at the start of this ride; it's fairly moderate but there's no warm-up. The climb gently winds its way north through rolling mountains. Around MM 9, you'll top out and start into a 5-mile descent to the Colorado River and the town of State Bridge, where you'll find the basics.

At State Bridge, you can turn right (northeast) on Trough Road (CR 1), for a side route over roughly 10 miles of pavement. Continuing on CO 131, it's 4 miles of huge rollers to McCoy (no services) and the start of another 9 miles of sustained, moderate climbing.

You'll top out at MM 29, and then it's 4 miles on moderate, rolling terrain to the town of Toponas at MM 33. (Note the port-a-potty at MM 31. Now, I've seen a lot of bathroom facilities on pass summits and at campgrounds, but this is just odd. I'm sure it meets needs, but it looks very random. I had to laugh. Anyway, restroom at MM 31.) For the continuation of CO 131, see Route 130 (p. 276).

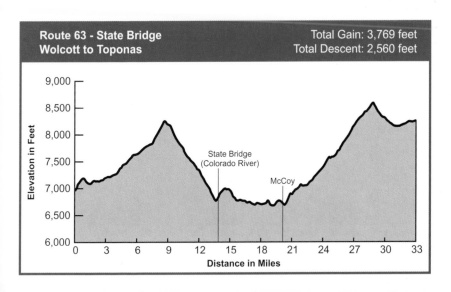

Route 63 - State Bridge
Wolcott to Toponas

Total Gain: 3,769 feet
Total Descent: 2,560 feet

State Bridge (Colorado River)

McCoy

Route 64

McCLURE PASS
CO 133: PAONIA TO CARBONDALE

59 Miles • Moderate

The Paonia area is full of rolling, sage-covered hills and valleys filled with farm fields. You can cover your basic needs in this area, as well as find bike stuff at the Paonia Peddler downtown. There is a plethora of local fruit to be found at nearby orchards as the summer progresses. Many orchards sell right from their driveways, and the produce is always cheap and delicious. The ride up CO 133 to McClure Pass is magnificent as you make your way toward The Raggeds.

From Paonia, it's 9 miles to Somerset. The road is decent with a good shoulder, but watch for rumble strips. As you ride through Somerset, you'll see a prime example of a small town that has completely integrated with the local industry—mining. Somerset is very quaint, but has no services except for the Portal Bar and Grill.

At MM 24, a sign indicates that it's 32 miles to Redstone and 49 miles to Carbondale. The slightly rolling terrain continues with little or no shoulder for the next 7 miles to Paonia Reservoir. You will cross railroad tracks in a couple of spots, and all the way from Paonia the road is gently climbing. As you come around a left-hand bend, you'll encounter a stunning view of the reservoir below and The Raggeds above the valley. By MM 27, you'll be climbing moderately beside the long, narrow lake.

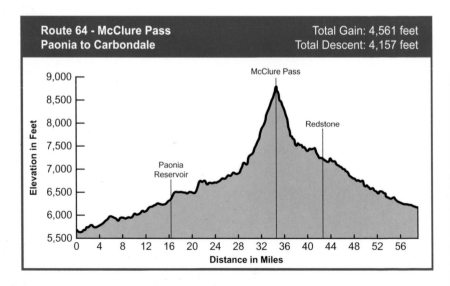

Route 64 - McClure Pass
Paonia to Carbondale
Total Gain: 4,561 feet
Total Descent: 4,157 feet

At MM 34, the vegetation starts changing to an alpine environment as the road climbs, and by MM 38 the climbing becomes more sustained. The aspen groves and wildflowers will astound you in this beautiful alpine valley.

You will reach the summit of McClure Pass (8,755') at MM 43, where you'll find a small parking lot and not much else. The descent begins right away and is very fast and abrupt. A right-hand bend in the road reveals an incredible scene—the Elk Mountains above and the Crystal River Valley below. The road is wide open, with one big, left-hand corner at the bottom near MM 46. Expect grades of more than 8 percent on this descent.

The views are amazing as you ride along the Crystal River, with very steep mountains rising thousands of feet on either side of the lush valley floor.

You will reach the fantastic town of Carbondale (6,181') at MM 67. Small and quiet, Carbondale offers a very nice coffeehouse on Main Street, and next door you'll find a great little bike shop. In an area heavily influenced by Aspen and its glitter, Carbondale is determined to stay "real." After living in Aspen for several years, I find Carbondale's low-key atmosphere very comforting. There are many quality routes in this area.

Looking north from McClure Pass

Route 65

FRYING PAN ROAD
FR 105/FR 505: BASALT TO END OF PAVEMENT

34 Miles • Difficult

It's hard to rate rides in the Aspen area. They're all high quality, with varied terrain and spectacular scenery. Frying Pan Road is the second longest route (the first is Independence Pass, Route 68, p. 148) and offers the most diverse terrain. It's way off the beaten path, so if you want to avoid the crowds of Aspen or Glenwood Springs then this one's for you. In Basalt, you'll be able to replenish yourself, and Ajax Bike and Sport can take care of your bicycle.

Head through Basalt on Midland Avenue, and veer left (east) onto Frying Pan Road (look for the sign). By MM 3, you'll be cruising on a very mellow, winding road that ever-so-slowly gains altitude, meandering alongside the Gold Medal fly-fishing waters of the Fryingpan River. Sandstone buttresses line the steep slopes of this secluded, gorgeous river valley.

At MM 12, about a mile of solid, moderate climbing leads you to the dam and a fine view of Ruedi Reservoir, a long lake in a mountain setting. By MM 17, you'll be at the top of this 5-mile climb, and the views just don't stop! After 4 miles or so of fast, winding descent, you will be in Meredith, which has a bar that might be open. Past Meredith, the road rolls for 5 more miles to the junction with FR 505. Take this road, which climbs gently for another 5 miles to the dirt. The road is narrow here, but very peaceful—definitely in the boonies.

NOTE: Mile markers become scarce later in this route. MM 29, several miles before the dirt, is the last one I saw.

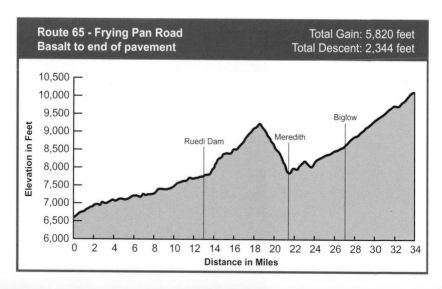

Route 65 - Frying Pan Road
Basalt to end of pavement
Total Gain: 5,820 feet
Total Descent: 2,344 feet

ROARING FORK VALLEY

Lying between Glenwood Springs and Aspen, CO 82 accesses many high-quality routes. The Roaring Fork Valley is incredibly beautiful, and every road provides excellent cycling conditions and phenomenal views. Every road, that is, except CO 82 itself. While the views on "Killer 82" are amazing, the road has been under construction forever and has heavy, high-speed traffic. At the time of this printing, there were some cycling-access restrictions on CO 82, so ask around or contact the Colorado Department of Transportation (303-757-9982) before riding. CDOT even has a website, www.sh82.com, where cyclists and other users of CO 82 can find out which detours are in place for both sections of the highway and the frontage Lower River Road. Aspen, Carbondale, Basalt, and Glenwood Springs all have bike shops that can inform you of current restrictions. Of course, in time, the roadwork will be done and all will be well in the valley.

While the towns in the Roaring Fork Valley are in fairly close proximity to one another, they couldn't be more different in character. Glenwood Springs is a fairly large town located right on I-70. It has lots of amenities and a friendly, home-town feel that welcomes visitors. Carbondale and Basalt are small and quiet, and both can provide the basics and a bit more. Routes 66A–B originate at "old" Snowmass, a little town just up the valley from Basalt.

Routes 67A–E center around the famous resort towns of Snowmass Village and Aspen. Snowmass Village is situated within the ski resort. The valley is narrow and somewhat steep, and ski lifts run right through the village. There are even skier bridges over the roadways, taking "ski-in, ski-out" to an optimum level of convenience. The scenery is incredible as the Elk Mountains rise right out of this little town.

The world-class resort town of Aspen is always bustling, and when it comes to activities and events as well as dining and accommodations, the sky is the limit. Having called Aspen home for several years, I must say it's a very exciting town and unlike any other in Colorado. While there isn't a lot of mileage to be had in the Aspen/Snowmass area, it is all top quality and makes for some great cycling.

Roaring Fork Valley (Routes 66A–B and 67A–E)

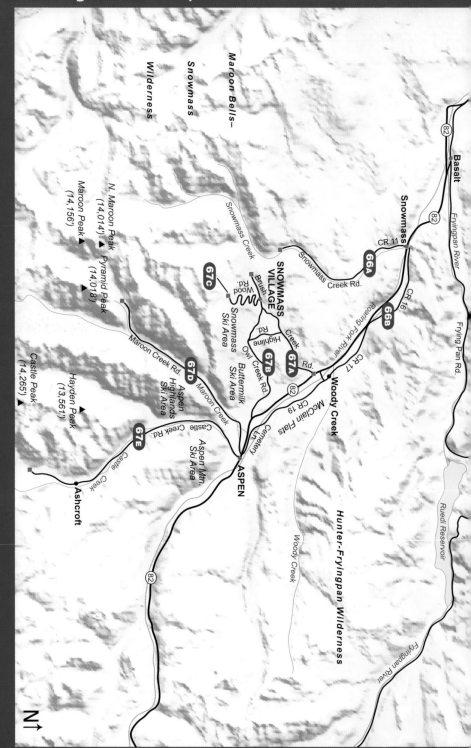

Snowmass Bells–
Wilderness

Maroon Bells

Basalt

82

Snowmass

CR 11

66A

Snowmass Creek

Snowmass Creek Rd.

CR 16

66B

N. Maroon Peak
(14,014')

Maroon Peak
(14,156')

Pyramid Peak
(14,018')

67C

Wood Rd.

Brush

SNOWMASS
VILLAGE

Roaring Fork River

Snowmass
Ski Area

Highline Rd.

Owl Creek Rd.

67B

67A

Creek

Rd.

CR 17

Woody Creek

Fryingpan River

Frying Pan Rd.

Maroon Creek Rd.

Buttermilk
Ski Area

82

McClain Flats

CR 19

Ruedi Reservoir

Castle Peak
(14,265')

Hayden Peak
(13,561')

67D

Aspen
Highlands
Ski Area

Maroon Creek

Cemetery

Hunter-Fryingpan Wilderness

67E

Castle Creek Rd.

Aspen Mtn.
Ski Area

ASPEN

Castle Creek

Ashcroft

82

Woody Creek

Fryingpan River

N→

Route 66A

SNOWMASS CREEK ROAD
CR 11: SNOWMASS TO END OF PAVEMENT

Approximately 8 Miles • Easy

Four miles south of Basalt on CO 82, you will find the old town of Snowmass, basic supplies, and a junction with Snowmass Creek Road (CR 11). Turn right (south). The route gently winds and rolls through some beautiful countryside along Snowmass Creek with views of the Elk Mountains to the south. Snowmass Creek Road is in good shape and has no shoulder, but traffic is very light.

A bucolic setting defines this ride along Snowmass Creek

For another nearby route, check out Woody Creek Backroads (Route 66B, below).

Route 66B

WOODY CREEK BACKROADS
CR 16/CR 17/CEMETERY LANE: SNOWMASS TO ASPEN

Approximately 15 Miles • Easy

This great route is an excellent way to get from the old town of Snowmass to Aspen while avoiding CO 82. Snowmass is 4 miles south of Basalt, has basic supplies, and is the junction of CO 82, CR 16, and CR 11 (Route 66A, above). If you're coming from Basalt, turn left (north) onto CR 16 (Lower River Road). You'll immediately cross a very cool bridge over the Roaring Fork River and start to head southeast toward Woody Creek. This road gently rolls and winds its way along the river through some absolutely gorgeous scenery.

NOTE: As of this printing, a 5-mile stretch of Lower River Road was closed for construction. Detour via the multi-use trail along the railroad right-of-way, accessible either from Basalt or Snowmass. Visit www.sh82.com for details.

About 5 miles south of Snowmass, you'll come to a three-way intersection; a right turn (west) here would take you across the river to CO 82. Continue past the intersection and the road number will change to CR 17. A few more miles, and you'll pass Woody Creek Tavern (on the right) where you can get whatever you prefer to drink. About a half mile down the road, you will find another three-way intersection with access to CO 82. Turning right (west) at this intersection is a great way to hook up with Brush Creek Road (Route 67A, below). Continue on CR 17 past this intersection, and you'll soon be climbing a short, fairly steep hill barely a mile in length. The road number will change to CR 19 (McClain Flats Road), and you'll find yourself on McClain Flats—the scene will blow your mind. The Elk Mountains are spread out before your eyes, and all four of the Aspen/Snowmass ski mountains loom in view. In a few more miles, you'll head down a short, steep hill and cross the Roaring Fork River, then head up a short, steep hill to where the road flattens out and the name changes again; now it's Cemetery Lane. Another mile or so, and you'll be at a junction with CO 82 where a left turn (east) will take you into town, less than a mile away.

Route 67A

BRUSH CREEK ROAD
CR 10: CO 82 TO END OF ROAD

6 Miles • Moderate

Brush Creek Road is in excellent shape, with no shoulder to speak of. Traffic can be a bit busy at times, since Snowmass Village is a popular resort, and this is the main road into the village. Brush Creek Road junctions with CO 82 about 5 miles north of Aspen; there is a great back way to get to this junction from Woody Creek (Route 66B, p. 141). From CO 82, Brush Creek Road starts climbing. About 3 miles up the road, you'll come to a three-way intersection with Highline Road, which connects to Owl Creek Road (Route 67B, opposite). To continue on Brush Creek Road, turn right (west) at the intersection and ride by the Snowmass Club Golf Course (on your left). The road will gradually get steeper as you go, but it never gets too bad. You'll climb all the way to the end of the road and pass through Snowmass Village, where you can find basic supplies and a bit more.

Route 67B

OWL CREEK ROAD
CR 12: BRUSH CREEK ROAD TO ASPEN

8 Miles • Moderate

Owl Creek Road is a fun route that involves a mile or so of crater-riddled dirt. It's my favorite way from Snowmass Village back to Aspen. There are two ways to get to Owl Creek Road from Snowmass Village, either from Brush Creek Road (Route 67A, opposite) or from Highline Road via Brush Creek Road. This route starts at the intersection of Owl Creek Road and Brush Creek Road east of town and just before the golf course. Turn left (east) onto Owl Creek Road and ride past the fire station. The road is in great shape but has no shoulder. Traffic isn't bad, however, as this is not the main route through the village.

Wind your way on a fast descent for about a mile to a three-way intersection with Highline Road. A left (north) here will take you about a mile downhill to Brush Creek Road. To continue on Owl Creek Road, veer right through this intersection and start climbing up a moderately steep grade for about a mile. At the top, the pavement will end, and you'll fly down a modest descent on a straight dirt road with lots of potholes. Watch out! After the pavement starts again, the descent will continue and get a bit steeper as you wind your way down to the Roaring Fork Valley roughly a mile away. You'll cruise flats for about a mile to CO 82, where you will be just a few miles from Aspen. A right turn (south) onto CO 82 will bring you into town.

NOTE: At the time of this printing, CO 82 between Owl Creek Road and Aspen was off-limits to cyclists. However, a multi-use bike path has been established on the east side of CO 82. Go to www.sh82.com for details.

Route 67c

WOOD ROAD
Brush Creek Road to end of road

3 Miles • Difficult

You shouldn't try this sufferfest unless you're prepared. About 4.5 miles up Brush Creek Road (Route 67A, p. 142) from CO 82, you will see a sign pointing to the Village Center. This can be a confusing intersection, so keep your eyes open. Turn left (south) at the Village Center. Immediately after you turn, you'll see a sign for Wood Road. Veer left (east) onto Wood Road and start climbing. The road gets very steep and there are eight switchbacks along the way; it's a beautiful setting and well worth the effort. The descent is a bomb, but be wary of side traffic, as there are many homes along the way.

Route 67d

MAROON CREEK ROAD
FR 125: Aspen to end of road
Fee required: $5/bike, $15/vehicle
Closed to vehicle traffic between 8:30 a.m. and 5 p.m.
Closed in winter

11 Miles • Moderate

Beginning at an elevation of 7,900 feet, this route is sublime—period! If you come to Aspen, you must ride this road. It's only about 11 miles and well worth the $5 fee to pass the tollgate. "Tollgate? What the heck?" Yes, you must pay for this one. I was appalled when I saw this new development, but the famous Maroon Bells area gets overrun every year, and there's just not much room in this narrow valley. If left to the "human condition," this road would be a traffic jam every day. Your ticket is good for five days. The road is closed to vehicular traffic between 8:30 a.m. and 5 p.m. So, except for shuttle buses and the occasional auto, you'll have it to yourself. If that doesn't make the five bucks worth it, just wait till you get to the top!

At the western edge of Aspen is the intersection of CO 82, Castle Creek Road, and Maroon Creek Road (the road you want). This intersection has a

Maroon Creek Road closes to vehicular traffic during the day,
so get ready to have a gorgeous ride almost to yourself

I remember an Aspen Velo Club race here. It was two laps on this climb. At the suggestion of a friend, I launched off the front of the pack at the bottom of the first climb. This was my favorite road for interval training at the time—short, high-intensity efforts punctuated with rest—and I knew every inch. So did the others, of course.

By the top I was a couple of minutes off the front. When I passed the pack going the other way, they had a good mile to go to the top and would hopefully never catch up to me. I was tired but felt I had it in me. When I got to the turnaround at the bottom, I almost fell off my bike when I found Tom Hayles, who was then the Colorado Category II state champ, right behind me. That's when fear set in. I was riding out of my league and he was about to school me.

He gained the front at the start of the second climb and put it in the big chain ring. My jaw dropped, but this was no time to show my hand. I switched to my big chain ring and followed. I put my head down and hammered until I could feel no more, and then the real work started. Absolutely delirious, I sucked his wheels for all it was worth. In the end, he barely squeezed 100 feet out in front of me.

My second place that day put me nearly 7 minutes ahead of the entire pack and won me a lot of respect. Tom, if you happen to read this, I must thank you for such suffering. It did a lot for me as a young rider.

roundabout, so pick your road as you ride through and head on up toward Aspen High School. It's a quick, moderate climb of about a half mile. You'll ride by Aspen Highlands ski resort and hit a short, steep descent to T-Lazy-7 Ranch, where you'll start into moderate climbing for a couple of miles to the tollgate. Here the fun begins, and you can see the valley closing in around you. There's just enough room for the road and Maroon Creek to get through as you start up this immaculate pavement with no shoulder.

By now you have surely seen the massive, jagged peak up ahead. This is Pyramid Peak (14,018'), and you will be climbing to its base. The climbing undulates a bit as you go but remains moderate; you can really fly up this road.

Toward the top, you'll get a view of monumental proportions. (When you hit the parking lot, you will also see why the traffic must be controlled.) The Maroon Bells—two fourteeners—rise up from the valley floor like two impenetrable walls. The descent is tremendous and fast, fast, fast. Wide open with no traffic, it only takes a few minutes. And you'll be grinning from ear to ear at the finish.

Route 67E

CASTLE CREEK ROAD
FR 102: ASPEN TO END OF PAVEMENT

12 Miles • Moderate

There are very few loop routes in the Aspen area. Out-and-back routes are standard here, and this one is no exception. It's just another ride up an incredibly beautiful, narrow river valley surrounded by alpine peaks. Life can be soooo boring, can't it?

Head west out of Aspen on CO 82 (the main drag), and just as you are leaving town you'll come to a roundabout intersection. As you go around the intersection, pick the turn for Castle Creek Road.

The terrain gently rolls as you start up this great, but narrow, road with no shoulder (7,900'). By MM 1 a broad peak with a pointed summit looms ahead. That's Hayden Peak (13,561'), and you'll be riding past it on your right toward the end of this pavement.

Mile markers on this road are sporadic at best, and the road winds its way up a series of moderate rollers as it gains elevation. This valley is narrow and deep with just enough room for the road and Castle Creek. The mountains on either side rise abruptly, with impressive ridgelines that seem to scrape the sky. At MM 10, a view opens up to the south and you will begin to see your destination. At MM 11, you'll reach the Ashcroft Ski Touring center. The road rolls a bit through here as it continues to climb gently, and it ends soon after you reach MM 12. (There is a short piece of pavement ahead that is closed to motorists, but it's hardly a half mile long.)

The descent back to Aspen on this road is very fast with a few moderate rollers you'll have to work for. Some of the corners you rode through on your way up are a bit sharp on the way down, so be careful. There is no room here for mistakes.

Route 68

INDEPENDENCE PASS
CO 82: ASPEN TO US 24

44 Miles • Difficult

Independence Pass is one of the monster climbs in Colorado. It ascends from roughly 8,000 feet to an elevation of more than 12,000 feet in just 17 miles. This route is a must if you plan to be in the area. During the years I lived in Aspen, I think I must have ridden this pass some 50 or 60 times. I never lost the love for it. If you ride Independence Pass, remember that it climbs well above treeline, requiring some extra precautions. (See pp. 16–19 for some thoughts on mountain cycling and gear.)

Head east out of town on CO 82 (Main Street), which makes a couple of 90-degree turns as it winds through town. Follow the signs. As you leave town, the road gently rolls along for a couple of miles on good pavement with no shoulder. At MM 45, you'll reach Difficult Campground. Here the climbing starts. It's a bit steep for the first couple of miles as you ride along the Roaring Fork River toward the Collegiate Peaks Wilderness. Just before MM 47, there's a short break in the climb as you approach the gate.

The highway department closes this road at the gate in winter, but you can ride around the gate to the snowline in spring and fall. These are enjoyable times to visit because there is no traffic, but watch for debris in the road. In the spring, giant snowblowers cut through from both sides (usually the first part of June) and the result is vertical walls of snow several feet high on either side of the

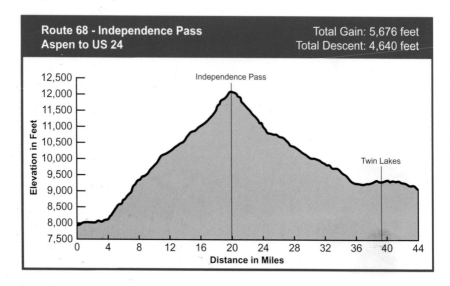

Route 68 - Independence Pass
Aspen to US 24

Total Gain: 5,676 feet
Total Descent: 4,640 feet

road. It is a unique experience to ride through this winter wonderland just after the pass opens.

The climb continues after the gate. If you are not a climber, you're about to get schooled because the road immediately becomes a steep, consistent ramp for about a mile, after which it backs off slightly. By MM 48, you'll be riding through blind corners with *no* shoulders. The road gets very narrow in places, and the traffic can be heavy on this popular scenic drive.

At MM 49, the curves get sharp and, in a couple of spots, there is barely room for two vehicles to pass one another. If you are heading uphill here, I suggest riding in the middle of the road and only moving over for oncoming traffic. Why would I say such a thing? Because I've seen motorists lose their side-view mirrors in this section by scraping the side of an oncoming car. If you get caught in this situation, it's lights out for you—not the car. Your only other option is off the cliff at the edge of the road! It's a very fast, blind descent through here, so be careful. Believe me, drivers will try to pass you on this stretch. No matter what, hold your ground.

Independence Pass affords views of high alpine wonderland

Past these curves the road remains very narrow in spots but generally affords a better view of what's ahead. It is very cozy, and the aspen trees are, as always, visually pleasing. The grade through this section is moderate, and there is some slight rolling as you approach Lost Man Campground around MM 55.

Just after the campground, you'll reach the first major switchback. The grade steepens as you approach treeline. By MM 56, the road levels out into some slight rollers with an uphill trend. You'll see alpine meadows ahead with the peaks of the Sawatch Range looming large above. At MM 58, you can see the road ahead as it climbs up the last headwall. You may think you're almost done, but it's a grunt, and the altitude starts to become a factor. If you are feeling bad, this last push will crush you!

You'll come to the last major curve before heading up a steep ramp abruptly winding its way up the mountainside. The views open up and you can see the Elk Mountains to the right (west). If you are feeling good, this is where you want to throw it into the big chain ring so you can really fly to the top, about 2 miles ahead.

The summit of Independence Pass (12,095') is wide open, with the interior of Colorado spread out before your eyes. The Collegiate Peaks are to your right (south), the Hunter–Frying Pan Wilderness Area is to your left (north), and the Lake Creek Valley can be seen far below to the east—that's where you are headed. On the summit, you'll find a parking lot and bathrooms.

The descent is spectacular—very fast with some steep sections and sharp corners. The first hairpin comes right away. You'll be going about 50 miles per hour, so be ready; the corner is nearly 180 degrees. After the turn, there is another fast section, followed by a very sharp, steep switchback. Next, there's more flying as you plummet toward Lake Creek and Twin Lakes. About 5 miles down from the summit, you'll ride around a left-hand bend as the mountainside drops away to reveal the valley below. You'll careen down a huge ramp to the valley floor. At the bottom (MM 66) is another very sharp corner, after which the road flattens out considerably. By MM 68, you'll be cruising through gradual, downhill rollers.

You'll arrive in Twin Lakes at MM 81. It's not really a town, but there is a small general store with gas, a great sandwich shop, and a couple of places to stay overnight. This area is very peaceful compared to Aspen on the other side of the pass. I highly recommend the cozy, family-run Nordic Inn, where you can enjoy a beer and a home-cooked meal as you gaze at the mountains. From Twin Lakes, it's 6 more miles to the junction with US 24, with a couple of nice rollers along the way.

There are many excellent routes in the area around this side of the pass, especially around Buena Vista (Route 69, opposite; Route 78, p. 170; Routes 82–84, pp. 178–180) and Leadville (Route 59, p. 129; Route 62, p. 133; Route 70, p. 152).

Route 69

ARKANSAS HEADWATERS
US 24: LEADVILLE TO BUENA VISTA

35 Miles • Easy

Leadville is a fairly good-size mountain town where you'll find the basics. As you head south of town on US 24, you'll ride beside the headwaters of the Arkansas River along a nice stretch of gently rolling highway. The peaks of the Sawatch Range tower above to the west with Mount Elbert (14,433'), Colorado's highest peak, in full view. Near the midpoint of the ride you can stop at Balltown, at the junction with CO 82, for basic services. The road is not bad, the shoulder varies in width, and it's a fairly straight shot except for a few bends around the town of Granite (no services). It's a total of 35 miles to Buena Vista, where you can find the basics and a bit more. For more routes around the Buena Vista area, see Route 78 (p. 170) and Routes 82–84 (pp. 178–180).

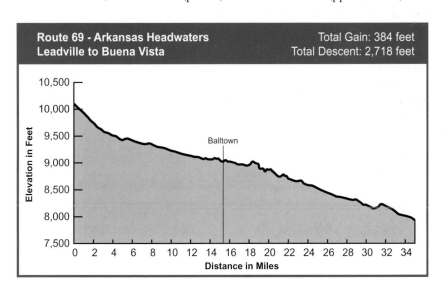

Route 69 - Arkansas Headwaters
Leadville to Buena Vista

Total Gain: 384 feet
Total Descent: 2,718 feet

Route 70

TURQUOISE LAKE ROAD LOOP
FR 104: LEADVILLE TO LEADVILLE

17-Mile Loop • Moderate

Most of this ride around Turquoise Lake is above 10,000 feet with some excellent, moderate climbing. Head west out of Leadville on West 6th Street, which becomes Turquoise Lake Road. (There are a few other pieces of pavement back here, so it can be confusing.) About 3 miles from town, you'll cross some railroad tracks. Shortly after the tracks, the road will fork; go right (northwest). This is the start of the loop. After a short incline, you will reach Turquoise Lake. Here you can go straight across the dam or turn right to go around the lake. Either way, you'll see fantastic views.

If you cross the dam, FR 104 starts with some gentle, uphill rollers that eventually become more sustained. After about 4 miles of climbing, you'll see a sign for Hagerman Pass (a dirt road). At this point, you begin a 2-mile, fast descent to the west end of Turquoise Lake, which now appears much larger than it did at the dam. After about 2.5 miles of sustained climbing, you'll be back above the lake, but this time you'll be on the north side. Eight more miles of fast riding and you'll return to the railroad tracks west of Leadville.

The altitude of this loop makes it more challenging. It's a great leisurely ride or an awesome training and interval loop to really gauge your fitness level. The annual "Lap the Lake" bike race takes place here every June, sponsored by the Lake County Recreation Department (719-486-4226).

Early season snow dusts the area surrounding Turquoise Lake

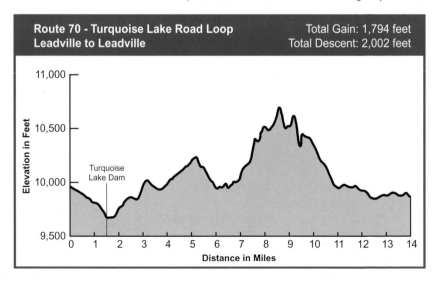

REGION 4

INTERMOUNTAIN SOUTH

You won't find a whole lot of roads going through this part of Colorado. Instead, you'll encounter lots of open country with exceptionally beautiful mountain ranges and some of the most pristine areas in the state. There are several high passes and some moderate climbs and rollers in the southern mountains as well. Gunnison, Crested Butte, Salida, Montrose, Lake City, and other great mountain towns provide all of the accommodations and supplies you'll need. Notable routes in the region include Hermit's Rest (Route 73, p. 161), The Gate (Route 74, p. 163), Cottonwood Pass (Route 78, p. 170), and one of Colorado's finest and least-known passes, Slumgullion Pass (Route 75, p. 165).

ROUTES

Afternoon thunderstorms can be a daily phenomenon during Colorado summers

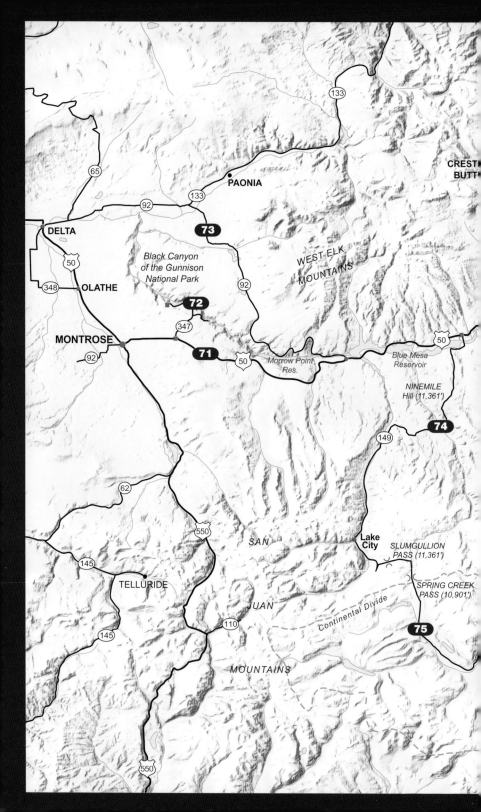

Route 71

CERRO SUMMIT
US 50: MONTROSE TO GUNNISON

65 Miles • Moderate

Montrose has services to meet all your basic needs and offers gorgeous, sweeping panoramas of the southern mountains. A wall of peaks known as the San Juan Mountains stretches across the southern horizon. There is not a more rugged or vast expanse of wilderness in all of Colorado. For rides south of here, refer to the Southwest routes (Region 6, p. 182).

Head east on US 50, on what is a spectacular route in its own right. The start of the ride in Montrose is at about MM 92. The road is wide with plenty of shoulder as you ride through lush, green meadows surrounded by rolling hills of sage and wildflowers. The road rolls very slightly, slowly gaining altitude.

Moderate climbing begins at MM 101, and you will see a sign that reads, "Cerro Summit 4 Miles." From here the climb is constant, with lots of room, and you'll be surrounded by rolling hills and very little tree cover. You'll reach Cerro Summit (7,800') by MM 105. After about 7 miles of fast, wide-open descent, you will be in Cimarron, where you'll find gas, a small grocery store, and a cafe. From Cimarron, it's 19 miles to Sapinero (basic services). But first enjoy a mellow descent into the town of Pleasant Valley, where you'll find a small store and camping (approximately MM 115). You'll have amazing views as you come down from Cerro Summit, and the Pleasant Valley area is no exception.

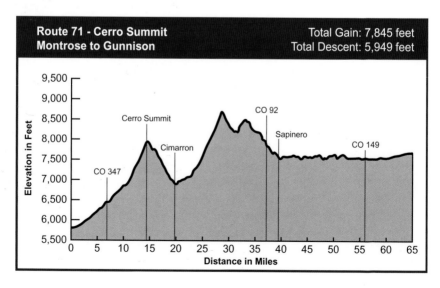

Route 71 - Cerro Summit
Montrose to Gunnison

Total Gain: 7,845 feet
Total Descent: 5,949 feet

At MM 117, as you bottom out and start a moderate climb of about 4.5 miles, you'll find beautiful, rolling mountains accented by aspen groves. Incidentally, the shoulder on this route comes and goes. When it's there, it's excellent; otherwise there's not much room, so stay alert.

You'll top out shortly at MM 121 and start a moderate descent into a small canyon with no shoulder. At MM 124, you'll begin climbing moderately to the Blue Mesa Dam. As you pass the junction with CO 92 (see Route 73, p. 161) around MM 131, you'll be treated to incredible, sweeping views of Blue Mesa Reservoir. It's 2 miles from here to Sapinero and another 15 miles to the east end of the Blue Mesa Reservoir—a welcome oasis surrounded by arid hills with sporadic aspen groves. The road gently rolls along the reservoir against this beautifully stark backdrop. From the east end of the reservoir, it's another 9 miles on flat road into Gunnison.

Gunnison is a good-size college town where you'll find all of your basics. For other routes in this area, refer to The Gate (Route 74, p. 163); Slumgullion Pass–Spring Creek Pass Combo (Route 75, p. 165); Cottonwood Pass (Route 78, p. 170); and Monarch Pass (Route 81, p. 177).

One last word of advice about this route: Watch for rumble strips!

The view from the lower slopes of Cerro Summit

Route 72

SOUTH RIM DRIVE, Black Canyon of the Gunnison National Park
CO 347: US 50 TO END OF ROAD
FEE REQUIRED: $4/BIKE, $7/VEHICLE

Approximately 15 Miles • Moderate

The Black Canyon has been called the "Yosemite of Colorado" because of the sheer cliffs that plummet nearly 3,000 feet down to the Gunnison River. One of the deepest, most narrow canyons in North America, this place is truly a natural wonder.

South Rim Drive (CO 347) will take you on an amazing ride along the rim, where views and drop-offs will send chills down the back of your neck. The road is about 15 miles long and starts with a moderate climb from its junction with US 50, 7 miles east of Montrose. As with any national park or well-known scenic route, I don't suggest riding here on peak summer weekends as the area will be clogged with traffic and pedestrians. The road is generally in great shape with a varying shoulder.

CO 347 heads north from US 50. It's 6 miles or so to the park entrance, and in that distance you'll climb nearly 2,000 feet. The climb isn't too bad, and the views to the south are phenomenal. Once you're in the park, the terrain is mellow, and you'll ride just over 8 miles along the canyon rim to the end of the road near High Point.

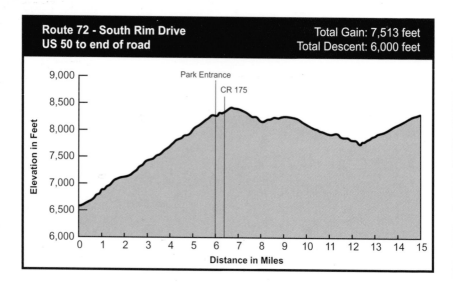

BONUS: East Portal Road (CR 175) is a difficult 5.5 miles from South Rim Drive to the Gunnison River. If you want a sufferfest, this one's for you. Just past the entrance to the park, you'll find a right turn (south) onto East Portal Road. This road is kept in pretty good shape with a varying shoulder. It is, however, closed in the winter. The terrain starts out pretty moderately, but soon you'll start plummeting to the Gunnison River on 16-percent grades with many sharp switchbacks along the way. Once at the bottom, you have no way out but up! Of course, if you lose your nerve, you can always stick your thumb out.

Route 73

HERMIT'S REST
CO 92: US 50 TO DELTA

72 Miles • Difficult

The road from Blue Mesa Reservoir to Delta is a spectacular piece of pavement that winds its way high above the northeastern edge of the Black Canyon of the Gunnison. Monster rollers with long climbs and descents rule the day on a route suited for those with a healthy appetite for hard work. The views from this road are absolutely superb. I highly recommend a stop along the route at Hermit's Rest, MM 55, to take it all in. Several thousand feet below the highway lies Morrow Point Reservoir, a narrow, deep lake that stretches like a snake for miles. To the south, green pastures edge up to the Uncompahgre National Forest, and the entire southern Rockies fill the horizon.

Don't forget to look down as you ride past Morrow Point Reservoir

The start of this route is at the junction of CO 92 and US 50. This junction is at the west end of Blue Mesa Reservoir, and CO 92 is the road that crosses the Blue Mesa Dam just west of Sapinero. At the visitor center/marina in Sapinero you can get the basics.

As you start on CO 92, there's a small descent to the dam with a pullout and an outhouse on the other side. After the dam, you'll start to climb some monster rollers, gradually gaining altitude as the Black Canyon, below, begins to plummet into the depths of the earth. This makes for some staggering drop-offs on the roadside.

By MM 65, the road is in great shape with little or no shoulder. After a nice descent, you'll cross Curecanti Creek, and then find more of the same—huge rollers. At MM 55, you'll reach Hermit's Rest, which boasts a view beyond words. You need to see this one for yourself. As you continue on your way toward Delta, the route settles into a moderately rolling descent of just under 20 miles into Crawford.

The town of Crawford sits at 6,520 feet and has very basic supplies. From here, the vegetation becomes a bit sparse, and the summer temperatures can be high. The road is fairly straight, in great shape, and has a good shoulder. It is 11 miles to Hotchkiss and 31 miles to the beginning of CO 92 in Delta, where you'll find the basics and a bit more.

If you are heading to Paonia, I recommend an alternate backroad from Crawford. On CO 92 just north of Crawford, you'll see a right-hand turn for CR 39.00. This road leads you into Paonia the back way with very little traffic. CR 39.00 eventually turns into CR 39.50 before coming to a "T" intersection. Go right on J.75 Dr.; this will take you into Paonia. It's about 15 miles from Crawford to Paonia. Both of these towns have basic services.

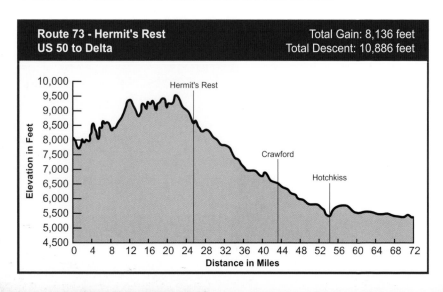

Route 74

THE GATE
CO 149: GUNNISON TO LAKE CITY

53 Miles • Difficult

Located up in a high, windswept valley next to the Gunnison River, the town of Gunnison feels like a remote outpost of sorts. But don't be fooled. Gunny is home to Western State College, and the town is full of young, sports-oriented folks. To the north lie Crested Butte, one of Colorado's best and least-known ski resorts, and the rugged Elk Mountains—home to the Maroon Bells–Snowmass Wilderness. To the east, nestled in the Sawatch Range, are the Collegiate Peaks Wilderness (see Monarch Pass, Route 81, p. 177) and Monarch ski area. To the west is Blue Mesa Reservoir—a mecca for boating, fishing, and hanging out. To the south, you will see the high, rolling hills of the Powderhorn Wilderness, which you will skirt on your way to Lake City.

As you make your way out of Gunny (west on US 50), the route is very flat and slightly downhill, winding its way along the Gunnison River toward Blue Mesa Reservoir. It's 9 miles to the junction with CO 149. Turn left at this junction, and cross the bridge where the Gunnison River empties into the reservoir. It's really quite a sight to come around the corner and see the bridge with the reservoir behind it—you'll wonder where the heck the road is going! This is a rare treat in Colorado, as very few roads in this state cross over any significant bodies of water.

About 2 miles after the bridge (MM 115), just when you think you'll be riding along the lake, the road takes an evil left turn and abruptly begins a long, sustained grind up Ninemile Hill. You guessed it—9 miles of climbing! As the road gains altitude, the terrain starts to change and becomes an amazing landscape of rolling hills dotted with aspen groves, pine trees, and wildflowers. Don't forget to look back as you're riding up for a beautiful view of the Blue Mesa Reservoir and the Elk Mountains beyond.

Sage and lupine cover the hills along CO 149

After MM 111, the grade backs off a bit and starts into some large, gradually rolling terrain as the route ascends the summit of Ninemile Hill (9,011'), just before MM 105. There is a pull-off and a chance to take in incredible, distant views. Although you've topped out on Ninemile Hill, you will continue to gain elevation as you start into some very large and somewhat steep rollers on your way to the ride's high point at MM 104. At 9,060 feet, you'll have a great view of the La Garita Wilderness and San Luis Peak (14,014'). From here, the road plummets into a screamin' downhill with big, wide corners.

Just after MM 101, you'll reach Cebolla Creek and the turnoff to the small town of Powderhorn—don't blink or you'll miss it. There are no services here or anywhere else between Gunny and Lake City. The road immediately starts climbing and a mile later launches into a steep headwall beyond which it undulates up and down with large rollers as you proceed toward your next high point.

At MM 96 and the junction with CR 26, you'll hit your second summit. Next comes another rippin' downhill, leading you through a wonderful, aspen-laden valley then abruptly dumping you into the Gateview Valley at MM 93. The road is in great shape and you won't find much traffic back here.

As you come around a left-hand bend at the bottom of the descent, you will see "The Gate" at MM 89. "What the heck is The Gate?" you ask. In the Gateview Valley are two cliff faces, one on either side of the road. Here the valley narrows just enough for the river (the Lake Fork of the Gunnison) and the road to pass through. This is the gateway to Lake City and the La Garita Wilderness. After passing through The Gate, the terrain changes rapidly into more of an alpine environment. The road also changes, as the rest of your route will consist of small, uphill rollers with flat sections in between.

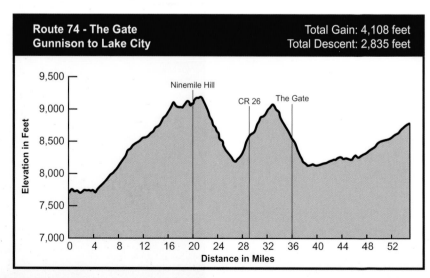

Route 74 - The Gate
Gunnison to Lake City
Total Gain: 4,108 feet
Total Descent: 2,835 feet

As you approach Lake City, the valley gets narrower and becomes canyon-like with bizarre and spectacular volcanic rock formations everywhere. The rollers become shorter and steeper as well. Around MM 81, the road heads down to the river where there is just enough room for you and the aspen trees. It's very lush and cozy along this stretch. A few more rollers, and you'll find yourself riding into Lake City at MM 73. (For more on Lake City, refer to Slumgullion Pass–Spring Creek Pass Combo, Route 75, below.)

Route 75

SLUMGULLION PASS–SPRING CREEK PASS COMBO
CO 149: LAKE CITY TO CREEDE

52 Miles • Difficult

Nestled deep in the eastern San Juan Mountains are two of Colorado's most out-of-the-way towns, Lake City and Creede. These two holdouts from the mining era have managed to hang on and become beautiful little summer havens. Lake City lies hidden in a small valley surrounded by the Weminuche Wilderness, the Big Blue Wilderness, and the Powderhorn Primitive Area. The only way in (other than by 4-wheel drive) is a formidable climb through The Gate (Route 74, p. 163) from Gunnison, or via this route from Creede over Slumgullion and Spring Creek Passes.

I find it very easy to sit on the porch at Poker Alice (the best coffee in Lake City) and forget that the rest of the world even exists. There are many eateries in town, as well as several places to stay. You will feel quite at ease wandering the streets in this quaint, friendly little hideaway. San Juan Mountain Bikes (CO 149 and Ocean Wave Drive) can help you in a pinch with a road tube or wheel truing, but it's mostly a mountain-biking shop. However, it does carry a lot of backcountry gear and clothing. It's right behind the Lake City Bakery, which should be your first stop for espresso and morning sweets.

The other side of this route takes you to Creede, another small, quaint little town. Practically buried at the foot of Mammoth Mountain, this little paradise has everything you need. Pay a visit to San Juan Sports for your biking necessities.

Tucked away between Lake City and Creede is one of Colorado's best-kept road-cycling secrets: CO 149. Every mile of this short-but-sweet highway is worth the effort. From its spectacular junction with US 50 just west of Gunnison all the way to Creede, this road offers challenges for every level of

Southerly view from Spring Creek Pass

cyclist. CO 149 from Lake City to Creede climbs over two very majestic passes, Slumgullion and Spring Creek. The round-trip from Lake City to Creede and back is formidable, with a lot of climbing. Of course you can do any portion you desire, but just be aware that there are no services between the two towns.

The start of this ride is in Lake City at MM 72 on CO 149, heading south and east toward Creede. The road has no shoulder, but it's in great shape and starts climbing immediately as you leave town on moderately rolling terrain. You'll hit the first headwall about 2 miles in as the road winds its way along the Lake Fork of the Gunnison River toward Lake San Cristobal. This climb is steep and sustained. An incredible view of the San Juans opens up as you ride above the valley floor.

About 3.5 miles into the ride, you will see Lake San Cristobal, Colorado's largest natural alpine lake. The lake was formed some 700 years ago when a massive mudslide broke loose from Mesa Seco to the east, essentially damming the Lake Fork of the Gunnison River. You'll be cycling through this mudslide area for much of the climb up Slumgullion Pass.

Just past MM 67, the Lake San Cristobal overlook, the climb mellows out a bit for a mile or so. About 6 miles into the ride, you'll pass a sign marking 4 miles to the summit. Here the road gets steep again—time to pay the piper.

Not far from MM 64, there is a turnoff (left) for Windy Point. The short (0.1 mile), paved road leads to a small parking lot with great views and plaques describing the scene—a good place for a snack. There is a restroom as well.

About 10 miles from the start is Slumgullion Pass (11,361'), your first summit (no facilities). You'll then start dropping into the low point between Slumgullion and Spring Creek Passes. The road opens up a bit, giving you more room. You'll lose about 1,000 feet here. There's a big corner at MM 59; it's a fun one when you're really flying. Four miles from the summit, the road flattens as you approach a beautiful high valley—and the ride only gets better! When you cross Rambouillet Creek and pass Oleo Ranch, you'll be at the bottom (MM 57).

Two miles of sustained, mellow climbing up the valley brings you to the Continental Divide and the top of Spring Creek Pass (10,901'). You'll find a parking lot, an outhouse, and picnic facilities, but no camping. Noteworthy, however, are the interpretive plaques describing area name origins and history —very cool! The Colorado Trail is also accessible from this summit.

The descent to Creede begins gradually with mellow, downhill rollers that soon become fast along a paved shoulder. This road is a riot! Eventually the descent gets steeper, but after MM 51 it mellows again. The downhill here carries you along Big Spring Creek into another large, high valley with tremendous views. Near MM 48, you can take a 3-mile detour on paved FR 510 which accesses a parking lot, campgrounds, outhouse, and an overlook of North Clear Creek Falls, then returns you to CO 149.

A short climb later, a view of Brown Lakes State Wildlife Area and Rio Grande Pyramid will appear. At this point the road drops steeply, and soon after, the view to the left reveals Bristol Head—a magnificent cliff face that dominates your ride down into Antelope Park. The creeks from these mountains form the headwaters of the mighty Rio Grande, which will accompany you the rest of the way into Creede. Riding through the beautiful Antelope Park can be difficult, however, due to the heat and high winds. At its best, it's an absolutely beautiful mountain valley hidden away from the rush of the outside world. In good conditions, you can really fly.

MM 43 begins this fast section into Creede, but the town is still 21 miles off, so pace yourself. Those heading back to Lake City may want to turn around here. If you're staying in Creede, or you have a shuttle driver, you're all set. Just open it up, clean out your carburetor, and empty your gas tank as you pedal your butt off. My friend Rick and I did this route from Creede to Lake City and back. Ouch!

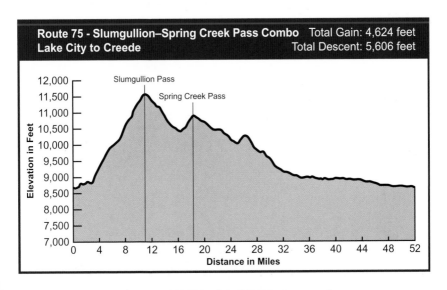

Route 75 - Slumgullion–Spring Creek Pass Combo   Total Gain: 4,624 feet
Lake City to Creede   Total Descent: 5,606 feet

Route 76

WAGON WHEEL GAP
CO 149: SOUTH FORK TO CREEDE

22 Miles • Easy

South Fork is a quiet mountain town with the basics. It's also the start of the Silver Thread Scenic Byway, which extends all the way to Lake City. Along this stretch, CO 149 is mostly flat with very gradual inclines that lead you along the Rio Grande. The pavement is in great shape, but there is little or no shoulder. It's 22 miles to Creede and very pretty as you ride through the Rio Grande Palisades, a section of rock cliffs along the road. This makes a great 44-mile out-and-back ride.

For more on the area around Creede, refer to Slumgullion Pass–Spring Creek Pass Combo (Route 75, p. 165). For more on South Fork, refer to Wolf Creek Pass (Route 92, p. 196).

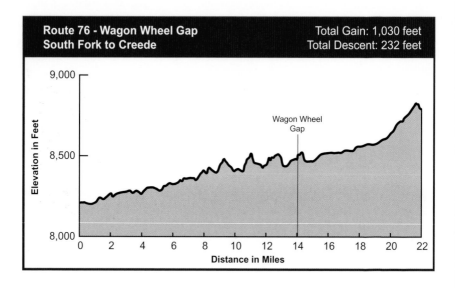

Route 77

EAST RIVER VALLEY
CO 135: GUNNISON TO CRESTED BUTTE

28 Miles • Easy

The only paved road between Gunnison and Crested Butte is CO 135 and it can be busy. It's a mellow route with a few moderate rollers and a general uphill trend into Crested Butte—a quintessential mountain town. On the way your only stop is Almont, where you'll find campgrounds and basic services. Once you're in Crested Butte, you won't have many choices for pavement, but the incredible beauty (and Camp 4 Coffee on Elk Avenue) makes up for it! Mountain biking was born in "The Butte," so that's what the town's all about, but there are other road routes out of Gunnison; see Cerro Summit (Route 71, p. 158), The Gate (Route 74, p. 163), Slumgullion Pass–Spring Creek Pass Combo (Route 75, p. 165), Cottonwood Pass (Route 78, p. 170), and North Pass (Route 79, p. 174).

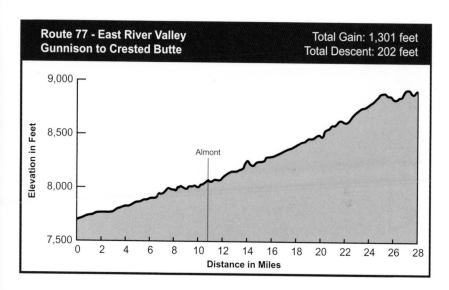

Route 77 - East River Valley
Gunnison to Crested Butte

Total Gain: 1,301 feet
Total Descent: 202 feet

Route 78

COTTONWOOD PASS
FR 306: BUENA VISTA TO COTTONWOOD PASS

20 Miles • Difficult

This ride over Cottonwood Pass begins in Buena Vista and the setting is one of grandeur. The Sawatch Range extends like a wall from Vail to Salida and contains 15 peaks over 14,000 feet in elevation. The Cottonwood Pass road winds directly over this wall. As Colorado rides go, Cottonwood Pass is a top-notch representation of pass-riding at its best and includes a bonus for the adventurous.

Buena Vista is a great base for multiple pass excursions if you don't wish to camp. In addition to riding Cottonwood Pass from here, you can enjoy Independence Pass (Route 68, p. 148), Monarch Pass (Route 81, p. 177), Poncha Pass (Route 82, p. 178), and Trout Creek Pass (Route 84, p. 180). You

Riders negotiate a dirt road on the west side of Cottonwood Pass during the Ride the Rockies annual tour

can also find campsites in all directions, as well as forest roads for backcountry camping. With a large grocery store and several restaurants, Buena Vista offers everything you'll need. Coffee lovers should check out Bongo Billy's at the south end of town on US 24. If you're looking for a bike shop, The Trailhead, on the north end of town, can help. For a healing soak, head up Cottonwood Pass Road (CR 306, or Main Street in town) to Cottonwood Hot Springs, or turn left off Cottonwood Pass Road onto CR 321 just as you leave Buena Vista to find Mount Princeton Hot Springs.

Cottonwood Pass Road is one of the few roads I'd never been on prior to this guide, and one of the adventures I looked forward to most. I was not disappointed; in fact, I was astonished. How did this one get away from me for all of these years?

I'd always thought it was dirt, and it is—partly. The Buena Vista side of the pass is paved to the top, and it's one of Colorado's finest pass roads, with some of the steepest grades you'll find in these parts and a rip-roaring descent back into Bueny. Cottonwood offers many challenges, even for experienced riders. The road is closed in the winter, so if you're riding this route check with the highway department, the sheriff, or a local business before committing.

The start of this route is in town at the junction of US 24 and CR 306 (Main Street). Heading west toward the big peaks, the road out is straight and climbs very gradually for the first 4-plus miles—a very nice warm-up. At this point, you'll start into some moderately rolling terrain as the road begins to wind its way up into the mountains. You'll notice why Cottonwood Creek got its name—it's chock-full of trees providing welcome shade.

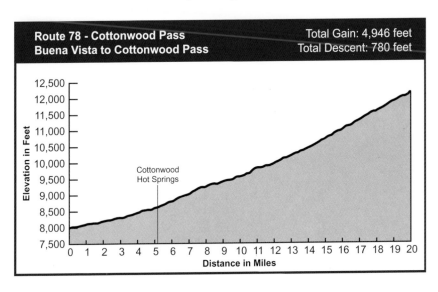

Five miles into your ride (there are no mile markers on this side of the pass), you'll reach Cottonwood Hot Springs. The hills will become formidable as you climb up the pass. Approximately 8 miles into it, you'll top out on a rather large roller as you go by Rainbow Lake. Look up to your right to see Mount Yale at 14,196 feet.

For the next few miles, you'll continue with large uphill rollers. Near mile 12, you'll pass the gates where the road is closed in winter. From this point on, the real work begins. You'll encounter 10-percent grades— some of Colorado's steepest on pavement—mixed with moderate climbing.

The first major switchbacks start about 15 miles into the ride, and from here on out the climb will continue in this fashion. Around mile 16.5, the landscape begins to open up, affording you tremendous views of the Collegiate Peaks, the Sawatch Range, and the Continental Divide. By mile 18, you'll really start to see your summit. The road ahead is more of the same—lots of switchbacks!

With its summit at 12,126 feet, Cottonwood Pass is one of Colorado's highest paved roads. The trip up takes you over approximately 19.5 miles of pavement. There are no facilities up here, but there is a large pullout and a nice sign to pose beside for pictures.

I had a unique experience while documenting this road. You may have heard of Ride the Rockies, an organized cycling tour where, if you win an entry by lottery, you get to ride a six-day route through Colorado with full SAG support, including aid stations with food, music, and games.

I knew that Ride the Rockies was coming over Cottonwood Pass on the day I was documenting it. I knew that I would see 2,000 cyclists on the route, and I knew that there would be some supportive folks up on the pass on this day. But nothing prepared me for what I was about to witness. There was loud music blasting and a deejay hosting silly games like "The First One to Run Up the Hill and Get the T-shirt Out of the Tree Can Have It." There were fajitas, sandwiches, and refreshments. I spent the whole day on top of that pass, watching all kinds of riders on all kinds of bikes having all kinds of fun. This tour is a fantastic thing to be a part of, and I highly recommend it.

Ride the Rockies participants convene at the aid stations

BONUS: Continue down the other side toward Gunnison. The west side of this pass is dirt from the summit for about 15 miles down to Taylor Reservoir. The road number changes at the summit to FR 209. If you are hungry for some more climbing, you can head down this road and turn around whenever you wish. If you are riding through to Gunnison, be wary, as road conditions will vary. The road is good, as far as dirt roads go (especially if its been graded recently), but it can be heavily washboarded. It is steep and has lots of sharp switchbacks.

When you reach the reservoir, turn left onto FR 742. The pavement starts again—with a good road to the dam and then a beat-up road with no shoulder —and leads down through Taylor Canyon to Almont, another 21 miles away. At Almont, turn left onto CO 135. From here, it's 11 gentle, downhill miles to Gunnison, where you will be able to take care of most of your needs.

EXTRA BONUS: If you love adventure, this is for you. Get a support driver to meet you in Buena Vista, and ride from Gunnison over Cottonwood Pass. This is an absolute classic, and the descent into Buena Vista is not to be missed. It's an arduous task with 45 miles of climbing to get to the summit. If you choose this direction, Almont—10 miles from Gunnison—is your last service stop until Buena Vista. I recommend a spare tire and tube, as well as extra H_2O in case you're stranded. This road does get a fair amount of traffic if you need to hitch a ride, but don't count on it. I've left the description of the climb vague to preserve the adventure for you. Have at it!

Route 79
NORTH PASS
CO 114: Saguache to US 50

62 Miles • Moderate

Saguache (pronounced *sa-watch*) is an interesting crossroads town. It lies on the flats of the San Luis Valley, nestled at the foot of the Cochetopa Hills. The view east across the valley of the Sangre de Cristo Range is breathtaking. The Sangres stretch north to south, containing nine of Colorado's 54 fourteeners. This range also boasts some of the tallest vertical gains; these summits rise nearly 7,000 feet from the floor of the San Luis Valley.

Saguache has the basics—very basic. You might find a quiet little cafe, as businesses come and go. You won't find a bike shop here or any services on the rest of the route. You will be riding through the Colorado "outback." Camping is available off of BLM roads, and there is a campsite up toward North Pass (also called North Cochetopa Pass).

CO 114 is your road for this ride. Its begins in the middle of Saguache, where it intersects with US 285. As you roll west out of town, you will enter a wide, flat valley along Saguache Creek. To the right are the Cochetopa Hills, and off to the left are the La Garita Mountains. The road is very straight, ever so gradually climbing up the valley—don't forget to look behind you, as your view of the Sangre de Cristos really opens up. After about 4.5 miles, the road starts into some gradual uphill rollers around MM 57. By MM 54, you will be pedaling through a gently rolling valley, eventually coming to big meadows of

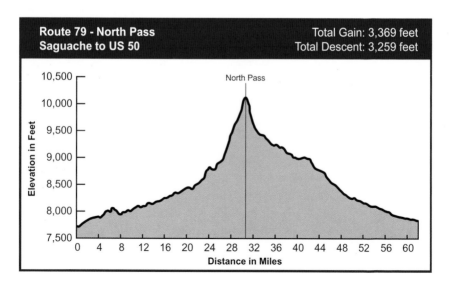

Route 79 - North Pass
Saguache to US 50

Total Gain: 3,369 feet
Total Descent: 3,259 feet

sage, wildflowers, and grasses with thick pine forests above. It is very peaceful back here.

At MM 45, you can see where you are headed—up into the forest toward the Continental Divide. The bridge at Saguache Creek is at MM 41. You will soon start the climb up North Pass. If you look right at MM 38, you'll see a peak in the distance. That peak is Long Branch Baldy (11,974'), and it sits on the Continental Divide. At MM 35, a sign indicates it's 4 miles to the pass summit. This is where the meat of the climb starts, and it continues moderately to the summit. The road is in excellent condition with a small shoulder.

You'll reach the summit (10,149') at MM 31. There are no facilities, but there is a

As it makes its way up North Pass, CO 114 twists its way through varied terrain

pull-off with a couple of maps displayed. As you start down toward Gunnison, the road is very fast and somewhat steep with wide-open corners but no shoulder to speak of. At MM 29, the road flattens a bit. As you ride along West Pass Creek near MM 27, the terrain changes to gradual, downhill rollers. Saguache Park sits at MM 26. If you look to your left, you'll see a rare roadside view of the La Garita Mountains and San Luis Peak (14,014'), Colorado's most remote fourteener.

After Saguache Park, the road starts heading down Cochetopa Canyon. Here you'll find a gently winding valley road. It's not quite a canyon, but the valley is still closed in, with many rock walls dotting the route. This is a very enjoyable (and fast) section of the ride. Around MM 10, you'll be working your way down out of the hills and into the Tomichi Creek Valley. You reach the end of the route at the junction of CO 114 and US 50. Gunnison is 8 miles west on US 50.

Route 80

QUARTZ CREEK
CR 76: Parlin to Pitkin

15 Miles • Moderate

Twelve miles east of Gunnison, you'll find a quiet little crossroads called Parlin. There is a very cool, old market with an eclectic mix of goods as well as a nicely cluttered assortment of antiques and random memorabilia. The folks here are friendly and make great espresso. The gas pumps, however, were empty when I visited.

At Parlin, you'll find CR 76, which heads northeast to Pitkin. The road is fairly narrow, with little or no shoulder, and it's a bit hacked-up. Sounds great to me. You'll go by the ghost town of Ohio at about 8.5 miles. From there it's another 6.5 miles of pavement before this road turns to dirt at Pitkin, where you can find the basics, but that's about it.

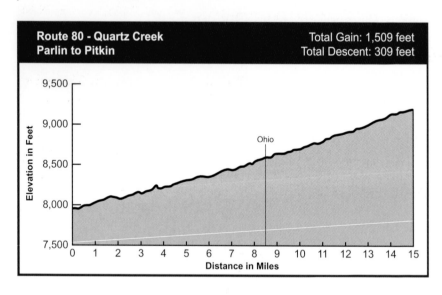

Route 80 - Quartz Creek
Parlin to Pitkin

Total Gain: 1,509 feet
Total Descent: 309 feet

Route 81

MONARCH PASS
US 50: SALIDA TO GUNNISON

60 Miles • Difficult

Salida, the "Crossroads of Colorado," is famous for its Arkansas River rafting. Located at the southern end of the Sawatch Range, the town is nestled at the foot of this great climb for cyclists.

Salida offers all you need. Otero Cyclery has lots of gear as well as a cool collection of Red Zinger/Coors Classic leader jerseys. And I highly recommend Absolute Bikes; check out its collection of old bikes. Scot Banks will be glad to tell you all about them if you visit the shop (conveniently located next to Bongo Billy's—an ideal coffee stop). Salida has plenty of lodging and is near camping options in all directions.

From Salida, take US 50 west to Poncha Springs—about 5 miles on flat road with an excellent shoulder—where you'll reach US 285. Stay on US 50 (to the right) toward Gunnison and Monarch Pass. US 50 is in great condition here, with a small shoulder and a slight incline as it heads out of Missouri Park and up near the headwaters of the South Arkansas River.

In Maysville (MM 212), you'll find camping but nothing else. The road is winding now. The hills get steeper at MM 206, as you start into the meat of the climb. A sign indicates 6 miles to the summit!

At MM 205, you'll find the Monarch Mountain Lodge and an outcropping of condos. Now the road becomes steeper, averaging a 6-percent grade that remains fairly sustained to the summit. Monarch ski resort is at MM 201.

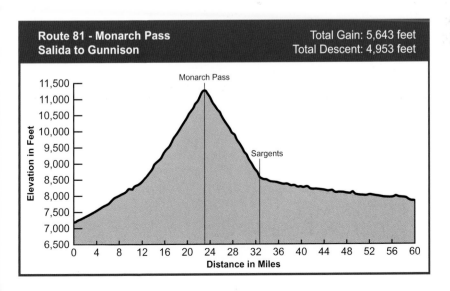

Route 81 - Monarch Pass
Salida to Gunnison
Total Gain: 5,643 feet
Total Descent: 4,953 feet

The summit of Monarch Pass (11,312'), at MM 200, is a Continental Divide crossing with a large parking lot, gift shop, and food. The Monarch Crest gift shop boasts some of the most kitschy, random items you can find anywhere. If you feel like parking your bike, you can even take a scenic gondola ride up to the top of the mountain above Monarch Pass.

The road heading down the pass toward Sargents and Gunnison is in great shape, but it is steep and winding with no shoulder. By MM 195, you will be in the middle of a screamin' descent—lots of fun. You'll wind your way along Agate Creek, and forested, rolling mountains will surround you all the way into Sargents (MM 190) at the bottom of a consistent, 10-mile descent. This little town is an oasis composed of just a few buildings including a small grocery, a gas station, an auto shop, a post office, and a cafe.

From here, it's still 32 miles to Gunnison on a road that gently rolls through the Tomichi Creek Valley and into the very broad Gunnison River Valley.

Route 82

PONCHA PASS
US 285: BUENA VISTA TO SAGUACHE

65 Miles • Moderate

This section of US 285 is rarely congested, but the traffic that is here moves fast. The area accesses many top-quality routes, including an excellent,

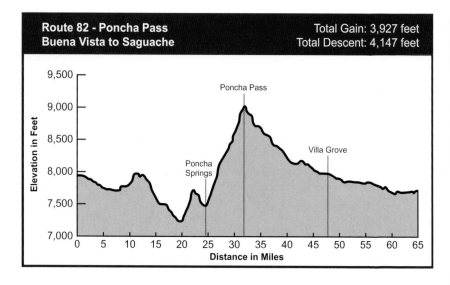

moderate climb up to Poncha Pass. (For more on Buena Vista, see Cottonwood Pass, Route 78, p. 170.)

Head south out of Buena Vista on US 24 on a flat, wide road with a huge shoulder. It's 2 miles to the junction with US 285. Once you pass this junction, it's 22 miles to Poncha Springs. The road is generally flat, but there are a few moderate rollers along the way. The views are astounding, as the Sawatch Range towers above to the west and contains many peaks over 14,000 feet in elevation. This is a spectacular valley!

Poncha Springs has the basics, but if you want more, Salida can take care of all your needs. It's about 5 miles east on US 50. There's two excellent bike shops in Salida. (For more on the Salida area, see Monarch Pass, Route 81, p. 177.)

As you ride south through Poncha Springs, you'll cross a bridge over the South Arkansas River at about MM 125 and begin an excellent moderate climb of 7 miles. Although it's a moderate climb, the road gets steeper near the top. The summit of Poncha Pass is at 9,010 feet, and there are no services on top.

The descent is very moderate and short, because the San Luis Valley on the south side of the pass is at a higher altitude than Poncha Springs. If you continue on, it's another 17 miles to Villa Grove (*very* basic services) on a straight road with an excellent shoulder.

The San Luis Valley is absolutely massive, and although there are some gradual rollers, the road is mostly flat. The Sangre de Cristo Mountains, on the eastern edge of the valley, are incredible. It's 17 miles from Villa Grove to Saguache (basic services), with fantastic views along the way.

Route 83

MOUNT PRINCETON HOT SPRINGS LOOP
BUENA VISTA BACKROADS
Approximately 21 Miles • Easy

Head west on Main Street (CR 306, or Cottonwood Pass Road) in Buena Vista, and in about a mile turn left and take CR 321 south. This is a mellow road with light traffic that takes you to the historic Mount Princeton Hot Springs—definitely worth a stop. Make an aesthetic little loop with a short, steep climb as you pass the hot springs and take a left turn onto CR 162. In about 4 miles you'll reach US 285, where another left turn will return you to Bueny, via US 285 and US 24, in about 8 miles. You can reverse the route by taking US 24 then US 285 south to Nathrop, then turning right (west) onto CR 162 to the hot springs. Go right (north) from here to head back into Bueny via Cottonwood Pass Road.

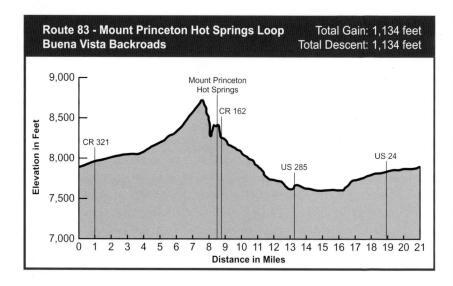

Route 83 - Mount Princeton Hot Springs Loop   Total Gain: 1,134 feet
Buena Vista Backroads   Total Descent: 1,134 feet

Route 84

TROUT CREEK PASS
US 285/US 24: BUENA VISTA TO ANTERO JUNCTION

16 Miles • Moderate

Trout Creek Pass is an excellent, sustained, moderately steep climb. The road is in great shape, but it's a major thoroughfare with a lot of truck traffic and not much shoulder. It's worth the effort—just be cautious.

Head south from Bueny on US 24. The road is flat, wide, and busy with a huge shoulder. Two miles south, you'll find the junction with US 285 at a "T" intersection. Turn left onto US 285/US 24 and cruise through Johnson Village, a very basic town with a truck stop as testament to the traffic you can expect through here.

The climb starts abruptly just past Johnson Village, and the road is in great shape. The shoulder comes and goes. It's 12 miles of fairly steep and sustained climbing. The views of the Sawatch Range to the west (behind you) are staggering; 14,000-foot peaks line the horizon from north to south. The summit of Trout Creek Pass (9,346') has a pullout but no services.

A moderately steep climb delivers you to Trout Creek Pass

The descent down the east side of the pass to the split of US 285 and US 24 at Antero Junction is barely a mile. (For more routes on the east side of Trout Creek Pass, refer to the Front Range South section of this guide, p. 74.) You can cruise flats on the east side, in South Park, for miles on end before heading back over Trout Creek Pass.

If you ride back to Johnson Village, the descent down the west side of the pass is phenomenal. The road is very fast and wide open, with no sharp corners of any note.

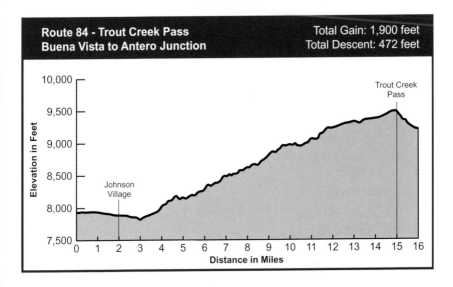

REGION 5

SOUTHERN COLORADO

The southern region of Colorado is dominated by the massive San Luis Valley. It is the largest mountain valley in Colorado—nearly 50 miles across and almost 90 miles long—and is surrounded by astounding views of the bordering mountain ranges. The Sangre de Cristo Mountains to the northeast rise nearly 7,000 feet (one of Colorado's highest vertical gains) and stand like a wall from north to south. The less massive Culebra Range lies to the southeast, while the great San Juan Mountains loom to the west.

Supplies in the San Luis Valley itself will be pretty basic, and the town of Alamosa is your best bet for variety. To the east over the Culebra Range, in Trinidad and Walsenburg, you can find a bit more in the way of supplies, but these small towns are still somewhat limited. Nestled in the San Juans to the west you will find Pagosa Springs, which can provide the most diverse array of supplies for your needs.

Many routes lie within the San Luis Valley, most of them fairly flat on long, straight roads. The mountains bordering this valley, however, contain several great, challenging pass rides. Notable routes include Cucharas Pass (Route 88, p. 190); an excellent double pass, Cumbres Pass–La Manga Pass (Route 90, p. 193); and Wolf Creek Pass (Route 92, p. 196).

ROUTES

Skunk cabbage along the fantastic route up Cumbres Pass, Route 90

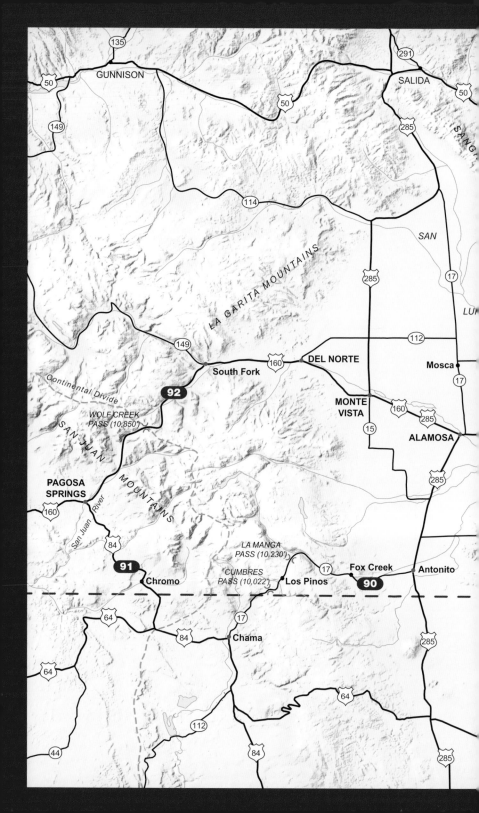

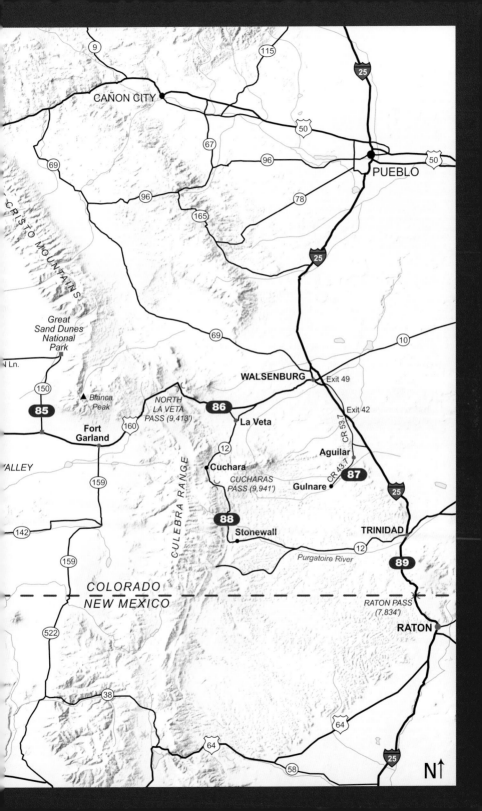

Route 85

GREAT SAND DUNES NATIONAL PARK
CO 150: US 160 TO PARK ENTRANCE

18 Miles • Easy

Trapped up against the Sangre de Cristo Mountains (northeast of Alamosa) is a sea of giant sand dunes covering more than 37,000 acres. The scene is surreal, to say the least— 700-foot dunes nestled up against 14,000-foot peaks. Their otherworldly beauty is well worth riding to see. Hiking up these dunes at sunset is an experience you won't forget, and a workout to boot! CO 150 ends shortly after the park entrance, and you can camp at the dunes for $10 a day. The regular entry fee is $3 per person. You'll also find fantastic views of the dunes and a general store outside of the park boundary. Head north on CO 150; you'll find its junction with US 160 some 12 miles west of Fort Garland. It's about 16 miles to the park entrance from here, a nice, slightly rolling ride. You can also head east from CO 17 just north of Mosca on 6N Lane (it's about 19 miles to the park entrance).

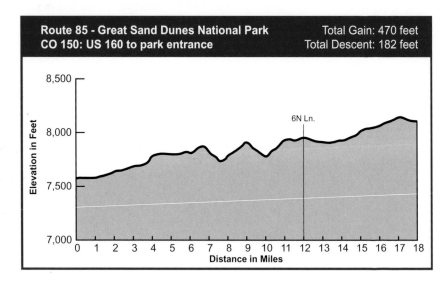

Route 86

NORTH LA VETA PASS
US 160: FORT GARLAND TO WALSENBURG

47 Miles • Moderate

Way down in southern Colorado just east of the San Luis Valley is a little-known continuation of the Sangre de Cristo Mountains called the Culebra Range. It's truly one of the secret gems of Colorado. Staggeringly beautiful and lacking crowds, this area provides two outstanding mountain rides—this one, and Cucharas Pass (Route 88, p. 190).

The town of Fort Garland lies in the southeast corner of the San Luis Valley, 26 miles east of Alamosa. The town sits up against the Sangre de Cristo Mountains on US 160, which is the road you want. Fort Garland has the basics of food, gas, and drinks.

You'll head east along Sangre de Cristo Creek with Blanca Peak (14,345') and her companions at close watch. This busy stretch of US 160 has a large shoulder, is in great shape, and offers spectacular mountain vistas as you ride up into the aspen groves atop the pass. The first 10-plus miles east from Fort Garland consist of very gradual, sweeping rollers heading up into the mountains. It can be a very hot start, as the San Luis Valley can be like an oven in the summer months.

At MM 270, as you continue east, you'll enter an alpine landscape, and the temperatures will start to drop a bit. Now the climb really begins. As you wind

CR 450 makes a nice detour off US 160 to the town of La Veta

your way upward at MM 276, the terrain opens up and you will see the pass road above. At this point, there's a moderate descent into the upper valley, and then it's back to gentle climbing.

About 21 miles out of Fort Garland, you'll arrive at the North La Veta Pass summit (9,413'—no services). You cannot escape this vista: Rough Mountain and Mount Maestas (both over 11,000') dominate the view like a roadblock over the summit.

At MM 282, you will come to a tremendous descent for a few miles, and then the grade will mellow through rolling downhill terrain toward Walsenburg. As you approach MM 285, you'll see a commanding view of the Spanish Peaks to the southeast.

At about MM 288, you can turn right on CR 450 for a short detour to the small, quaint town of La Veta. It's 4 miles of old road to La Veta, where you can get basic supplies. This road has a lot of character—watch for potholes! As you ride into town, you'll find Main Street (CO 12), which you can take north for 5 miles to get back to US 160. It's then 11 more miles on US 160 to Walsenburg.

If you don't ride into La Veta, just continue east on US 160 past CR 450, and then past the junction with CO 12. The terrain gradually mellows out as you roll into Walsenburg, a great little town. With the prairie to the east, the landscape here is quite different from the mountains. This town has all you need and is a good base for this ride and other rides in this region, whether you're going one way or round-trip.

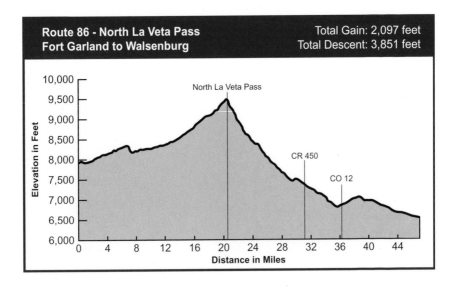

Route 87

WALSENBURG BACKROADS
I-25 FRONTAGE/CR 53.7/CR 43.7

23 Miles • Moderate

Some great, major routes out of Walsenburg appear in this guide, but here are a few of the more obscure roads in the area. Head south out of Walsenburg on US 85 for about 1 mile to I-25 and Exit 49. Cross over the interstate to the east side and head right (south) on the frontage road to Exit 42 (near Pryor). The road is in good shape and gently rolls along. Ride south on I-25 for 1 mile to Exit 41, get off, and head south on CR 53.7. A small country backroad is what you will find, and a good part of the road is paved with old concrete slabs that have grass growing out of the cracks—classic cycling! The road is pretty hacked up, there's no one out here, and it's about 17 miles from Walsenburg to Aguilar. As you ride through Aguilar, you'll find it almost like the backwoods. There may or may not be any services (don't depend upon them), though there is a liquor store. Turn right onto Main Street, where you'll see a sign pointing to Gulnare. Head through town—a couple hundred yards—and take a left on CR 43.7 (San Antonio Avenue). You'll head into a beautiful valley with a decent road but no shoulder. No traffic either. The pavement ends about 6 miles out of Aguilar, and the views and solitude are worth the effort. Gulnare is another few miles on bad dirt, so turn around once the pavement ends for a nice ride back to Walsenburg.

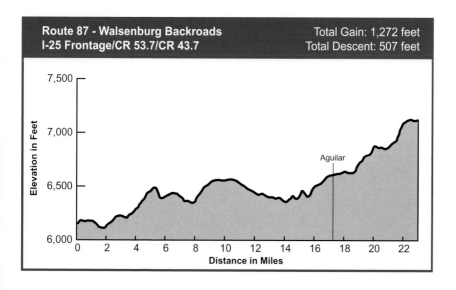

Route 87 - Walsenburg Backroads
I-25 Frontage/CR 53.7/CR 43.7

Total Gain: 1,272 feet
Total Descent: 507 feet

Route 88

CUCHARAS PASS
CO 12: TRINIDAD TO LA VETA

65 Miles • Difficult

Few cyclists know about this place. Tucked away in the far southeastern Front Range, just west of Trinidad and Walsenburg, sits the Culebra Range. Elegant ridgelines peer from above as you ride through incredible pastured valleys dotted with lakes, aspen groves, and pine forests. This route is simply sublime from its start in Trinidad to its finish in La Veta—absolutely stunning!

Trinidad is a good-size town that will cover all of your needs. CO 12 is your road. It's 32 miles to Stonewall at the bottom of the south side of Cucharas Pass, then another 33 miles to La Veta. The beauty begins immediately as you rise above the prairie on your way past Trinidad Lake and up into the Culebra Mountains. You will climb moderately as you ride a gently winding road up the somewhat narrow Picketwire Valley along the Purgatoire River.

When you ride into Stonewall, you'll immediately be mystified by the beauty and aware of the origin of the name. It doesn't get more aesthetically pleasing than this. As you cycle through the town (a couple of buildings, including the Satisfied Bear general store), you will be surrounded by green pastures with the Culebras above you and a 100-foot stone wall slicing its way across the South Valley. The Stonewall rock formation is more than a mile long and about 15 feet thick. Streams flow from all directions as you ride through a small gap in this wall and head north toward Cucharas Pass.

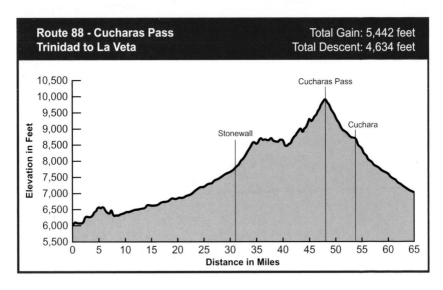

Route 88 - Cucharas Pass
Trinidad to La Veta

Total Gain: 5,442 feet
Total Descent: 4,634 feet

The Devil's Stairsteps, or the Great Dikes of the Spanish Peaks, near La Veta

At MM 37, the climbing becomes more formidable, with rolling, winding terrain up to Monument Lake (about 4 miles from Stonewall)—there's great camping here! You'll get a tremendous view of the Spanish Peaks to the northeast as you ride on. North Lake, at MM 30, is a small reservoir tucked away in the hillside. The road is excellent, with little or no shoulder, and the varied, rolling terrain persists as you continue toward the summit.

At MM 26, you hit big rollers! Steep, too! But the real climbing begins at MM 24.5, where you will encounter some steep sections on the last 2 miles to the summit. You'll reach the Cucharas Pass summit (9,941') at MM 22.5.

Five miles or so of top-quality, steep, sustained descent take you into the town of Cuchara and the bottom of this pass at MM 17. Cuchara is a side-of-the-road kind of town, with a couple of restaurants and other basics. It's very cool, and a great place to enjoy a brew.

From here, continue down to La Veta through moderately rolling terrain past the several large rock formations known as Devil's Stairsteps (a.k.a. Great Dikes of the Spanish Peaks). Soon after Devil's Stairsteps, you'll cross over three streams within a short distance of each other; this area is called Three Bridges. The road flattens out, and a long, fairly straight section of a few miles leads you into La Veta.

La Veta is a quaint little town with a nice city park, across from which you will find a small bakery with great coffee. For other needs, try Walsenburg, some 11 miles northeast on US 160. For another great route in this area, check out North La Veta Pass (Route 86, p. 187).

Route 89

RATON PASS
I-25: TRINIDAD TO RATON, NM

21 Miles • Moderate

A fantastic road that gets no press, I-25 south from Trinidad is definitely worth doing. Traffic can be heavy, as this is a major highway, but you'll have plenty of shoulder. Views are awesome as you ride by Raton Mesa and Fishers Peak Mesa on your way up to the pass, which sits right on the border. Beautiful, rolling mountains and lots of forest characterize this ride. The climb is moderate and sustained, and it begins as you leave town. It's about 13 miles of climbing to Raton Pass (the New Mexico state line, at 7,834 feet), and there are no services until you reach the town of Raton. From the pass, it's about 8 miles of fast descending to Raton, making for a solid climb on the way back if you choose to do it.

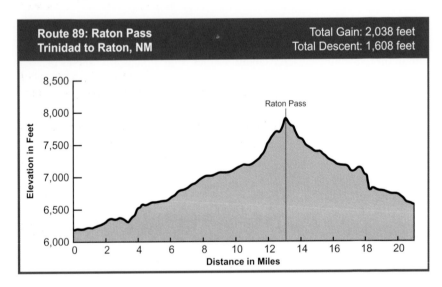

Route 89: Raton Pass
Trinidad to Raton, NM

Total Gain: 2,038 feet
Total Descent: 1,608 feet

Route 90
CUMBRES PASS–LA MANGA PASS COMBO
NM 17/CO 17: CHAMA, NM, TO ANTONITO
48 Miles • Difficult

In many of the southern mountain ranges of Colorado, you can find places where crowds are nowhere to be found. The southern San Juan Mountains are no exception. Straddling the Colorado–New Mexico border lies one of Colorado's highest-quality bicycle routes. The road between Chama, New Mexico, and Antonito, Colorado, is spectacular. CO 17 winds its way high up into these mountains. Riding the long, sweeping, high-altitude rollers between these two passes, you'll be treated to incredible views of mellow, wandering ridgelines and lush, forested mountainsides dotted with a brightly colored carpet of wildflowers. It is a great out-of-the-way place to go, with a lot of campsites and BLM camping options. Camping up on the passes is exceptional!

If you're in the San Luis Valley to the northeast, you can access this route at Antonito (basic services) on US 285, about 30 miles south of Alamosa. Chama, on the other hand, is a bit more substantial and has a couple of restaurants and a basic grocery store. All it's missing is a bike shop and espresso. I suggest driving south from Pagosa Springs on US 84 for 49 miles to Chama and parking your car there. From Chama, you can bust out an out-and-back that you won't soon forget.

Home to the Cumbres & Toltec Scenic Railroad (C&TS), Chama is full of Old West history and is a must for train buffs. In fact, one thing you have to watch out for on this ride is train tracks. CO 17 crosses the C&TS tracks

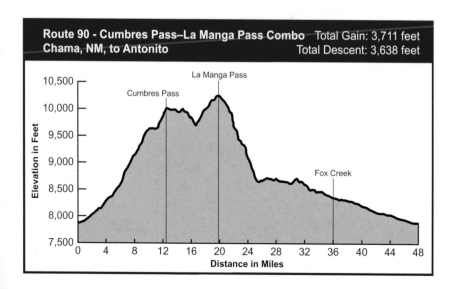

Route 90 - Cumbres Pass–La Manga Pass Combo   Total Gain: 3,711 feet
Chama, NM, to Antonito   Total Descent: 3,638 feet

A remnant of a bygone era at Cumbres Pass

several times. Most crossings are mellow, but if you are coming downhill, I suggest you slow down or jump them.

The start of this route is at MM 2, just north of Chama. For the first several miles, the road climbs very gently with some rollers, meandering along Wolf Creek. The view is of beautiful, open hillsides and rolling mountains. Just before MM 7, you'll reach your first railroad crossing. The road is in great shape, with a wide shoulder. As you head farther along, the rollers gradually become more pronounced, and the views open up. There are no major peaks in these mountains, just mellow, rolling ridgelines that barely peak up over treeline. Huge, open alpine meadows full of skunk cabbage and wildflowers abound, bordered by aspen groves and pine forests. And if you see what appears to be a forest fire, don't panic. It's probably smoke from the train on its way up the valley.

At about MM 8, you'll reach the Colorado state line (on the New Mexico side). At this point, the mile markers go back to zero. The shoulder also disappears here. In fact, there's little or no shoulder, with moderate, sustained climbing from here on out.

Just before MM 3 (in Colorado), you'll cross the tracks again. Use caution, and watch out for people photographing the train at these crossings; they often cannot hear you coming, and you might startle them! After these tracks, you'll come around a big corner and start some serious climbing. Here the views really open up, and you'll see why I speak so highly of this road.

At approximately MM 4, you'll reach the summit of Cumbres Pass (10,022'). At its elevation, the summit is a strange place to find a train yard. But there is one—very cool. You'll also find a parking lot and maybe some water up here. Watch out for a multiple-track crossing—it can damage your rims.

From the top of Cumbres Pass, you'll head into a gradual, rolling descent along Cumbres Creek. Soon, the road drops steeply into Los Pinos (MM 8). You can stop into the Rendezvous Steakhouse in Los Pinos to enjoy a great steak dinner in what looks like the middle of nowhere. There are no other services.

After Los Pinos, you'll enter into a section of mellow, uphill rollers all the way to the summit of La Manga Pass (10,230'), just after MM 11. Nothing here but beauty! Seven-percent grades begin at MM 12, and there are some very tight corners for about 4 miles until you drop into the Conejos River Valley. The descent ends abruptly, and the gradual, downhill rollers into Fox Creek and beyond are very fun and fast. There is a restaurant in Fox Creek where you can get water and a bite to eat.

I usually don't go into Antonito, although I ride in the valley for a while to loosen my legs for the climb back up La Manga. If you're riding back to Chama, you'll want to assess your energy level, as climbing out of this valley can really put the hurt on. It's your call when to turn back.

Route 91

NAVAJO RIVER
US 84: PAGOSA SPRINGS TO CHAMA, NM

48 Miles • Moderate

One of the best routes out of Pagosa Springs, this great ride heads into New Mexico and hooks up with CO 17 (Cumbres Pass–La Manga Pass Combo, Route 90, p. 193). US 84 rolls moderately through some beautiful out-of-the-way countryside on its way to Chama, New Mexico.

It's 24 miles to Chromo, Colorado, where you can find basic services. Another 5 miles will take you to the New Mexico state line. Follow the valley road about 6 miles on US 84 to the junction with US 64, then continue east (left) on US 64/US 84 for 12 miles to the junction with NM 17. Turn left (north) onto NM 17 and ride another mile to reach Chama. Chama is a small, friendly town with the basics and a couple of restaurants.

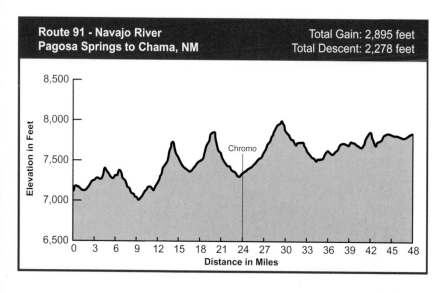

Route 91 - Navajo River
Pagosa Springs to Chama, NM
Total Gain: 2,895 feet
Total Descent: 2,278 feet

Route 92

WOLF CREEK PASS
US 160: Pagosa Springs to South Fork

42 Miles • Difficult

This one is a classic! Wolf Creek Pass (10,850') is a monster climb. The setting is spectacular, and the road is in excellent shape. This route starts in Pagosa Springs (7,079')—a fairly good-size town where you'll find the basics and a bit more. See Routes 91 and 93, pages 195 and 204, for other great rides in this area.

As you head out of town to the northeast on US 160 (MM 145), you will be cycling along the San Juan River. The road rolls along moderately and has an excellent, wide shoulder. At MM 153, you'll descend from a roller into a beautiful valley, and encounter alpine terrain as you slowly gain altitude. Here you can begin to see where you're headed—huge cliffs with a mountain backdrop. It's incredible!

Shortly after MM 156, you'll see the road starting up the pass. This can be an intimidating sight, as there are several switchbacks and it looks steep. It is steep! There's moderate climbing to MM 158, and soon you'll come around a big left-hand bend with a sign that reads, "Wolf Creek Pass Summit 8 Miles." This is where the work begins. From here on, the road continuously becomes steeper. You'll be in the thick of it as you pass MM 159. A few switchbacks take you up the first headwall of Wolf Creek Pass.

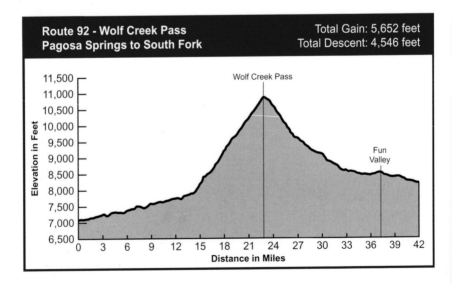

Route 92 - Wolf Creek Pass
Pagosa Springs to South Fork

Total Gain: 5,652 feet
Total Descent: 4,546 feet

By MM 161, you're out of the switchbacks. The incline backs off a bit, and the road straightens into a gently winding, moderate climb. It is very constant, however, amounting to a long, steady grind of about 5 more miles to the top. The shoulder remains very wide with lots of room. If you look ahead at MM 165, you'll see a low point in the mountains. That's where the pass road cuts through. MM 167 is the summit of Wolf Creek Pass. There is a large pullout but no facilities as you cross the Continental Divide.

NOTE: At publication date, the east side of Wolf Creek Pass was under construction, and it was a mess with long delays. I suggest you check with the sheriff's office or the locals before you pick this one.

On this descent, you'll start heading down right away. There are awesome views of the southern Weminuche Wilderness (pronounced *Wim-en-ooch*). A few very fast corners and you'll pass Wolf Creek ski resort, where you can probably find water if you need it, but they have no summer services that I'm

Steep grades are the norm on the way up Wolf Creek Pass

*A*s a chef for most of my working life, I would often work nights until 10 or 11 p.m. Many times I would leave work and drive up to a trailhead, preferring to wake up and already be out in the woods.

One night while driving over Wolf Creek Pass on the way to the Sangre de Cristo Mountains, I saw an odd sight—a cyclist plugging away at the pass. It was well after midnight and pouring rain. "Geez, man, what's up with that?" I said to the guy I was with. "Some people are just not all there."

As if that wasn't enough, shortly after we saw another rider, then another. "Freaks, I tell ya!" Not sure what to think, we drove on. Then we saw a SAG vehicle (support car), and it all became perfectly clear.

Livin' large on the side of the sag wagon was the acronym RAAM—Race Across America. We were stunned. I knew this race existed, but seeing it gave the ride a whole new meaning. These cyclists were in the middle of 10 or more days of nonstop riding from coast to coast.

I always say that, just when you think you're good at something, someone is sure to put you in your proper place!

---

aware of. Around MM 168, the road straightens into moderate, winding terrain, but it is still very fast—a bomb of a descent. Next, you will head through the snowshed, a tunnel created to allow avalanches to run over the road without blocking passage. As with all tunnels, this snowshed can be dangerous. Be wary of rocks, potholes, and ice. Ice can be present in any mountain tunnel for as much as two-thirds of the year. And even though most tunnels are lit, they're still dark. After the snowshed, the descent steepens a bit—fantastic, wide-open road.

Around MM 173, the grade backs off, and a shoulder is hard to come by. Up to this point, Wolf Creek is a top-quality out-and-back from Pagosa Springs. From here, however, traffic is usually heavy, as US 160 is a major thoroughfare, and speeds are high with a lot of blind curves. For these reasons, I do not recommend riding the lower east side of Wolf Creek Pass.

If you do continue down the east side, you'll soon pass Fun Valley, an RV campground. You might think to yourself, "Isn't that…? Well, that looks like…could it be?" Yes, in fact, it is! The same Fun Valley from the Chevy Chase movie *National Lampoon's Vacation*—it really does exist! It looks like few changes were made for the movie. It's there in all its glory!

Soon after you pass Fun Valley, the shoulder returns, and you'll come to MM 184, the city limit for South Fork. It's a gorgeous valley as you cycle along the South Fork of the mighty Rio Grande. No good coffee here that I could find, but great cheeseburgers! For another excellent route in this area, see CO 149: South Fork to Creede (Route 76, p. 168).

REGION 6

SOUTHWESTERN COLORADO

This region of Colorado is utterly magnificent. The diversity of routes rivals those of the Front Range regions, but you won't have as much vehicular company on these flats, rollers, and high-mountain passes. The San Juan Mountains and their adjacent ranges contain an amazing array of serrated peaks and ridgelines as well as some of Colorado's largest wilderness areas. Down in these parts, you'll find Durango, Telluride, Silverton, Ouray, and Cortez, where your needs will be thoroughly met.

This region boasts some of Colorado's best weather, and you can find excellent cycling conditions throughout most of the year. Winters tend to be mild, and sunshine is plentiful. Notable routes in this region include the Coal Bank–Molas Pass Combo (Route 96, p. 214), Red Mountain Pass (Route 97, p. 217), Lizard Head Pass (Route 99, p. 222), and an incredible perennial tradition for extremists, the Death Ride Loop (Route 95, p. 212).

ROUTES

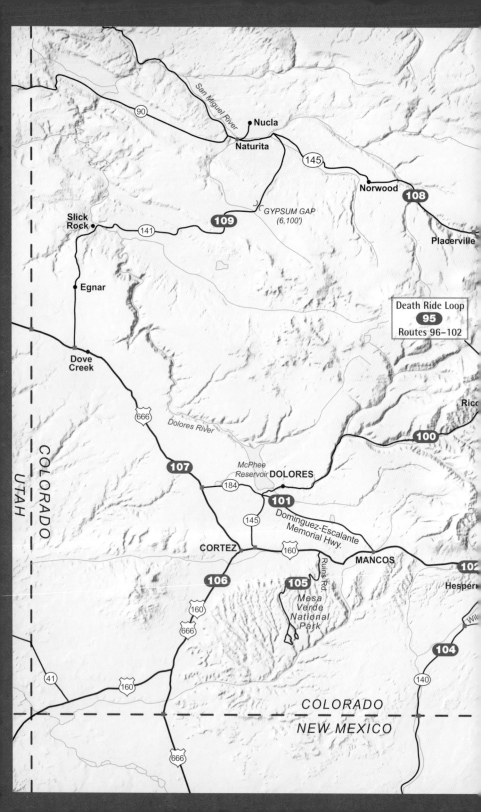

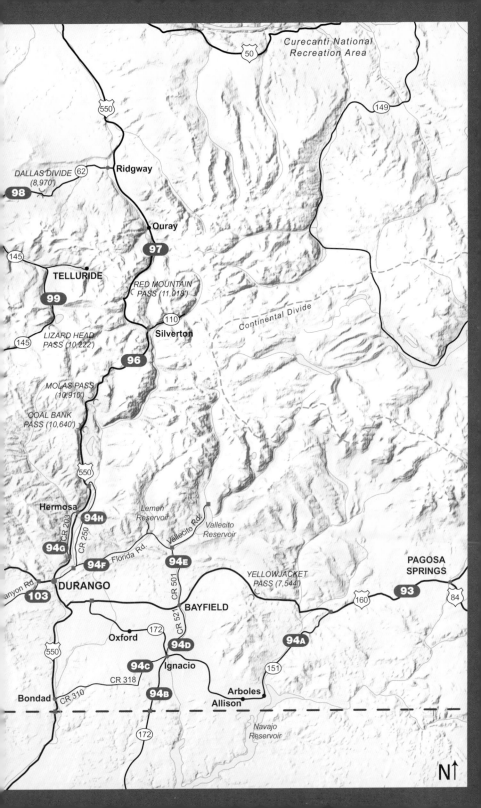

Route 93

YELLOWJACKET PASS
US 160: PAGOSA SPRINGS TO DURANGO

60 Miles • Moderate

Traversing from east to west, this section of US 160 remains the same for most of its length. The road is generally great and, as usual, the shoulder varies from wide to none. Moderate rollers of varying size dominate as you cruise through beautiful, meandering hills covered with subalpine and upland desert vegetation. Glimpses into the far southern landscape abound, and you'll find basic services and supplies along the way.

Pagosa Springs has all you need. But businesses seem to come and go, and the only good coffee that's stuck around over the years is at The Malt Shoppe on the east end of town near the junction of US 160 and US 84. Northeast on US 160 from Pagosa Springs is Wolf Creek Pass (Route 92, p. 196)—a monster of a climb. If you head southeast from Pagosa Springs, you'll find a beautiful route on US 84 to Chama, New Mexico, as well as access to the spectacular double-pass combo of Cumbres–La Manga (Route 90, p. 193).

Heading west out of Pagosa Springs, US 160 climbs somewhat steeply leaving town. This continues for a couple of miles but levels out a bit. The terrain seems endless as it rolls and winds toward Durango. About 17 miles west of Pagosa Springs and just east of Chimney Rock is the junction with CO 151 to Ignacio (Route 94A, p. 206). It's 24 more miles of moderate rollers to Bayfield, with one very large hill called Yellowjacket Pass (7,544'), a moderate 2-mile climb—no big deal.

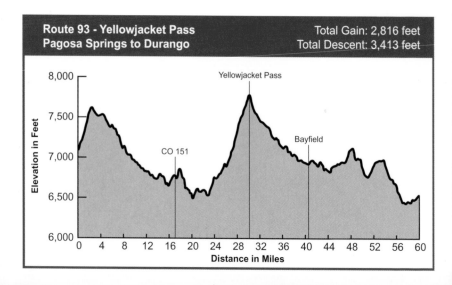

Route 93 - Yellowjacket Pass
Pagosa Springs to Durango

Total Gain: 2,816 feet
Total Descent: 3,413 feet

In between towns, you'll find several gas stations and food stores for your needs. Also, this road can be busy, as it is a major thoroughfare. A great crossroads, Bayfield has many options for cycling. To the north, Vallecito Road/CR 501 (Route 94E, p. 209) takes you to Vallecito Reservoir and is a gorgeous ride to a very quaint lakeside village. To the south is the Buck Highway/CR 521 (see Route 94D, p. 208) and a connection to CO 151.

From Bayfield, it's 19 miles of large rollers to Durango, where you'll find yourself in a cycling utopia. Whether you're a roadie or a mountain biker, you have many choices here.

Durango is the largest town in this region, with dozens of restaurants and many activities. Durango hosts several excellent bike shops and other sporting-goods stores. For general outdoor needs, I recommend Gardenschwartz Outdoors on Main Street. I've purchased many a toy from these folks over the years. You also have numerous choices for coffee and can probably find a cafe to suit your mood. If you really want to hang out, The Steaming Bean on Main Street is it.

For bike shops, try the Durango Cyclery. It's a small neighborhood-oriented shop with roadie roots and is the home of the infamous Death Ride (Route 95, p. 212). Mountain Bike Specialists on Main Street is Durango's largest bike shop and one of the Four Corners' leading event promoters, with hands in things like the Mountain Bike World Cup and the Iron Horse Bicycle Classic. Durango also hosts world-class mountain biking, and Mountain Bike Specialists' advocacy has been indispensable to area cyclists and mountain bikers for years. Mountain Bike Specialists is also the usual meeting place for the Durango Wheel Club, one of America's oldest cycling clubs. Sometimes as many as 50 or more cyclists will show up, and the group might contain Tour de France veterans or mountain-bike world champions. Don't bother to show up for a ride if you're not ready to suffer. In Wheel Club rides there is no such thing as a warm-up.

Other rides in the Durango area provide many options for linking roads and designing loops for your enjoyment. See Durango Area Backroads (Routes 94A–H, pp. 206–211) for details on many excellent routes.

Routes 94A-H

DURANGO AREA BACKROADS

For me, Durango is the ultimate mountain paradise. If you have any inclination toward the outdoors, there are few places in Colorado that compare. Durango's location is unique. If you like to play in the mountains, you have the largest expanse of them in the state, including several wilderness areas and hundreds of trails for hiking, running, and mountain biking. For water enthusiasts, the Animas River runs through town, and barely a half-day's drive will find you at the Dolores River or the San Juan River. The Grand Canyon is only five hours away by car, and Lake Powell is about six or so. If you're a rock climber, Indian Creek is just over two hours from Durango, along with countless other sandstone walls and towers. Durango itself boasts several excellent crags for your enjoyment. For skiers, there are several choices nearby from low-key to world-class, not to mention the backcountry runs. If you're looking for a resort, however, forget it. Here, you're in cowboy country, where dressing up means a pair of jeans without holes in them and your favorite pair of boots.

Durango was my home for nearly 13 years, and I could go on all day about it. The quality of rides is excellent, and the diversity is endless, ranging from short, mellow loops to epic, daylong routes. This area has it all. There are eight major climbs for cyclists within 100 miles of Durango, and if you count both sides of each climb, you can double that.

Route 94A

NAVAJO RESERVOIR
CO 151: US 160 TO IGNACIO

34 Miles • Easy

Start at the junction of CO 151 and US 160, about 17 miles west of Pagosa Springs, for this great southern route. There's plenty of peaceful countryside as you head gently down toward Navajo Reservoir on an excellent road with little or no shoulder. Eighteen miles from the start is Arboles, where the road heads toward the town of Allison, 3 miles farther. After Allison, it's 13 miles of straights and rollers to Ignacio, where CO 151 ends, and you can find the basics.

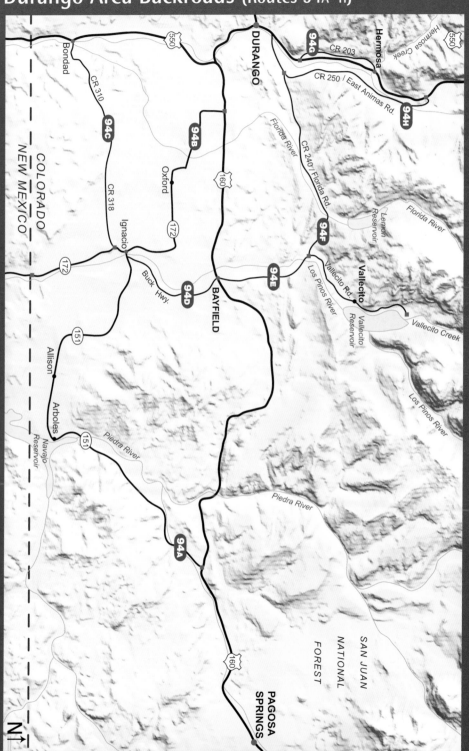

Durango Area Backroads (Routes 94A–H)

Route 94B

OXFORD CONNECTION
CO 172: US 160 TO NEW MEXICO STATE LINE

25 Miles • Moderate

Beginning at the junction of CO 172 and US 160, about 8 miles east of Durango, this is a great connection route. CO 172 heads south through a few miles of flats and then into some large rollers as it makes its way 16 miles to Ignacio, where you can get the basics and connect with other area routes. CO 172 continues south for 9 more miles to the state line. This highway can get a lot of traffic at times.

Route 94c

BONDAD
CR 318/CR 310: CO 172 TO BONDAD

16 Miles • Moderate

With spectacular views of southern Colorado and the San Juan Mountains, this stretch of road is beautiful. CR 318, which becomes CR 310, is in great shape and starts at a junction with CO 172 about a mile south of Ignacio. A few miles before you reach Bondad, you will start a very fast descent to the junction with US 550. There are basic services just south (left) on US 550.

Route 94D

BUCK HIGHWAY
CR 521: BAYFIELD TO IGNACIO

9 Miles • Easy

A fine way to get from Bayfield to Ignacio, Buck Highway (CR 521) is generally flat and very peaceful. Views go on forever, and summers can be hot! The road is good, with no shoulder and no traffic. You can meet all of your basic needs in Bayfield, or you can head to Durango (19 miles west on US 160).

Route 94E

VALLECITO ROAD
CR 501: BAYFIELD TO VALLECITO RESERVOIR

18 Miles • Moderate

Heading north from Bayfield at the stoplight on US 160, Vallecito Road (CR 501) is a great road with little or no shoulder that gently rolls along in the beautiful, quaint valley of the Los Pinos River. From here, it's about 10 miles to a junction with CR 240/Florida Road (Route 94F, p. 210), which is an excellent connecting road. Continue on CR 501 for about 5 more miles of gentle rollers to Vallecito Reservoir. The views around this spectacular lake are worth all the effort. The pavement ends just past the north end of the reservoir. There are basic services at the lake, including a few restaurants and two small grocery stores toward the north end.

NOTE: The Missionary Ridge Fire burned through this area all the way to the waterline in June 2002.

Following the 2002 Missionary Ridge Fire, the vegetation around Vallecito Reservoir will look far different than it appears in this 2001 photo

Route 94F

FLORIDA ROAD
CR 240: CR 250 TO CR 501

14 Miles • Moderate

For another local, classic route, Florida Road (pronounced *flor-EE-da*) is in fantastic condition, with a good shoulder at times. There can be some daily commuter traffic, but for the most part this road offers superb cycling conditions. From the start in east Durango at the junction with CR 250, Florida Road (CR 240) climbs gently, gradually increasing in grade. It's just over 3 miles of moderate climbing to Edgemont Ranch at the top. You'll ride moderate but sustained rollers from here, and the overall trend toward the east is slightly uphill.

About 12 miles from the start, you'll find Helen's Store, where you can purchase the basics and find some very nice down-home folks! Helen has grown many years young, and I can't say how much longer this wonderful little store will be around, so stop in and say "hi" when you ride by. (If you head straight past Helen's Store onto CR 243, you'll get a couple of miles of pavement and some steep climbing to Lemon Reservoir.) Florida Road turns right at the store and crosses the Florida River. Now the road climbs abruptly for about a half mile, then levels off and starts into a descent of a couple miles to CR 501. At this junction, you can go left to Vallecito Reservoir or right toward Bayfield (Route 94E, p. 209). Either way is excellent, but the ride to Vallecito Reservoir is particularly gorgeous.

You can usually find peaceful cycling along the Florida River, but avoid rush hour

Route 94G

WEST ANIMAS
CR 203: US 550 to Hermosa

7 Miles • Easy

Heading north from Durango, this road is a great way to avoid the traffic on US 550. You'll cruise through the Animas River Valley; it's lush and wide open, with distant views of the San Juan Mountains. Take US 550 (Main Street) north, a great road with usually plenty of traffic. Just over a mile out of town, look for a junction (no stoplight) where a left turn will put you on CR 203, a great road with less traffic but no shoulder. CR 203 gently rolls and winds along for some 7 miles before rejoining US 550 at Hermosa, which has basic supplies. This is a popular local loop when combined with CR 250 (Route 94H, below) and a bit of US 550 (Route 96, p. 214).

Route 94H

EAST ANIMAS ROAD
CR 250: Florida Road to US 550

13 Miles • Easy

Take a tour through the beautiful Animas Valley on this fun route. Rolling, forested hills surround you, the valley is wide and relatively flat, and you can enjoy views of the Needle Mountains. Head northeast out of Durango on Florida Road a couple of miles to a three-way intersection with CR 250; you can't miss it. (There's an excellent bakery on the northeast corner.) Go left (north) to get on CR 250 (East Animas Road), which is in good shape but has no shoulder. Still, traffic is pretty light. A short, fast descent leads to some mild rollers as the road winds its way north. You'll ride through some flats with a few 90-degree curves and across the Animas River via Baker's Bridge. Then it's barely a half mile uphill to US 550. Just before US 550 you'll see a KOA campground, which has water. Combine this route with CR 203 (Route 94G, above) for a nice loop, using a couple short sections of US 550 (Route 96, p. 214).

Route 95

DEATH RIDE LOOP (Routes 96–102 Combo)
US 550/CO 62/CO 145/CO 184/US 160

228 Miles • Very Difficult

You've probably figured out that the Death Ride is a long one—yes, indeed! Of the few insane one-day rides in this country, the Death Ride has got to be one of the finest. Down in southwestern Colorado is a scenic byway made up of several highways that form a loop called the San Juan Skyway. This loop is about 230 miles long and has more than 20,000 feet of climbing. Of the six major climbs along the way, four are high mountain passes of more than 10,000 feet in elevation. The weather can run the gamut from snow to sweltering heat, and the scenery is second to none. Every time I do the Death Ride, the countryside inspires me, as the route crosses every climate zone that Colorado has to offer. The Death Ride is never a race, and it's always a lot of fun.

Now I'll just give you a quick overview and refer you to the respective pages in this guide that cover each segment of the ride. Note that the segment descriptions don't always follow the same direction as the Death Ride but are written for the benefit of segment riders. Also note that in the Cortez-Mancos area, the Death Ride route represents just partial sections of Routes 100, 101, and 102.

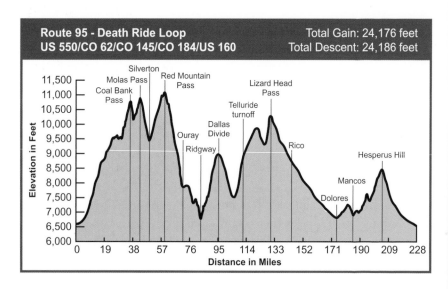

Route 95 - Death Ride Loop
US 550/CO 62/CO 145/CO 184/US 160

Total Gain: 24,176 feet
Total Descent: 24,186 feet

Finally, be aware that this loop is the most difficult route in the guide. If you're attempting the entire loop, make sure you start early, because it's easier to ride in the pre-dawn dark when you are fresh than to ride into the night when you are tired. Choose a long summer day, and get a support driver if you don't want to carry a ton of stuff or have to stop for supplies.

The ride traditionally starts in Durango in front of Durango Cyclery. The first leg is Durango to Silverton, discussed in the Coal Bank Pass–Molas Pass Combo (Route 96, p. 214). Next is Red Mountain Pass, between Silverton and Ridgway (Route 97, p. 217). Then it's over the Dallas Divide (Route 98, p. 220), where you'll ride your 100th mile and usually deal with some powerful headwinds. Next is Lizard Head Pass (Route 99, p. 222), a long, hard grind that can break you if you are feeling bad. Then from Rico, make a long slog to Dolores (Route 100, p. 224). CO 184 intersects at Dolores and leads to Mancos (Route 101, p. 225). Finally, the brutal stretch of US 160 from Mancos to Durango (Route 102, p. 226) is the last leg of the traditional route.

While you can find plenty of hard routes, this one certainly commands respect. Try it and let me know what you think.

---

*W*hile I was rinsing off 15 hours of sweat and dust in the shower, my eyes burned and every inch of me was experiencing either pain or numbness. I couldn't tell which. But I had a very large smile on my face as well!

Any avid cyclist understands these symptoms are the result of many miles of self-inflicted joy. I had done it: my first Death Ride! I barely recalled the 4 a.m. start in front of Durango Cyclery; it was dark and cold, and I didn't know who would actually show up. Far behind me was the hot coffee, passed to us through a car window at dawn, and the freezing rain on Lizard Head Pass, and having to push down on my thigh to help turn the pedals because my leg was cramping. I thought I was a goner. Somehow I pedaled through it.

The Death Ride is casual; it's not a race. There are usually two to 10 riders. In 230 miles, "Death Riders" conquer five major mountain passes and climb some 20,000 feet in 15 hours—if they're lucky. Some, like "Bicycle Bob," have completed this loop more than 10 times, and plenty of others have never finished. I am fortunate to have completed five out of six attempts. The ride is full of local legend—"fish stories" of past attempts and successes—and lore that goes back many years. Traditionally, in the last 30 miles, riders may "test" themselves by going "off the front," if they dare. As if you weren't testing yourself already!

Route 96

COAL BANK PASS–MOLAS PASS COMBO
US 550: DURANGO TO SILVERTON

49 Miles • Difficult

Begin on Main Avenue in Durango, which becomes US 550 as you head north out of town at about MM 21. After a short descent into the Animas Valley (less than a mile), you'll be on a flat road with an excellent shoulder and a gradual incline. Soon you'll see the Iron Horse Inn on the right. Look left here and you'll see a turn for CR 203 (Route 94G, p. 211), an alternate route north that hooks back up with US 550 about 7 miles north at Hermosa.

On US 550, however, you'll find fairly good road with a great shoulder and a few slight rollers along the way. In Hermosa, you'll find gas, food, and beer, as well as the best pizza in the Durango area at Mama's Boy. There's nothing else here; it really isn't much of a town. Past Hermosa and across Hermosa Creek (just before the railroad tracks), you'll see where CR 203 comes out. Cross the tracks, but be aware—this railroad crossing is very poor and crosses the highway at a bad angle. There is a lot of high-speed vehicle traffic here besides. After the tracks, the terrain begins to change. You'll start into some short, moderate rollers on your way to the junction with CR 250 at the KOA campground (MM 35). CR 250 is another excellent way through the Animas Valley.

Continuing on US 550, you'll head up an imposing ramp called Shalona Hill. It is steep and sustained. About 2 miles later the climb backs off, and you'll start into some moderate uphill rollers.

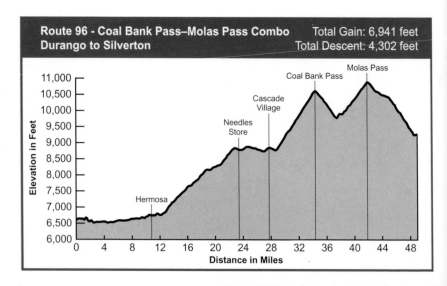

Route 96 - Coal Bank Pass–Molas Pass Combo   Total Gain: 6,941 feet
Durango to Silverton   Total Descent: 4,302 feet

The road to the base of the first pass is in excellent shape with a huge shoulder. Look right at MM 46, just before the top of a big roller. The Needle Mountains present a stunning panorama of alpine wonder. After a short, fast descent (less than a mile), you'll come to Needles Store, where you can get your basics. Good eats are also available at the Olde Schoolhouse Cafe on the other side of the highway. As you look ahead, the large, flat-topped peak on the north horizon is Engineer Mountain (12,968'). You'll see it later, on your left, when you summit Coal Bank Pass.

At MM 49, you'll reach Durango Mountain Resort (formerly known as Purgatory), where you can find limited services. It's all small, gentle rollers as you approach the base of Coal Bank Pass. Cascade Village is at MM 51, and the convenience store here is your last chance for food.

Now the climbing really starts. After Cascade Village, you'll descend for about a quarter mile and then head into the first major turn of the climb. At the base of the pass, the shoulder disappears and continues to come and go throughout the ride. Shortly after you start the climb, you'll see an astounding view of the West Needle Mountains. At MM 53, the sign reads: "Coal Bank Summit 4 Miles."

Seven miles in all, the climb is moderate and sustained, except that it backs off a bit near the top. Coal Bank Pass summit sits at 10,640 feet, where you'll find a small parking lot and a restroom.

The descent starts immediately, and the scenery will blow your mind, as the San Juan Mountains fill your entire view. It's 3 miles of steep, constant grades

to the low point between Coal Bank and Molas Passes. This is a rip-roarin' descent—very fast with some tight curves—and a nice grunt on the way back up! Just after MM 59, the climb to Molas Pass begins. Here, you will find yourself in the middle of an alpine wonderland surrounded by peaks, with nowhere to go but up. Around MM 60, a sign indicates 4 miles to Molas Pass Summit. This climb is also moderate but a bit easier than Coal Bank. The trees thin as you climb above 10,000 feet. At MM 63, you will see a large peak off to the right—Snowdon Peak (13,077')—

North Twilight Peak commands your attention as you ride the north side of Coal Bank Pass

T his route is full of road-cycling lore. Not only is it the start of the Death Ride Loop, but it is also the course for one of Colorado's longest-running road races, the Iron Horse Bicycle Classic. For decades, racers have challenged themselves on this route. The course record is under two hours, which is phenomenal given that this 50-mile race includes 30 miles of climbing. Non-elite racers enter as well, and I admire all of them. To voluntarily spend six or eight hours suffering on a course others complete in less than two takes a lot of perseverance!

and if you haven't looked behind you yet, please do. There is an incredible view of Engineer Mountain; you couldn't miss it if you tried. Its north face is a sheer, 1,000-foot-high cliff.

By MM 64, you'll reach Molas Pass summit (10,910'). If you thought that the views were astounding before, wait until you see this. Once again, the San

Juan Mountains span the entire horizon with unbelievable grandeur. You are now in the middle of Colorado's largest unbroken expanse of peaks. If you have ever hiked in these mountains, then you know that beyond the view from Molas Pass lie endless peaks and ridges, for much farther than the eye can see. This landscape is what kept me in Durango for so many years.

Fine fall weather provides ideal cycling conditions

The descent into Silverton is 7 miles. From the top of Molas Pass, the road is pretty wide open and fast. A couple of miles bring you to Molas Lake Campground, where a little general store might be open. After that, the road plummets aggressively into Silverton, and the shoulder comes and goes. The second half of this descent is fast and dangerous, with sharp corners, abrupt drop-offs, and very little room. One last, tight, 180-degree corner (just before MM 70) places you in the valley of Silverton, the very essence of an old Colorado mining town. You can find basics here as well as a genuine Rocky Mountain feel. It's a quirky little town whose residents are friendly. When you arrive, if you're like I am, you won't want to leave.

The only other way out of Silverton is via Red Mountain Pass—a monster of a road (see Route 97, opposite).

Route 97

RED MOUNTAIN PASS
US 550: RIDGWAY TO SILVERTON

34 Miles • Difficult

I suggest beginning this ride on the east end of Ridgway, at the junction of CO 62 and US 550. This approach allows you to enjoy 11 miles of fairly flat warm-up before the abrupt start of this grueling climb. The Big Blue Wilderness of the San Juan Mountains towers above on the left (east), and to the right (west) is the Sneffels Range with its serrated ridgelines. You can't miss Mount Sneffels (14,150'), a jagged, pyramid-like monster of a peak. Nestled in the midst of these mountains is Ouray. It looks like the road dead-ends on the south side of town, but if you look closely you'll notice a narrow road perched on the mountainside, winding its way mercilessly up into the canyon above. This is your road—one of Colorado's most classic and notorious rides.

Ouray has everything you need and is small enough that you can cruise the whole town on foot. There's great Italian food at Bon Ton, and don't forget Ouray Hot Springs—a large, year-round facility, and the perfect place to soak after a long ride. Stop at the visitor center north of town (just past the hot springs) for ideas on other things to do in this area.

You will notice right away that this climb doesn't even let you leave town before it starts. In fact, most of Ouray is on a big hillside. Main Street is US 550; take this south (uphill) through town. As you leave the business district, you'll

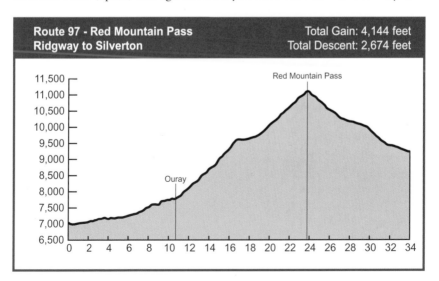

Route 97 - Red Mountain Pass
Ridgway to Silverton

Total Gain: 4,144 feet
Total Descent: 2,674 feet

immediately start grinding up several steep switchbacks. When you see MM 93, you'll have 13 miles to go before you reach Red Mountain Pass. You'll find the superb Amphitheater Campground up past the Box Canyon turnoff, just after the second switchback outside of town. Mountains tower around the camping area, and the view overlooks Ouray down below.

A few turns later after MM 92, the road opens up a little, and the grade mellows out considerably. You'll begin to see where you are going. From this point on, the road can get very narrow at times. Spectacular views of the Uncompahgre Gorge surround you. There are equally spectacular drop-offs on the edge of the road, with no shoulder and no guardrails. US 550 across Red Mountain Pass is not one of the safest roads for cycling, but the views and the experience are worth it. Just be mindful. The road is in fairly good condition, and traffic is usually very slow. A look ahead through the tunnel at MM 91 will reveal the rest of the route up the canyon. Don't be fooled—this is only the first half.

US 550 from Coal Bank Pass to Ouray has more than 150 snowslide paths that can potentially block the road. On the side of the road as you approach the south (or upper) end of the canyon near MM 89, you will see a snowshed that

Splendid late-afternoon light on US 550 along the way to Red Mountain Pass

lies in the path of the East Riverside Slide. The snowshed houses an emergency telephone. I've heard a tale of a snowplow that was swept from this road by an avalanche. The driver, after 18 hours of digging, finally got to the phone in the snowshed. A memorial on the road up ahead honors a fallen snowplow driver.

Just after the snowshed, there are four steep, short switchbacks, and then as quickly as it started, the climbing will end. Once again, don't be fooled— there's much more to come. This semi-flat section provides good prep time for the upper sections. About 2 miles of relative flats lead to an even steeper ramp of switchbacks and tight, narrow turns as the road snakes its way to the summit.

You will find the Idarado Mine and a bit of Colorado mining history at MM 82. Boy, some of these old miners' houses would be great fixer-uppers! Just past MM 81, the grade mellows out, and the summit of Red Mountain Pass (11,018') beckons. There are no facilities at the summit—the closest services are 11 miles down the other side, in Silverton.

The road descends steeply from the summit at MM 80. It's a bit narrow, with some abrupt corners during the first 1.5 miles as it winds along the head-waters of Mineral Creek. A magnificent vista opens up while you are riding through these turns, and you can see down into Mineral Creek Valley. After a big right-hand curve, the road plummets to the valley floor, with Sultan and Bear Mountain peaks presiding over your descent. The terrain in the valley rolls moderately with a fast downhill trend, and it's a 5-mile shot into Silverton, where you'll find the basics (plus a bunch of friendly locals).

Route 98

DALLAS DIVIDE
CO 62: Ridgway to CO 145

23 Miles • Moderate

Near and dear to my heart, this route has scenery that is second to none. It's simply gorgeous in this neck of the woods. (There are only so many words in my vocabulary to define beauty.) The entire time you're riding, you'll be looking at one of Colorado's most spectacular and rugged mountain ranges. The Sneffels Range is probably photographed more than any other in the state, and the peaks provide you with endless inspiration as you grunt up Dallas Divide. It's a moderate but sustained climb on an excellent road with a good shoulder.

The start of the route is in Ridgway, which sits in a beautiful valley along the Uncompahgre River. This small town can provide the basics and a little more. The San Juan Mountain Bakery has the finest shortbread cookies I've ever eaten as well as other goodies and excellent espresso.

Main Street in Ridgway is CO 62, and the road you want. As you leave town heading west, the road starts climbing abruptly, but only for about a mile. You'll top out and then head into some moderate, rolling terrain through Pleasant Valley on your way to the base of Dallas Divide. Here you begin to see the views I mentioned earlier, and if you're not impressed, then something's wrong with you.

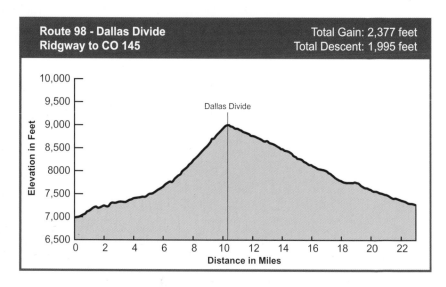

Route 98 - Dallas Divide
Ridgway to CO 145

Total Gain: 2,377 feet
Total Descent: 1,995 feet

*A*t the top of the first short hill out of Ridgway, I'm always reminded of one of my previous Death Rides, when eight of us were stopped because road crews were paving the road. We were at about mile 90 in the loop, it was about 90 degrees, and the fresh tar made it feel a lot hotter. And the fresh pavement was gooey—just our luck. So there we were, way over in the weeds, trying to steer clear of the "black glue" that we would have been scraping from our tires all week. Timing is everything!

About 4.5 miles into the ride, the climb starts and gradually steepens. This climb never gets too steep, but it is solid and sustained all the way to the top. The headwinds can be fierce up here and can turn this grind into gruel, but the scenery never quits.

At the summit of Dallas Divide (8,970'), there is a pullout but nothing else except for amazing panoramas of the Sneffels Range. This is a broad summit, and the descent begins gradually. It is a bomber downhill—not steep, but consistent—on a wide-open road for about 6 miles. Then the terrain backs off into gentle sloping road for another 5 miles. Shortly after MM 1, you'll come to the junction with CO 145, where there are no services. However, if you head left on CO 145 less than a mile from the junction, you'll ride into the small town of Placerville, which has a general store.

Views of the Sneffels Range make CO 62 over Dallas Divide an unforgettable route

Route 99

LIZARD HEAD PASS
CO 145: PLACERVILLE TO RICO

38 Miles • Difficult

Few places in Colorado inspire in me such a sense of the profound. The peaks are at once massive and humble, imposing and inviting, unrelenting and peaceful. Deep, lush valleys give way to towering peaks harboring year-round snowfields. Endless green meadows and miles of aspen groves dot a landscape of supreme majesty.

The route over Lizard Head Pass starts in Placerville, where you can find a small general store. As you head south, a gentle climb of about 10 miles becomes steeper near Telluride. The road is narrow, with many blind corners and no shoulder. Traffic can be heavy, so be careful. As you approach town, turn right at a "T" intersection to stay on CO 145. It's 12 miles from Placerville to this turn. Some cyclists may prefer to drive to Telluride and begin the climb up Lizard Head Pass from there.

Telluride is nestled in a deep, narrow, alpine valley and has a quaint, friendly atmosphere. In my 15 years of living just on the other side of the mountains from Telluride, I had never been there. When I did, I was pleasantly surprised to find a town that has maintained its integrity. The locals have been vigilant about preserving their town's beauty and tranquility. Telluride has won a place in my heart. You are sure to enjoy yourself in Telluride, as there are many first-rate amenities to choose from, but it is expensive.

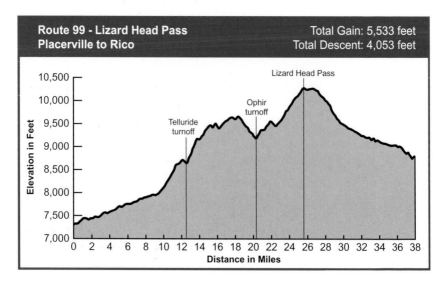

Route 99 - Lizard Head Pass
Placerville to Rico

Total Gain: 5,533 feet
Total Descent: 4,053 feet

If you are cycling past Telluride, you'll actually have to make a right turn to continue on CO 145 up Lizard Head Pass. Now the road widens and the shoulder comes and goes (mostly it goes). The Ophir turnoff is 9 miles away. Less than a half mile past the right turn, the road steepens considerably. If you're a "Death

Look for rock climbers on awesome Ophir Wall along the road to Lizard Head Pass

Rider" (Route 95, p. 212), you will now confront some of the most formidable mental challenges of your day.

The road climbs steeply for some 3 miles, at which point it levels out as you pass Telluride Ski Resort. The scenery here is staggering, with astounding views of Mount Wilson, Wilson Peak, and Lizard Head Wilderness to the west. The hillsides here are dotted with some magnificent homes—or ridiculous ones, depending on your point of view.

More climbing follows a short, moderate descent as you head to the turnoff for the town of Ophir. A very fast, steep descent of a mile or so brings you to the turnoff. You'll be treated to more insane vistas—peaks on the right, and the Ophir Needles, a well-known rock-climbing spot, on the left.

At Ophir (if you choose to make a pit stop), you'll find a post office and a small rock-climbing school where you can get some water. Continuing on CO 145, you'll start climbing again, and the terrain will level into some more rollers. This diverse route really puts you to the test! About 10 miles in, you'll see Matterhorn Campground. Here you will start the final grind up to the summit of Lizard Head Pass.

Eleven miles or so from the Telluride turnoff, you'll approach Trout Lake, with Vermilion Peak and Sheep Mountain looming to the east.

In a couple more miles you'll reach Lizard Head Pass (10,222'). On the summit, you'll find a parking lot, restrooms, and alpine paradise. From Lizard Head Pass, the 12-mile descent down to Rico (8,827') is relatively fast. The first couple of miles are moderate. The road steepens for a short time, and you'll ride through some fun, wide-open curves. From here, the route moderately descends through a few rollers as it winds along the Dolores River. As you get closer to town, you'll be cycling through a beautiful valley where the dense, forested ridges offer a bit of seclusion. You also get some excellent views of the Rico Mountains. A great, low-key place to relax, Rico has limited services.

Route 100

McPHEE RESERVOIR
CO 145: US 160 TO RICO

47 Miles • Moderate

S tart this gorgeous ride at the junction of US 160 and CO 145, a couple of miles east of Cortez—a medium-size town that is quiet, friendly, and can take care of most needs. The road becomes moderately rolling as you ride north on CO 145 through the farm fields of the Cortez area. It is a gradual climb to Dolores, 10 miles away.

In Dolores, you'll find the basics. Once you leave town, the surrounding terrain as well as the vegetation begin to change. As you continue north, the road winds along the Dolores River, and incredible aspen groves dominate the hillsides. The road rolls its way on a gradual climb of 37 miles from Dolores to Rico, where you'll find the basics.

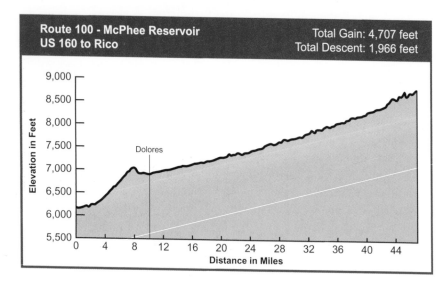

Route 101

DOMINGUEZ–ESCALANTE MEMORIAL HIGHWAY
CO 184: MANCOS TO US 666

27 Miles • Moderate

A great road with little or no shoulder, this short highway is hillier than the roads near Cortez. It sits up in the mountains, providing spectacular views of Mesa Verde and Sleeping Ute Mountain to the south.

It's about 18 miles from Mancos to the junction with CO 145 near Dolores. At this junction, you can go right for about a mile into Dolores, where you'll find basic services. If you go left instead, you'll soon come to a right turn— the continuation of CO 184. Take this right, and you'll pass a roadside food store. Nine more miles will bring you to the junction of US 666, where you'll find another store for the basics.

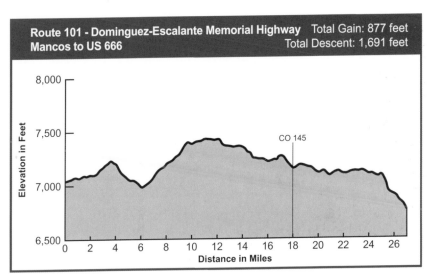

Route 101 - Dominguez-Escalante Memorial Highway   Total Gain: 877 feet
Mancos to US 666   Total Descent: 1,691 feet

Route 102

HESPERUS HILL
US 160: DURANGO TO CORTEZ

46 Miles • Moderate

West of Durango, US 160 starts with gently climbing terrain for a couple of miles before the grade begins to steepen into a solid climb up Hesperus Hill. A fast mile brings you down into the town of Hesperus, which boasts a roadside store for the basics. This 10-mile climb and short descent is an excellent out-and-back from Durango.

Continuing west from Hesperus, US 160 descends moderately for another 10 miles. This section is very fast with excellent shoulders for most of the way to Cortez. The bottom of the descent brings you to Cherry Creek, where a short, steep hill just over a mile long is your last obstacle before a fast descent brings you into Mancos, about 6 miles farther. Mancos is small and basic, but it has a couple of markets, and some great food can be found—just ask around.

Continuing west on US 160, roughly 6 miles of moderate rollers will bring you to the turnoff for Mesa Verde National Park and another astonishing ride (Route 105, p. 229). Home to Anasazi ruins and spectacular views, this national park charges an entry fee, but paying to ride in Mesa Verde is worth every penny. Continuing past Mesa Verde on US 160, you'll ride for about 10 more miles on a relatively flat road before reaching Cortez. Here you will be able to meet all of your basic needs.

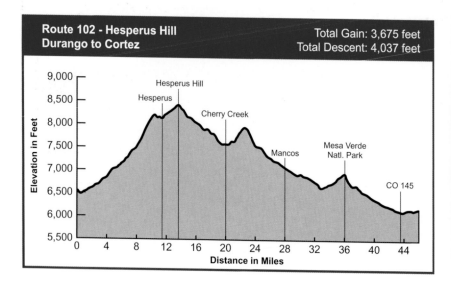

Route 102 - Hesperus Hill
Durango to Cortez
Total Gain: 3,675 feet
Total Descent: 4,037 feet

Route 103

WILDCAT CANYON ROAD
CR 141: US 160 TO CO 140

11 Miles • Moderate

Some excellent routes lie just west of Durango in the hills around Red Mesa. Wildcat Canyon Road is one of them, and it is in great shape with no shoulder. Traffic can be heavy during commuting hours, but the views are outstanding. Durango has everything you need in the way of supplies and accommodations. Just over 2 miles west of Durango on US 160, you'll see a left turn (southwest) onto Wildcat Canyon Road (CR 141). The road is a bit narrow with lots of curves as it cruises through the canyon, so be alert. You'll climb moderately for the first mile or so, then the road will mellow into some easy rollers with an uphill trend. Another couple of miles up the road, and you'll start into a fairly steep ramp just over a mile long. The road will curve abruptly to the left (west) at the top, which is the junction with CR 125. From here, the road straightens out and heads into some nice gentle rollers for the rest of the way to its junction with CO 140.

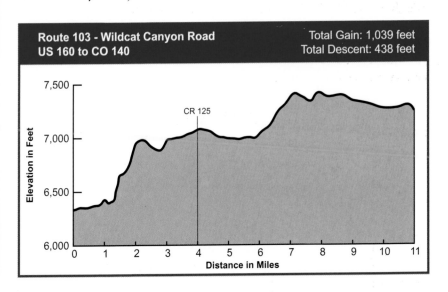

CO 140
HESPERUS TO NEW MEXICO STATE LINE

23 Miles • Easy

Start this route about 11 miles west of Durango at the junction of CO 140 and US 160, where you'll find the very small community of Hesperus and a food store with the basics. Head south on CO 140, which is fairly flat with a slight downhill trend. You'll find some small rollers along the way, and about 8 miles down the road (just before Breen) you'll see the junction with Wildcat Canyon Road—a great loop when combined with this ride (Route 103, p. 227). Continue south on CO 140, and another 15 miles will bring you to the New Mexico state line, with tremendous views the whole way.

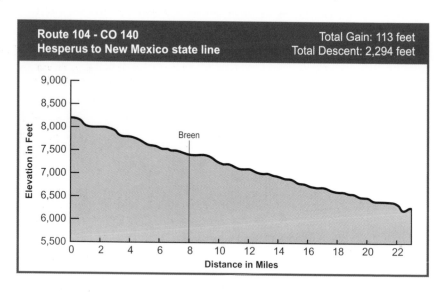

Route 104 - CO 140
Hesperus to New Mexico state line

Total Gain: 113 feet
Total Descent: 2,294 feet

Route 105

RUINS ROAD, Mesa Verde National Park
MANCOS TO END OF EAST LOOP
FEE REQUIRED: $5/BIKE, $10/VEHICLE

30 Miles • Difficult

If I were to write a cycling guide about the top 50 American road routes, I'd say Colorado could take credit for at least five, and Mesa Verde's Ruins Road is one of the finest. The desert unfolds to the west as the La Plata Mountains soar on the eastern horizon. You'll have lots of climbing at the start of Ruins Road, so I suggest you start this route in Mancos, 7 miles west of the park entrance, to warm up. Mancos has basic services and sublime views.

Expect lots of fast corners riding through the rollers of Mesa Verde National Park

US 160 from Mancos to the park entrance is in excellent shape with a large shoulder, but it can see a lot of high-speed traffic. As with any popular destination, reconsider plans to cycle Mesa Verde on the weekend in peak summer season, as the roads can be very busy. Approaching the park, you'll see the road as it climbs up the east rim of the massive mesa. Exit right off US 160 for Mesa Verde, then go left over the bridge. The road is in excellent shape, but the shoulder varies greatly. It's less than a mile of gentle uphill to the park gate; from here it's about 15 miles to the visitor center and about 23 miles to the eastern cliff loop at the end of the road.

After a few steep switchbacks, you'll pass MM 2. The road winds around the east side of the rim and heads up toward the top. As you ride this section, the views of the area are fantastic. At this point, you'll be well above the Mancos Valley. Just before MM 4, the road goes around a right-hand bend, through a shallow notch on the east rim, and into a secluded valley where Morefield Village is located. Here you'll find basics including food, gas, and restrooms.

After a half mile, you'll see a quarter-mile-long tunnel. This tunnel is not lit, and is just long enough for the darkness to be a bit sketchy. Headlights and taillights are good to have here. I wait for a break in traffic, or ask a motorist if I can ride in front of their car through the tunnel. On the descent out of the park, your speed renders the tunnel less of a problem—just be wary.

As you emerge from the tunnel, the road takes you through another narrow valley. Mesa Verde National Park has many narrow canyons and valleys, all running more or less parallel from north to south. All of these valleys, and the mesas in between them, sit atop the giant—Mesa Verde. Ruins Road cuts across this terrain from east to west along the north rim, creating a roller-coaster effect as it winds and rolls. As you continue, the views open up, providing some glimpses of where you are headed. From Morefield Village it's 11 miles to Far View Visitor Center, where you'll find more basics. The road rolls relentlessly as it climbs to the park's high point (8,571') just before Far View.

At Far View, you'll find the turnoff for the remote Wetherill Mesa Road, as well as supplies. Continuing past Far View, the terrain changes. The view from this area, Chapin Mesa, is astounding. The entire Four Corners region is spread out before your eyes! The route straightens out and begins a gradual descent for 6 miles to the end of the road. This section is deceiving; while it feels like a moderate descent, it is not. You will descend just as much as you climbed from Mancos, and the subsequent climb back to the park's high point can be a bit of a grind.

Out toward the end of Chapin Mesa, turn right at the first intersection for restrooms and water at the nearby museum. Heading back to this intersection, continue south for less than a half mile to another junction, this time of two short, scenic loops with incredible views of Anasazi cliff dwellings.

Turn left for the east loop. (Straight ahead takes you to the west loop.) The east loop takes you past the famous Cliff Palace. Also look for an Indian fry-bread stand at the south end to get the sustenance you'll need to get yourself back to Far View. Try the west loop, too. If you want a real bruiser of a ride, try this one as an out-and-back from Durango. It's a mere 120 miles round-trip!

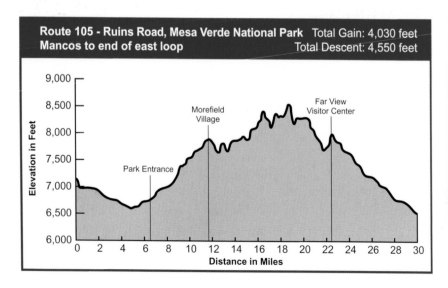

Route 106

FOUR CORNERS
US 666/US 160: CORTEZ TO NEW MEXICO STATE LINE

26 Miles • Easy

You will ride south into the desert and through the Ute Mountain Indian Reservation on this stretch of road—no more trees and very little H_2O. In cooler months, however, this scenic route can make for very pleasant cycling on relatively straight, gently rolling terrain. The canyons of Mesa Verde lie to the east for much of the ride. The road has a good but varying shoulder width, and there are a few services along the way. The Ute Mountain Tribal Park Headquarters are at the junction where US 160 and US 666 split.

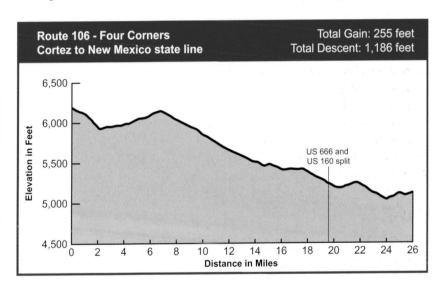

Route 106 - Four Corners
Cortez to New Mexico state line

Total Gain: 255 feet
Total Descent: 1,186 feet

US 666 and US 160 split

Route 107

DEVIL'S HIGHWAY
US 666: CORTEZ TO UTAH STATE LINE

43 Miles • Easy

Winding north from Cortez through moderate, rolling farm country, this highway passes plenty of food stops along the way. You'll also have incredible vistas of the majestic, faraway peaks of the San Miguel and La Plata Mountains rising above the horizon to the east. At 10 miles you'll reach CO 184 heading east to Dolores. It's another 25 miles to Dove Creek. Two miles farther on US 666 will bring you to the junction with CO 141—an excellent route toward Naturita (Route 109, p. 234). From this junction, it's 6 more miles to the Utah state line.

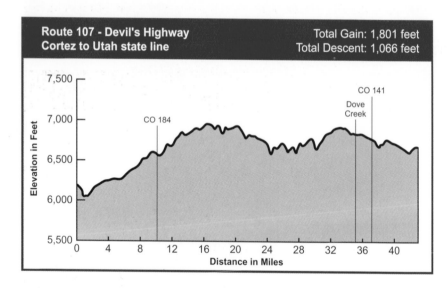

Route 107 - Devil's Highway
Cortez to Utah state line

Total Gain: 1,801 feet
Total Descent: 1,066 feet

NATURITA CANYON
CO 145/CO 141: PLACERVILLE TO NATURITA

37 Miles • Easy

Many people who live in this area commute to Telluride for work, so CO 145 can see some traffic. However, the farther west you ride, the less traffic you'll find. All in all, this is a nice, easy route. As you head out of Placerville toward Naturita, CO 145 winds along the San Miguel River, eventually climbing a bit to the flats around Norwood after about 17 miles. It is gentle, sloping terrain as you cycle through this agricultural and mining country. You will reach the small community of Redvale at about 26 miles. The road winds a bit as you approach Naturita. About 4 miles from Naturita, CO 145 junctions with CO 141, which will take you west into town. Naturita has the basics and boasts an espresso shop. There is some pavement north to Nucla, as well as other short connecting roads in the area. Have at it!

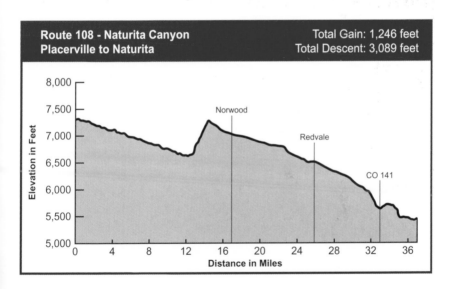

Route 108 - Naturita Canyon
Placerville to Naturita

Total Gain: 1,246 feet
Total Descent: 3,089 feet

Route 109

GYPSUM GAP
CO 141: US 666 TO NATURITA

61 Miles • Moderate

The landscape is vast near the town of Dove Creek, and you can see the Blue Mountains outside of Monticello, Utah, on the western horizon. Heading north from US 666, CO 141 is a straight road with moderate rollers. As you ride through these farm fields, the air is fresh and the sky extends forever.

Ten miles north of US 666 you'll reach Egnar, where there are no services. In fact, there's not much of anything. Up to this point, you will have been slowly gaining elevation, and at Egnar the road starts winding a bit. At MM 16 (16 miles north of US 666), you'll start a steep descent into Disappointment Valley. It's a 7-percent grade, and you'll plummet consistently for 6 miles. There are some pretty cool sandstone formations around here, and you'll ride through fairly sharp curves on your way down into the valley.

Lone Cone looms in the distance as you ride through Disappointment Valley

There's nothing in the town of Slick Rock, and from here it's 38 miles to Naturita. The descent levels out into some moderate, rolling terrain, and at MM 25 you'll be riding through Disappointment Valley toward Gypsum Gap. The magnificent, pointed peak to the right (southeast) is Lone Cone (12,613'). Up and over a few hills, and the road takes you through Gypsum Gap (6,100') into the Big Gypsum Valley.

When you reach Dry Creek Basin, you'll see views of the San Miguel Mountains to the southeast and the massive Uncompahgre Plateau to the north. It's big country out here, and a carefree feeling persists as you cruise along a gently descending road. Go left (west) when you reach the junction of CO 141 and CO 145, and 4 miles on a good mellow road will bring you to Naturita for basic services and espresso.

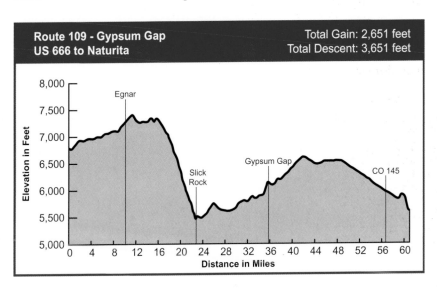

Route 109 - Gypsum Gap
US 666 to Naturita

Total Gain: 2,651 feet
Total Descent: 3,651 feet

REGION 7
WESTERN SLOPE

The Western Slope of Colorado has a vast and varied landscape. You'll find high mountains, huge mesas, lowland valleys, and arid hills and canyons. Grand Junction sits at the western edge of the Rocky Mountains and is the largest town in this region. Here you'll find all of your needs attended to. Other towns in the area include Meeker, Rifle, Delta, and Montrose, any of which can accommodate you with basic supplies. Summers can be hot on the Western Slope, but for the most part, you'll find excellent weather for much of the year, especially when other parts of Colorado are in a deep freeze. Notable routes in this region include Paradox Valley (Route 110, p. 240), Unaweep Canyon (Route 111, p. 242), Rim Rock Drive (Route 115, p. 247), and Grand Mesa Scenic Byway (Route 116, p. 249).

ROUTES

Rim Rock Drive in Colorado National Monument, Route 115

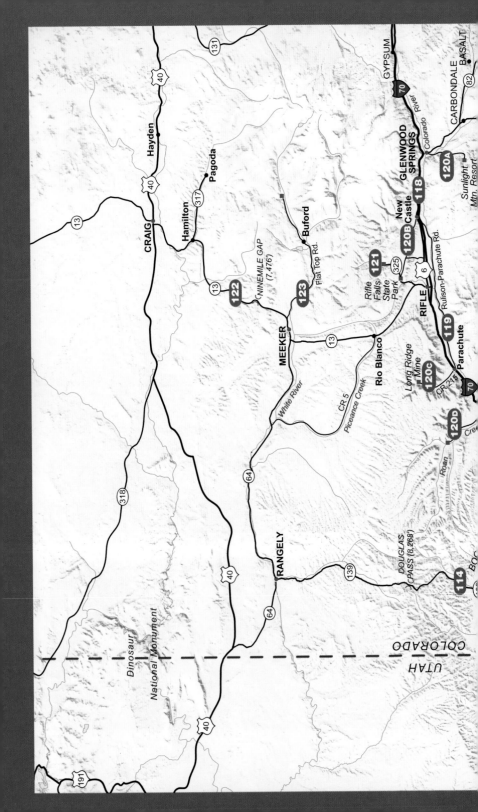

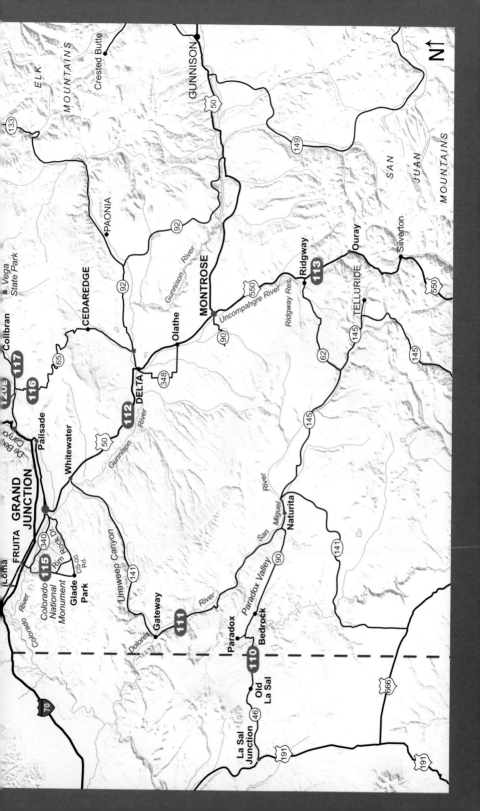

Route 110

PARADOX VALLEY
CO 90/UT 46: Naturita to La Sal Junction, UT

57 Miles • Difficult

In Naturita, you'll find the basics, including espresso. As you head west out of town, you'll wind along the San Miguel River on CO 141. Two miles out, you'll reach the junction with CO 90; go left (south). The road is great, with little or no shoulder, and climbs gently as you head toward the mouth of the Paradox Valley. After a gradual descent of about 20 miles through a seemingly desolate valley, you'll find the town of Bedrock. It's very fast toward Bedrock. (If you're coming the other way—ouch! It's not steep, but it's long and straight.) Sandstone cliffs several hundred feet high line the ridges on either side of the valley.

At Bedrock, you'll find a very basic store and nothing else. It's about 5 more miles to Paradox, and you may start wondering why you are riding this road; just be patient. At the turn to Paradox (MM 10), it looks like the valley dead-ends. The La Sal Mountains of Utah loom large overhead. Nowhere to go but up, and that's just what you'll do, as the road makes a sharp left hairpin and launches into a whole different type of ride. The road is narrow and of varying quality. Three miles of steep, consistent climbing follow, but you'll be rewarded with incredible views of the valley and the La Sal Mountains. As you descend along the La Sal Creek, the terrain becomes more and more like the canyon country of Utah—sandstone cliffs and formations everywhere.

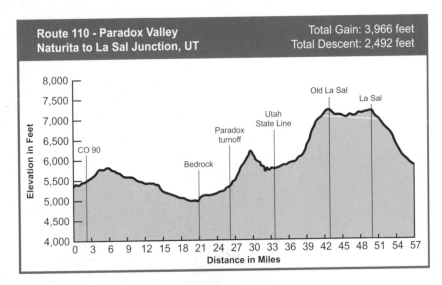

Route 110 - Paradox Valley
Naturita to La Sal Junction, UT

Total Gain: 3,966 feet
Total Descent: 2,492 feet

After MM 4, you'll find 3 miles of steep, winding descent before you ride through a beautiful, lush canyon. At the Utah state line, the road name changes to UT 46 and mile markers start with approximately MM 22, again counting down. Another steep climb of 9-percent grades greets you at MM 20 and continues for a few miles. At MM 18, the road begins to level off into the moderately rolling countryside around Old La Sal.

There's phenomenal beauty up here. It's hard to believe that Moab and Canyonlands National Park are just on the other side of these mountains. The road descends to meet UT 191 at La Sal Junction, but there are really no services to speak of out here.

BONUS: Back before your first climb (near Paradox at MM 10), turn right on CR 5.75 and go for about a mile until you reach Paradox. There are no services there. Main Street in this quaint little outpost is Road U-5. Take that west (left) for a couple of miles on a narrow country road and you'll come to another climb. This climb is short, sweet, and perfect after your climb to Old La Sal. It's 2 miles of grades, 10 percent and higher—very steep and usually strewn with dirt and rocks from rain runoff. Watch it on the descent; the pavement turns to dirt after a couple of miles.

It's canyon country near the Utah state line

Route 111

UNAWEEP CANYON
CO 141: NATURITA TO WHITEWATER

96 Miles • Difficult

Just west of Naturita on CO 141, you'll be cycling through nearly 20 miles of arid landscape along the San Miguel River. The scenery in this area is incredible. Along the ride, you'll catch views of some big country, and the canyon keeps getting deeper.

Hanging Flume, where the San Miguel River meets the Dolores River, is a point of interest worth mentioning. Here, the canyon walls drop several hundred feet below you, and high on the cliffs you'll see the remnants of a water flume built directly into the cliff face—an unusual reminder of Colorado's mining history.

Views of river-carved canyons distinguish this ride

About 5 miles later, you'll drop into the Dolores River Canyon itself. This is spectacular! Beautiful sandstone walls tower above this narrow canyon as you ride along the river.

You will reach the town of Gateway at MM 111—about 51 miles from your starting point. Here you'll find gas and a small grocery store. It is a mixture of mountains and mesas as you leave Dolores Canyon and begin the route through Unaweep Canyon, an amazing and remote place. As you ride along West Creek, the road gradually and moderately climbs toward the Unaweep Divide. The cliffs found here are some of Colorado's best and most secret rock-climbing spots! The Unaweep Divide is located about halfway between Gateway and Whitewater. It's unmarked; from here you will begin a gradual descent of more than 20 miles.

At MM 146, this descent becomes steeper but is still moderate. After 5 miles of sustained downhill you reach a valley called The Hunting Ground. Soon after you'll be in Whitewater; there is a basic market but not much else. Grand Junction, a large town with full services and amenities, is 10 miles northwest on US 50.

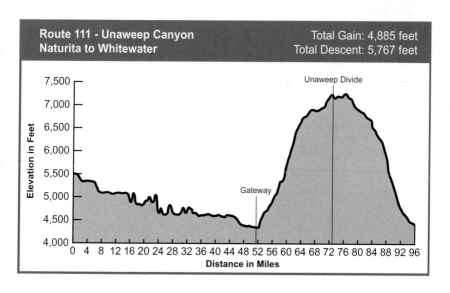

Route 112

GUNNISON RIVER VALLEY
US 50: GRAND JUNCTION TO MONTROSE

61 Miles • Easy

Grand Junction is a beautiful town with full services and excellent opportunities for cycling. US 50 is a great route from Grand Junction to Montrose. It's moderately flat, on a wide road with an excellent shoulder. Traffic is heavy and fast, but the views are incredible and there are plenty of services along the way. US 50 heads south from Grand Junction and follows the Gunnison River. It's 9 miles to Whitewater and another 31 miles to Delta, where you'll find basic supplies. It's 21 miles from Delta to Montrose, with stunning views the whole way. For routes around Delta and Montrose, check Route 64 (p. 136), Routes 71–73 (pp. 158–162), and Route 97 (p. 217).

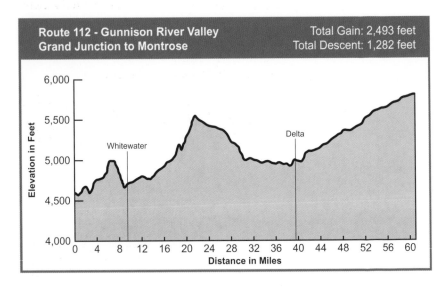

Route 112 - Gunnison River Valley
Grand Junction to Montrose

Total Gain: 2,493 feet
Total Descent: 1,282 feet

Route 113

RIDGWAY RESERVOIR
US 550: MONTROSE TO OURAY

37 Miles • Easy

Prepare yourself for a fantastic, mellow cruise. If you ride south on US 550 from Montrose, you'll have a difficult time watching the road, as the views of the Sneffels and Uncompahgre Ranges are absolutely mind-boggling. It is hard to rate the beauty of the scenery in Colorado, especially on a comparative basis, but if I were to subject this one to the old 1-to-10 scale, I'd have to say that it ranks a firm "20." The views in this area are some of the most awe-inspiring in Colorado. The road south from Montrose is mostly flat and straight. The traffic is heavy and fast, but you'll have room.

You'll see Ridgway Reservoir just before you reach the town of Ridgway. Twenty-six miles south of Montrose, Ridgway offers basic services and accesses an excellent route up Dallas Divide on CO 62 (Route 98, p. 220). Continue on US 550 for 11 miles to Ouray—a cool little town with the basics. From here, you can extend your ride to include the spectacular climb up Red Mountain Pass (Route 97, p. 217) by continuing on US 550 south to Silverton.

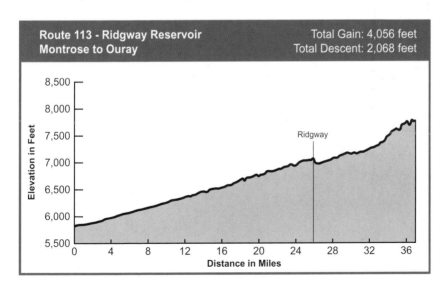

Route 113 - Ridgway Reservoir
Montrose to Ouray

Total Gain: 4,056 feet
Total Descent: 2,068 feet

Route 114

DOUGLAS PASS
CO 139: LOMA TO RANGELY

73 Miles • Moderate

This part of the state is Boonieville—nothing out here. CO 139 is generally in great shape, with a varying shoulder, but don't count on any services. The route is also great as an out-and-back from Loma (about 18 miles west of Grand Junction) to the top of Douglas Pass (8,268'), which is about 70 miles round-trip.

As you approach the climb, the arid terrain of the Book Cliffs turns to forest. The pass itself is an excellent, winding climb of moderate length and steepness through some gorgeous rolling hills. Farther north toward Rangely, the road straightens and flattens out. The landscape becomes arid once again. In Rangely you can find the basics.

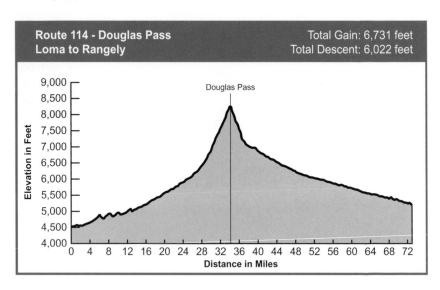

Route 114 - Douglas Pass
Loma to Rangely
Total Gain: 6,731 feet
Total Descent: 6,022 feet

Route 115

RIM ROCK DRIVE,
Colorado National Monument
Grand Junction to Fruita
Fee required: $3/bike, $5/vehicle

Approximately 30 Miles • Difficult

In all of Colorado there is no route like Rim Rock Drive. It has gained notoriety among cyclists for a few reasons. This loop was part of the now defunct Coors Classic Bicycle Race (formerly Red Zinger), and the route also appears in the movie *American Flyer*. Nicknamed "Tour of the Moon" because of the sandstone cliffs and formations along the way, it climbs high above Grand Junction, with sweeping vistas of the Western Slope. There are many narrow sections and several short tunnels. It's quite a grind, and the temperature can be very hot in this semiarid landscape. I do not recommend it on weekends, when traffic can be heavy and slow.

From Grand Junction, head west on Broadway (CO 340) and cross the Colorado River; signs point the way. Turn left on Monument Road just after the Colorado River. It's about 4 miles of gentle rollers to the monument entrance.

There are no mile markers on this route. The climbing begins past the entrance, becoming steep in spots. The rock walls and the warm color of sandstone are appealing against the blue sky. After about 3 miles with several switchbacks, on narrow road with no shoulder, you will see the first tunnel. If vehicles are behind you, make sure they see you; get in the middle of your lane and make them wait. The tunnels are short.

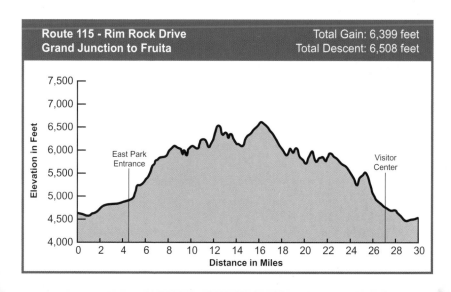

Route 115 - Rim Rock Drive
Grand Junction to Fruita
Total Gain: 6,399 feet
Total Descent: 6,508 feet

Roadside view from Rim Rock Drive

Four miles from the entrance there is a bonus ride to Glade Park if you turn left (southwest) onto Road DS-00. Past the Glade Park turn, the climb backs off into moderate, uphill rollers, and, in a little over 3 more miles, you'll pass a sign: "Elevation 6,640 ft." This is the high point of the monument.

As you continue winding along you'll get glimpses down into the heart of the monument. The drop-offs are insane, and the sandstone cliffs and formations are incredible. On the west side of the park, you will find yourself in a small, secluded, canyonlike area. A gentle climb of a couple of miles takes you to another high point, where the views open up in all their glory.

After this second high point, you'll start descending toward the monument's west gate. Tight corners, unsettling drop-offs, and great views abound. Soon you'll see the visitor center, where you can get water. The road continues to drop sharply, and you'll ride through two short tunnels in the midst of several tight, sharp switchbacks before arriving at the park's west entrance.

Just past the west entrance is the junction with CO 340. Go north at the junction for 3 miles to Fruita—a town with services and a good bike shop. You can also turn right on CO 340 and end up where you started instead of going into Fruita. You'll ride this section of CO 340 about 9.5 miles back to its other junction with Monument Drive.

BONUS: Four miles from the monument entrance, turn left on Road DS-00, which moderately rolls and winds its way south and west. Enjoy beautiful mesas, a good road with no shoulder, and serious solitude. It is 5 miles to Glade Park and its small store. The road continues 10 miles beyond—an excellent addition to an already spectacular ride.

Route 116

GRAND MESA SCENIC BYWAY
CO 65: I-70 TO CO 92

62 Miles • Moderate

Grand Junction is a relatively large town where you will find all you need before heading east on I-70 about 17 miles to its junction with CO 65, the starting point for this ride.

As you head up a narrow valley on CO 65, the road is in good shape, but the shoulder comes and goes. The road winds along for 10 miles to its junction with CO 330 (see Route 117, p. 251). The scenery here includes cottonwood trees along Plateau Creek and some sandstone formations. After you pass the junction, it's 2 more miles on CO 65 to Mesa, which has a general store and gas. There is no shoulder, but the road is good.

By MM 47, you're in a subalpine zone. Aspens, pines, and meadows await as you climb higher. The views open up and by MM 45, the reality of the vertical gain sets in. Grand Mesa is the largest flat-topped mountain in the world and one of Colorado's highest vertical gains in a single paved climb.

The climb is generally moderate the whole way, and at MM 42 you'll pass Powderhorn Resort. You can get water at the restaurant, which is open in the summer (Wednesday through Saturday). At MM 40, you'll find a roadside restroom. The road then winds through three moderate switchbacks, and at MM 38 drops away abruptly—you can see all the way to Utah.

Around MM 37, the climbing backs off. Expect moderate rollers as you cross the top of Grand Mesa. After MM 33 you'll see an elevation sign (10,839').

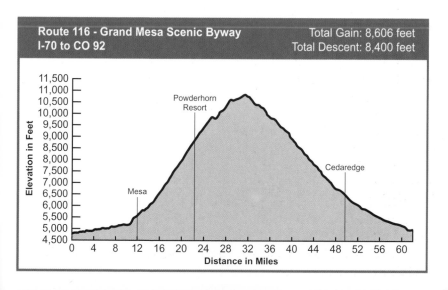

Route 116 - Grand Mesa Scenic Byway
I-70 to CO 92

Total Gain: 8,606 feet
Total Descent: 8,400 feet

At about MM 28, you'll come to the Grand Mesa Lodge, where you can load up on basics. Island Lake will soon be in view. You would never believe the number of lakes up here—more than 200! The forests hide most of them.

By MM 24, you can see the San Juan Mountains stretching across the southern horizon. If you know these amazing peaks, you can rattle off their names one by one as you peer across nearly 100 miles of ridgeline.

At MM 21, you'll be on a long descent into Cedaredge, at MM 12. This little town has all the basics plus espresso. There are 12 more miles of gentle, down-sloping road to the junction with CO 92, where there are no services. (Delta is just a few miles west on CO 92, however, and has basic services.)

When I was working on this guidebook, I thought the area around Grand Junction was just arid country full of dry scrub. But when I went there to document the road on Grand Mesa, I was surprised to find aspen and pine forests. Aspens only grow between 8,000 and 10,000 feet, and Grand Junction sits at only 4,600 feet. I hadn't realized that the summit of this flat-topped mountain is around 11,000 feet in elevation and that hundreds of lakes dot the mesa. For the cyclist, that means nearly 6,300 feet of vertical gain from Grand Junction! There are roads that are higher in elevation, but only one other route in the state has this kind of vertical gain. I was beside myself—just stunned—as I rode up it.

Grand Mesa, the world's largest flat-topped mountain

Route 117

VEGA RESERVOIR
CO 330: CO 65 TO VEGA STATE PARK

23 Miles • Moderate

This is an exquisite road tucked away below the northern slopes of Grand Mesa. The scenery at the junction of CO 65 and CO 330, about 10 miles from I-70's Exit 49, is otherworldly. Sandstone formations rising above this secluded little valley distinguish it from the surrounding terrain.

It's 11 miles to the town of Collbran on a mellow, rolling road that is in excellent condition with no shoulder. In Collbran, at MM 11, you can find the basics. The landscape changes to beautiful, forested, rolling mountains and lush green valleys, with Grand Mesa looming to the south. Collbran itself is immaculate—this town has a real sense of pride.

It's 12 more miles to Vega State Park. As you ride along this beautiful valley, lush gives way to more lush. After a nice, moderate climb of a couple of miles you will see the dam. As with all state parks, you must pay to get in.

The pavement goes around the north side of the reservoir and turns to dirt, but it's a great little loop back to the dam and well worth it. There is only about a mile more pavement past the park entrance, so if you don't want to ride dirt, then turn around and head back here.

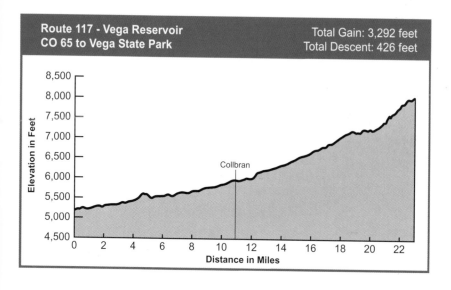

Route 117 - Vega Reservoir
CO 65 to Vega State Park

Total Gain: 3,292 feet
Total Descent: 426 feet

Route 118

GRAND HOGBACK
US 6: GLENWOOD SPRINGS TO RIFLE

27 Miles • Easy

Glenwood Springs is a great town and has all the supplies you'll need. None of the side roads heading west out of Glenwood go through, so you will have to ride on I-70 until Exit 109, about 7 miles west of town. Here, US 6 divides from I-70 and provides an excellent frontage road with mellow, rolling terrain on a slight downhill trend as you descend the Western Slope of the Rockies. You'll travel through a break in the Grand Hogback at New Castle, then to the town of Silt on your way to Rifle. These towns have basic supplies. For rides north of Silt and Rifle, check out Route 121 (p. 260) and Route 124 (p. 268); for a route to the south, see Route 119, (p. 253).

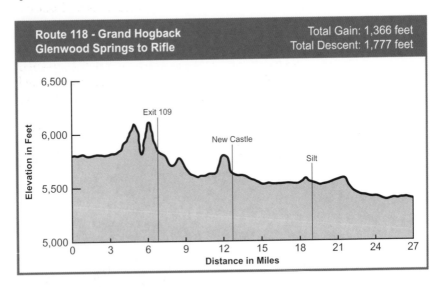

Route 118 - Grand Hogback
Glenwood Springs to Rifle

Total Gain: 1,366 feet
Total Descent: 1,777 feet

Route 119

RULISON-PARACHUTE ROAD
NEW CASTLE TO PARACHUTE

Approximately 34 Miles • Easy

A bunch of county roads lie on the south side of I-70 between Glenwood Springs and Grand Junction. Most of them are unpaved, but one east-west route west of Glenwood Springs is on pavement most of the way. The road is in pretty good condition, with no shoulder, hardly any traffic, and basic services. You'll encounter many intersections and side roads, and the road numbers will change several times, but if you stick to the pavement you should be able to get through without too much confusion. The mileage through here is approximate, so watch the road signs. The DeLorme *Colorado Atlas & Gazetteer* (see Appendix E) will be very helpful for this section.

About 11 miles west of Glenwood Springs and just east of New Castle on I-70 is Exit 105. If you exit to the south here, you'll find CR 335. Turn right (west) and cruise along the Colorado River through a beautiful, open valley toward Silt. About 7 miles or so west on CR 335, you'll come to a three-way intersection with CR 311. You'll want to stay right (west) to stay on route and continue west on CR 311 for just over a mile to the next intersection, this time

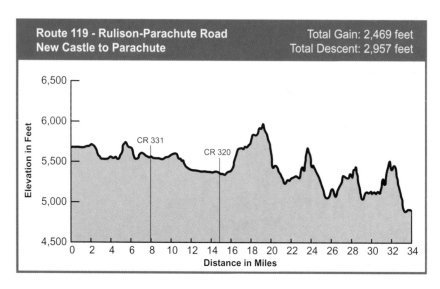

Route 119 - Rulison-Parachute Road
New Castle to Parachute

Total Gain: 2,469 feet
Total Descent: 2,957 feet

with CR 331. A right turn (north) here will take you into Silt, where you can find basic supplies (about a mile away). If no supplies are needed, go straight (west) at this intersection and you will be on CR 331. Continue west on CR 331 for barely a mile to yet another three-way intersection with CR 346. Head straight (west) through this intersection and you will stay on CR 346 until Rifle, about 7 miles away. Just south of Rifle, you'll come to a "T" intersection with CR 320; here a right turn (north) will take you under I-70 (at Exit 90) about a half mile into Rifle, where you'll find basic supplies.

If no supplies are needed then turn left (south) at this "T" intersection and you'll be on CR 320, which will immediately curve to the right (west). Eventually the road will be labeled Rulison–Parachute Road/CR 320; this may help if you get confused. Soon you'll start climbing moderately for a few miles and run into some short dirt sections in fairly good condition. You'll be climbing up onto Taughenbaugh Mesa, and the views of the surrounding area and the Colorado River down below are quite beautiful.

Stay on CR 320 through the climbing and some easy rollers to a "T" intersection with CR 309 in about 7 miles. Turn left (west) and follow CR 309 through easy terrain back down to the river for about 8 miles to a 4-way intersection with CR 308 and CR 301. Turn right (west) onto CR 301 and make another right turn (west) onto CR 300, where you will cross the Colorado River and I-70 (at Exit 75) as you head into Parachute. You will come into town on CR 215, and you can take care of your basic needs here.

Routes 120A–E

GLENWOOD SPRINGS AND GRAND JUNCTION AREA BACKROADS

I don't recommend riding on I-70 unless you have to, and sometimes you have to. Fortunately, there is an excellent shoulder on the stretch of interstate between Glenwood Springs and Grand Junction. And where the interstate is off-limits to cyclists, there is usually a side road to be found. From Glenwood to Grand Junction, you'll have many choices for alternate routes.

Route 120A

SUNLIGHT MOUNTAIN
CR 117: GLENWOOD SPRINGS TO SUNLIGHT MOUNTAIN RESORT

12 Miles • Easy

Heading west out of Glenwood Springs, take 27th Street down across the Roaring Fork River and veer left (south). The climb begins moderately and forks after a couple of miles. Go right on CR 117. It's about 12 miles from town to Sunlight Mountain Resort. The climb is moderate with some gentle rollers and a steeper section at the end. The road is great, with no shoulder and very little traffic, as it's tucked out of sight in the hills west of Glenwood Springs and Carbondale. The Sunlight Mountain Inn can provide you with the basics, as well as beer.

CR 117 climbs gently to Sunlight Mountain Resort

Glenwood Springs and Grand Junction
Area Backroads (Routes 120A–E)

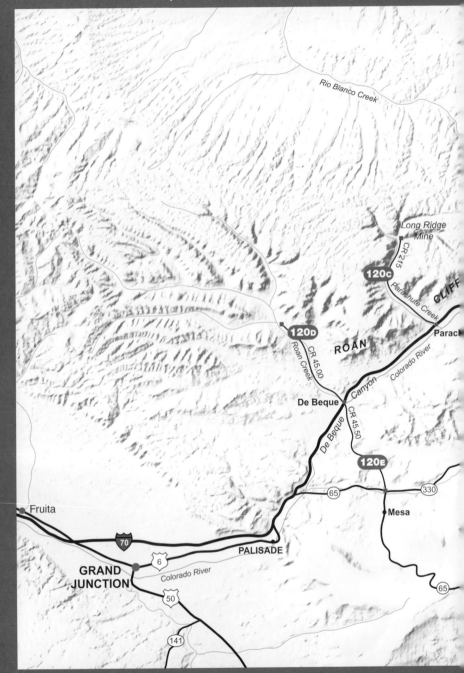

Rio Blanco Creek

Long Ridge Mine

CR 215

120C

Parachute Creek

CLIFF

120D

ROAN

Parac

Colorado River

Roan Creek

CR 45.00

De Beque

De Beque Canyon

CR 45.50

120E

Fruita

65

330

Mesa

70

6

PALISADE

GRAND JUNCTION

Colorado River

50

141

65

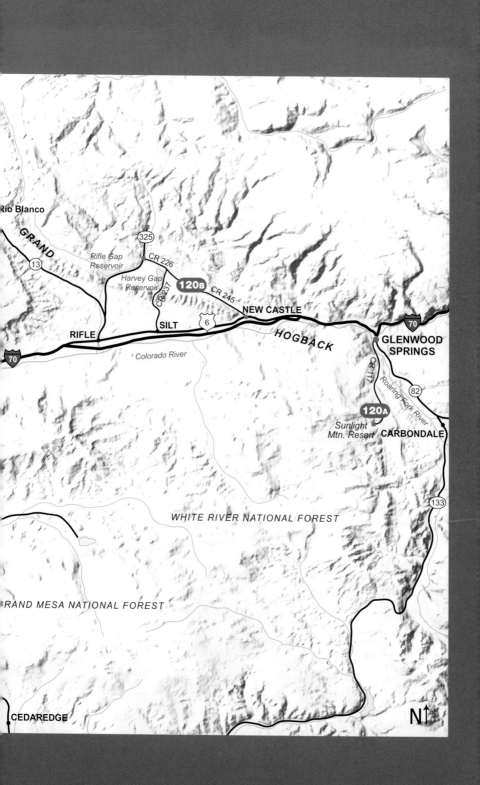

Route 120B

HARVEY GAP RESERVOIR
CR 245/CR 226: New Castle to CO 325

15 Miles • Easy

Beautiful, quaint backroads in the hills north of New Castle make up this route. Head north from the west end of town on CR 245. There is moderate, rolling terrain and no traffic. Seven or so miles in, you'll come to CR 226; take this, as CR 245 turns to dirt as it continues north. In a few more miles, you'll pass CR 237 on the left; it heads into the town of Silt (basic supplies) after going past Harvey Gap Reservoir. A ride of about 5 more miles on CR 226 takes you to the junction with CO 325.

Route 120c

LONG RIDGE MINE
CR 215: Parachute to Long Ridge Mine

15 Miles • Easy

A small town several miles west of Rifle, just off I-70 (Exit 75), Parachute has basic supplies. CR 215 is a fun little route that heads north from Parachute toward the Long Ridge Mine, near the Roan Plateau. The countryside here as you ride along Parachute Creek is pretty arid. You'll find a very gentle uphill trend with some subtle rollers and several small ground swells along the way. CR 215 is basically deserted except for occasional mining vehicles; it's a wide road with plenty of room and in fair condition. The road dead-ends at the mine—there are no services. It's a fast ride back to Parachute, with really nice views.

For a glimpse of mining country, head north from Parachute on CR 215

Route 120D

ROAN CREEK VALLEY
CR 45.00: DE BEQUE TO END OF PAVEMENT

11 Miles • Easy

D e Beque is a small town with basic supplies in a beautiful setting beside the Colorado River. It is located about 13 miles west of Parachute right next to I-70 at Exit 62. CR 45.00 heads north from De Beque along Roan Creek with the Roan Cliffs on your right (east). The terrain has a gentle uphill trend. The road is in good shape, with no shoulder and very little traffic. You'll find no services where the pavement ends.

Route 120E

DE BEQUE CANYON BYPASS
CR 45.50/CO 65: DE BEQUE TO PALISADE

Approximately 32 Miles • Easy

W est of Rifle, De Beque is next to the Colorado River and I-70 (Exit 62). You will find basic supplies here, and Grand Mesa looms large to the southeast.

If you want to get from De Beque to Palisade, CR 45.50 is the way to start. You can take I-70 the whole way, but I don't recommend it: Things get a little tight through De Beque Canyon, and then there are the Beaver Trail Tunnels, where bicycles are not permitted. A bike path skirts the tunnels, but it's not very pleasant. CR 45.50 heads south across I-70 at Exit 62. It's a great road in pretty good condition. There's no shoulder but little traffic.

The terrain is pretty flat and straight for a couple of miles, then it starts to climb and roll very moderately up into the foothills around Grand Mesa. The views are fantastic, and you'll see some funky sandstone formations as you get closer to the junction with CO 65. There are no services at the junction, but if you go left (south) for 2 miles on CO 65, you'll find the town of Mesa, where you can get basic supplies. To continue on to Palisade, you'll need to turn right (west) at the junction with CO 65 and proceed for about 10 miles to where it intersects with I-70 at Exit 49. Get onto the interstate and head west for about 7 miles into Palisade, where you'll find basic services.

Route 121

RIFLE FALLS
CO 13/CO 325: RIFLE TO RIFLE FALLS STATE PARK

Approximately 15 Miles • Easy

Rifle is a basic, low-key town just off of I-70 at Exit 90. There's a bike shop here called The Patched Tire. Head north from Rifle on CO 13 for about 3 miles to the junction with CO 325, on the right. Continue north on CO 325 for about 12 miles as the route gently rolls and climbs to Rifle Falls State Park. At MM 2, an incredible rock "fin" juts from the ground—pretty cool. Rifle Gap Reservoir, at MM 4, is beautiful. The pavement ends at Rifle Falls State Park.

Beautiful views and light traffic accompany you to Rifle Falls State Park

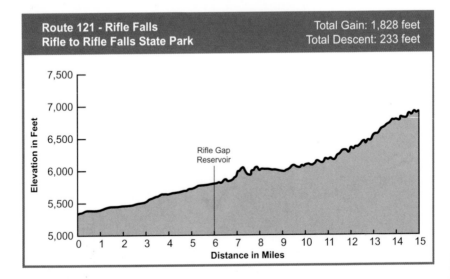

Route 122

NINEMILE GAP
CO 13: RIFLE TO CRAIG

89 Miles • Moderate

Heading north from Rifle on CO 13, the road is curved and rolling. The pavement is a bit hacked up in places. By MM 10 you'll be on an incline, with moderate, sustained climbing to MM 16. Then you'll top out onto some long, gradual rollers.

At MM 19, you'll reach the town of Rio Blanco (no services). If you turn left onto CR 5, you'll find about 35 miles of great pavement heading northwest, hooking up with CO 64 west of Meeker. It's 23 miles of mellow rollers on CO 13 from Rio Blanco to Meeker at MM 42. You will find the basics in this small, peaceful community.

The 35-mile stretch of road from Meeker to Hamilton is in good shape, but there's no shoulder. About 5 miles out of Meeker you'll start an easy 4-mile climb through the Danforth Hills to Ninemile Gap. Then you'll ride on easy, rolling terrain mixed with some flats and straights. Continue through Hamilton on CO 13 and you'll find more mellow cycling with some very gentle rollers and curves. From Hamilton, it's 13 miles along the Yampa River to Craig, where you can get basic supplies. For other routes in this area, check out Harper's Corner Scenic Drive in Dinosaur National Monument (Route 124, p. 268) and Craig to Steamboat Springs (Route 125, p. 269).

Back at Hamilton, there's a junction with CO 317. If you crave more pavement, head east here for 12 miles to Pagoda. The road is good with no traffic, but there are no services in Pagoda.

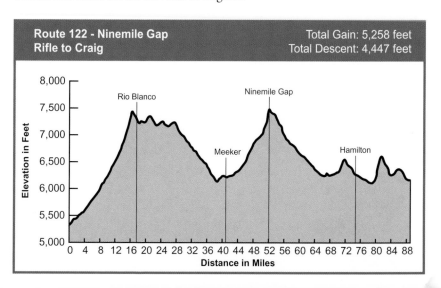

Route 122 - Ninemile Gap
Rifle to Craig
Total Gain: 5,258 feet
Total Descent: 4,447 feet

Route 123

FLAT TOP ROAD
CR 8: MEEKER TO END OF PAVEMENT

Approximately 30 Miles • Easy

This road is Meeker's finest route, and you can find basic supplies in town. You'll gently roll and wind your way to the town of Buford in a gorgeous valley at the foot of the Flat Tops Wilderness, then continue about 10 miles to where the pavement ends.

From CO 13 east of Meeker, hang a right onto Flat Top Road (CR 8). In Buford, you'll find a small grocery store and a coffee stand, of all things. I could not believe it—espresso in Buford!

As you continue to the end of the paved road, the valley will become more and more picturesque. The aspen groves here are some of the largest I've ever seen. In case you didn't know, an aspen grove can appear to contain hundreds of trees, all of which are really one organism. Yes, that's right—an aspen grove is one of the world's largest organisms!

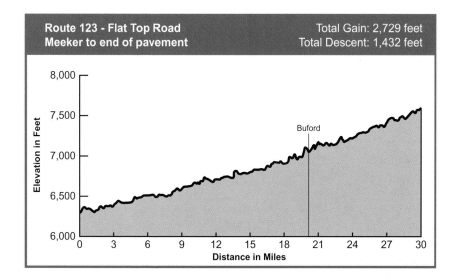

Route 123 - Flat Top Road
Meeker to end of pavement

Total Gain: 2,729 feet
Total Descent: 1,432 feet

Idyllic scenery along the road to Buford

REGION 8

NORTHWESTERN COLORADO

The northwestern region of this guide covers two very distinct environments. The eastern section boasts gorgeous alpine settings in the Park and Gore Ranges. On the west side of these ranges lies Steamboat Springs, where you'll find plenty of supplies, skiing and other activities, and accommodations. The routes around Steamboat are mostly moderate and filled with rollers and flats as well as fantastic views of the surrounding area.

The climate in the region's western section is arid, and the landscape consists of mostly treeless, rolling hills. Very few people live out here, and there's lots of empty countryside. Summers are sizzling and winters are frigid, but spring and fall are nice times to tour the area. Craig is small and has basic supplies. The Elkhead Mountains lie to the northeast and provide some beautiful views and lots of solitude. As you head west, supplies and services become minimal and scarce. The mountains and canyons of Dinosaur National Monument in the far northwest are spectacular and well worth the trip.

Notable rides in northwestern Colorado include Harper's Corner Scenic Drive (Route 124, p. 268), Elk River Road (Route 126, p. 270), Twenty Mile Road (Route 128, p. 272), Rabbit Ears Pass–Muddy Pass Combo (Route 129, p. 274), and Gore Pass (Route 133, p. 279).

Riders will love the wide-open landscapes of the Flat Tops Vista Route

Routes

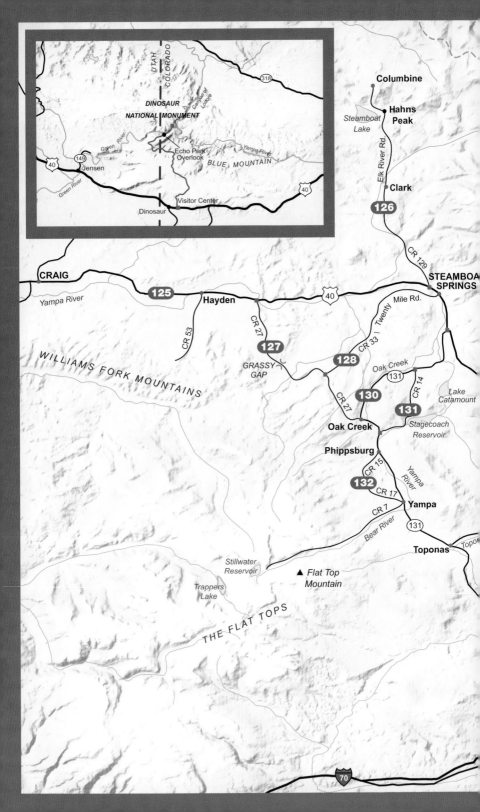

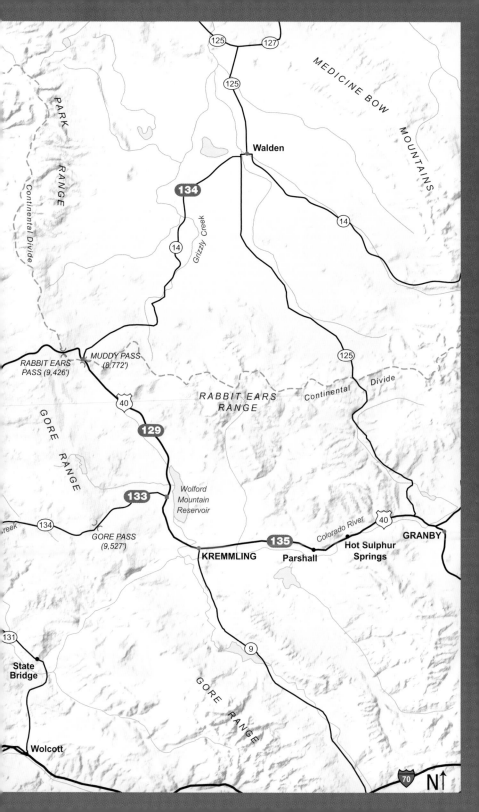

HARPER'S CORNER SCENIC DRIVE, Dinosaur National Monument
US 40 TO END OF ROAD

31 Miles • Moderate

The main road into Dinosaur National Monument from the south, Harper's Corner Scenic Drive lies about 90 miles west of Craig near the Utah state line in far northwestern Colorado. The views on this 31-mile stretch are well worth the effort to reach them, and the road is in good shape with a varying shoulder.

Two miles east of the tiny town of Dinosaur, where you can get basic supplies, is the monument's visitor center. Admission to Dinosaur National Monument is free on the Colorado side. The route starts here and heads generally north. You will climb more than 1,500 feet in the first 5 or 6 miles, then the road mellows out into rolling terrain. As you approach the monument boundary you'll cross west over into Utah, enter the monument, then wind northeast back into Colorado. Near the end of the road you'll reach the Echo Park Overlook, with a view of the canyons at the confluence of the Green and Yampa Rivers. A mile later the road ends at Harper's Corner and a nature trail.

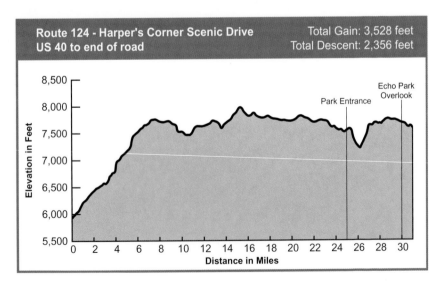

Route 124 - Harper's Corner Scenic Drive
US 40 to end of road

Total Gain: 3,528 feet
Total Descent: 2,356 feet

Route 125

YAMPA RIVER VALLEY
US 40: CRAIG TO STEAMBOAT SPRINGS

42 Miles • Easy

Fairly small with basic services, Craig feels a bit like parts of Wyoming. The landscape is barren, with few trees and lots of small, rolling hills. From Craig (MM 92), it's 17 miles to Hayden, and from there, another 25 miles to Steamboat Springs. It's a great road with a nice shoulder. The terrain is typical of the area: gradual rollers, endless views of forested mountains and big, wide valleys filled with farm fields—very nice!

At Hayden (MM 107) you'll find the basics, and not much else. (South of Hayden is CR 53, a nice piece of pavement about 10 miles long.) As you head east out of Hayden on US 40, the road is very flat. At MM 112, you'll come to the junction with CR 27 (Route 127, p. 271).

US 40 to Steamboat Springs is pretty straightforward. You will be riding through gorgeous countryside along the Yampa River as you make your way into town.

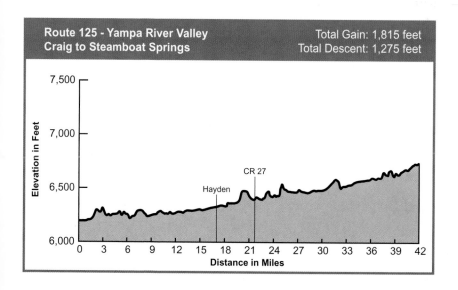

Route 125 - Yampa River Valley
Craig to Steamboat Springs

Total Gain: 1,815 feet
Total Descent: 1,275 feet

Route 126

ELK RIVER ROAD
CR 129: STEAMBOAT SPRINGS TO COLUMBINE

30.5 Miles • Moderate

Steamboat Springs is a major mountain resort that can meet all of your needs (check out Orange Peel Bicycle Service). It also offers some of the most unspoiled terrain in Colorado. There is not as much development in Steamboat as there is in the central mountains. Head out of Steamboat on US 40 going west toward Craig. Just outside of town (MM 131), you will see the sign for Hahns Peak. Head right (north) on Elk River Road (CR 129). Mile markers start at this junction.

You'll ride through farm fields and rolling, forested mountains for about 14 miles on this secluded road with no shoulder to speak of. You will find a decent shoulder as you approach Clark, however, and you can find the basics at—where else?—the Clark Store. At MM 19, you'll be climbing moderately until you top out at MM 21 and head into some large rollers.

At MM 23, you'll roll into the town of Hahns Peak, where you'll find the basics and a view of Steamboat Lake. The terrain changes a bit as you head up into the hills. You'll be in the boonies of northern Colorado—it's very peaceful out here. The road climbs moderately for about 5.5 more miles to Columbine, where you'll find a small store and the end of the pavement.

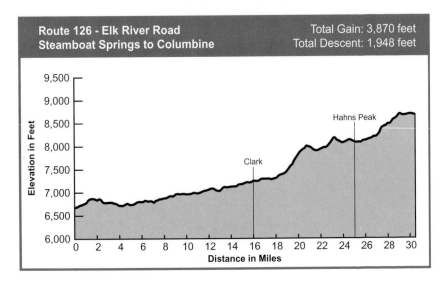

Route 126 - Elk River Road
Steamboat Springs to Columbine

Total Gain: 3,870 feet
Total Descent: 1,948 feet

Route 127

GRASSY GAP
CR 27: US 40 TO OAK CREEK

23 Miles • Moderate

A great road with no shoulder, CR 27 is a beautiful, rolling route through the hills southwest of Steamboat Springs.

CR 27 winds through the hills southwest of Steamboat Springs

Near MM 112 on US 40, you'll see a sign that reads, "Twenty Mile Road/Oak Creek 23 Miles." This is where the route begins. As you head south from US 40, the mile markers start at 23, and MM 0 will be at the route's end at Oak Creek.

The ascent to Grassy Gap is about 8 miles long. Here the long, white trunks of the aspens soar skyward in a fluorescent green plume, and in the fall, the golden color of the leaves offers a vibrancy that will resonate right through you. At MM 19, tremendous views abound as you look south across pastures to the Flat Tops Wilderness. You'll gradually gain altitude. A screamin' descent for the last 2 miles brings you to CO 131 and the town of Oak Creek, which has the basics.

For alternate routes in this area, check out Twenty Mile Road (Route 128, p. 272) and Oak Creek Valley (Route 130, p. 276).

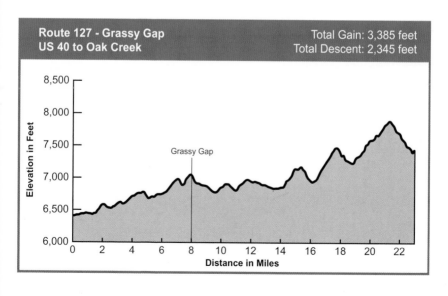

TWENTY MILE ROAD
CR 33: STEAMBOAT SPRINGS TO CR 27

Approximately 20 Miles • Moderate

Rolling through the hills southwest of Steamboat Springs, CR 33 is a fantastic stretch of road. It eventually hooks up with CR 27, where you will be able to go to the right toward US 40 and the town of Hayden, or left to Oak Creek and CO 131.

From Steamboat Springs, take 13th Street west across the Yampa River. A short, steep hill takes you immediately up above the valley, and the views of the Flat Tops Wilderness and the Steamboat area are most enjoyable. The road from MM 12 to MM 10 takes you through a nice little climb followed by a very steep descent of barely a mile.

At the bottom of this hill, the road turns to dirt. This is a very dangerous transition, so be ready to slow down if your handling skills are questionable.

Enjoying the bucolic scenery along CR 33

The dirt is good—a little washboard—and it's about 2 miles until the pavement starts again after a short, steep hill around MM 7. After another very steep, fast descent of maybe a half mile on pavement, you'll hit dirt again. This time the dirt starts in the middle of the downhill; it is extremely sketchy—watch out.

You'll ride a bit farther and then come to a "T" in the route. Go right to stay on CR 33. It's another 1.5 miles of dirt downhill to the pavement, and a few more miles on chip-seal (a mixture of gravel and tar), my least favorite road surface. (I'd rather ride a dirt road full of craters any day.) This takes you to the junction with CR 27 (Route 127, p. 271).

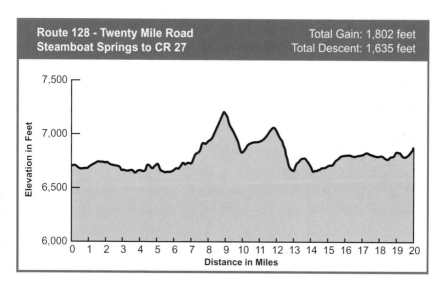

Route 128 - Twenty Mile Road
Steamboat Springs to CR 27

Total Gain: 1,802 feet
Total Descent: 1,635 feet

Route 129

RABBIT EARS PASS–MUDDY PASS COMBO
US 40: STEAMBOAT SPRINGS TO KREMMLING

52 Miles • Difficult

You can enjoy some tremendous countryside up in northern Colorado, with vast, rolling mountains and subtle alpine ridges stretching as far as the eye can see. This ride offers some excellent and varied terrain across two of northern Colorado's rare mountain passes.

The route starts in Steamboat Springs at about MM 135. Head south out of town on US 40 on straight road with a slight downhill trend. Traffic can be fast through here, but the shoulder is great. As you leave town, look ahead and a little to the left (southeast), where you'll see a rather daunting ramp of road heading up into the mountains—that's your road.

At MM 139, you'll start climbing toward Rabbit Ears Pass (9,426'). Excellent with a wide shoulder, the road offers consistent, moderate climbing and a great view down to Lake Catamount. After 10 miles of climbing at fairly substantial and consistent grades, you will reach the Rabbit Ears West Summit (9,400')—not to be confused with Rabbit Ears Pass, which is 8 more miles ahead.

After a while, you'll come to a long, straight section of road. This is the third, last, and longest of the straight sections, after which a gentle right bend curving into a more significant left bend will put you at the Continental Divide and the top of Rabbit Ears Pass. You'll find a pullout here but no services.

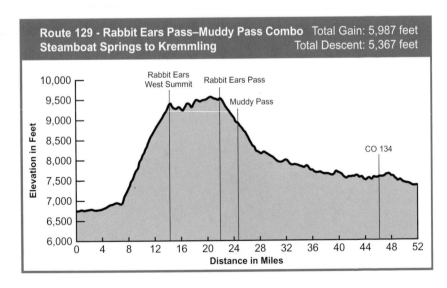

Route 129 - Rabbit Ears Pass–Muddy Pass Combo   Total Gain: 5,987 feet
Steamboat Springs to Kremmling   Total Descent: 5,367 feet

As you start down the other side, you will get 3 miles of solid descent to Muddy Pass (8,772'). Yes, a descent—Muddy Pass represents the high point of CO 14 at its junction with US 40, but it's still lower than Rabbit Ears Pass. Look up; you can't miss the Rabbit Ears.

Muddy Pass sits on the Continental Divide at MM 157. From here, US 40 heads south, bottoming out at MM 159. The terrain rolls moderately and the shoulder becomes smaller. By MM 161, it's high, rolling terrain with some flats mixed in. The countryside is beautiful. You'll come out of the trees into some arid, sage-covered hills, with the Gore Range to the right (southwest), and the Rabbit Ears Range to the left (southeast).

At MM 178 on US 40, you will reach the junction with CO 134, which accesses Gore Pass (Route 133, p. 279). From here, it's 6 more miles on US 40 to Kremmling, where you'll find basic services and espresso.

Wolford Mountain Reservoir stretches alongside US 40 in the flats north of Kremmling

Route 130

OAK CREEK VALLEY
CO 131: STEAMBOAT SPRINGS TO TOPONAS

40 Miles • Moderate

This route is a main thoroughfare with high-speed traffic and little or no shoulder. Sound fun? It's actually not bad. Every major mountain valley has this problem. CO 82 from Aspen to Glenwood Springs is far worse, and if you ride anywhere in the foothills or the Front Range, CO 131 will seem like a quiet country road—but be mindful.

Go south on US 40 from Steamboat Springs and turn right (west) onto CO 131. Ride a short, straight stretch, take a 90-degree left bend, and continue on more straights along the valley toward Oak Creek.

Not far from MM 62 is CO 131's first junction with CR 14, which is an excellent route to Stagecoach Reservoir (Route 131, opposite). Continuing on CO 131, it's nearly 12 miles of gently rolling terrain from the junction to Oak Creek, where you'll find the basics. See Grassy Gap (Route 127, p. 271) and Twenty Mile Road (Route 128, p. 272) for more Oak Creek routes in the area.

Two miles later you'll see where CR 14's southern terminus connects with CO 131. After another mile or so, you will reach Phippsburg and the junction with CR 15/CR 17 (Route 132, p. 278).

After about 6 more miles, you'll reach Yampa. A ride of 9 miles past Yampa delivers you to Toponas and the end of this route. Here you'll see the junction with CO 134 to Gore Pass (Route 133, p. 279). From Toponas, it's 20 miles to State Bridge and 34 miles to Wolcott at CO 131's junction with I-70 and US 6.

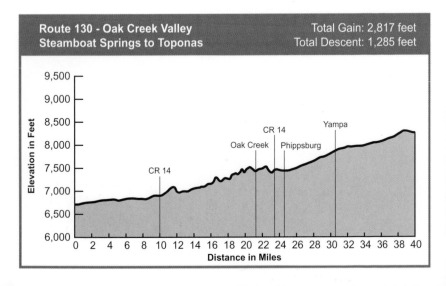

Route 130 - Oak Creek Valley
Steamboat Springs to Toponas
Total Gain: 2,817 feet
Total Descent: 1,285 feet

Route 131

STAGECOACH RESERVOIR
CR 14: CO 131 TO CO 131

11 Miles • Easy

The quiet countryside near Stagecoach Reservoir

Two miles south of the town of Oak Creek on CO 131, you will see a left (east) turn onto CR 14. This is a very enjoyable ride past Stagecoach Reservoir in a beautiful setting with excellent, rolling terrain. The route begins by heading northeast toward Steamboat Springs.

By MM 4, you are riding on moderately rolling terrain at the south end of the reservoir. Beautiful, forested mountains are plentiful as you cruise through the foothills of the northern Gore Range. After a couple of 90-degree corners, but before MM 11, you will come back out at CO 131 just south of Steamboat Springs.

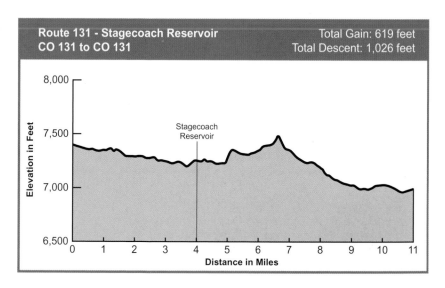

| Route 131 - Stagecoach Reservoir CO 131 to CO 131 | Total Gain: 619 feet Total Descent: 1,026 feet |

Route 132

FLAT TOPS VISTA
CR 15/CR 17: PHIPPSBURG TO YAMPA

Approximately 8 Miles • Easy

Perfect for cycling, this short route is an old road with no shoulder and little traffic. Popular with locals, the road heads into mellow terrain at the base of the Flat Tops Wilderness. It's absolutely gorgeous through here.

Starting in Phippsburg, the route heads south from town, where you'll ride through farm fields on moderate rollers with the Flat Tops commanding your view. Just before MM 3, you'll hit a short, steep downhill winding around a corner to the junction with a dirt road. There is usually a lot of gravel on this section of the road, making the corner very dangerous, so watch it. At this point, the road number changes to CR 17. Wildflowers rule in summer as you make your way into Yampa, where you can get the basics and find the junction with CO 131.

BONUS: From Yampa, take CR 7 southwest along the Bear River to Stillwater Reservoir for about 12 more miles of pavement.

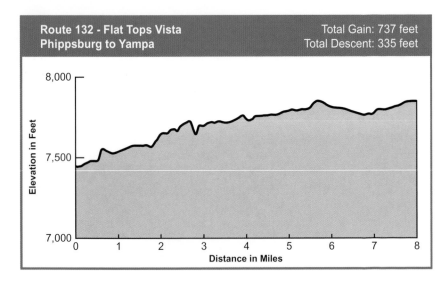

Route 133

GORE PASS
CO 134: US 40 to Toponas

26 Miles • Moderate

The forested hills of the Gore Range

This route starts at MM 26 on CO 134 at the junction with US 40, 6 miles north of Kremmling. You'll find mellow rollers and some flats on this road, which is a bit chunked up in some spots and has no shoulder. By MM 25, you'll be gradually winding your way up into the hills of the Gore Range. At MM 22, the climbing is moderate but sustained. The next sign reads, "Gore Pass Summit 6 Miles." In the next few miles, the road will undulate a bit, but it stays moderate.

The summit of Gore Pass (9,527') lies at MM 16. You'll find a campground but nothing else. On the descent at MM 12, you'll see beautiful, alpine meadows and aspen groves as you cross Rock Creek. By MM 7, after the west-side high point, you will be cruisin' a fast, very scenic descent along Toponas Creek to Toponas and the junction with CO 131 (Route 130, p. 276).

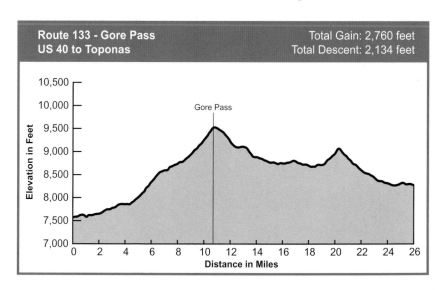

Route 133 - Gore Pass
US 40 to Toponas
Total Gain: 2,760 feet
Total Descent: 2,134 feet

Route 134

GRIZZLY CREEK VALLEY
CO 14: WALDEN TO MUDDY PASS

34 Miles • Moderate

This is a wonderful, leisurely route. Head south out of Walden on CO 125, and just outside of town you'll see the junction with CO 14; turn right (west). This route is so mellow that you can hardly call it a pass ride. The change in terrain is gradual and moderate. Eventually you'll be winding your way along Grizzly Creek to Muddy Pass (8,772') and the junction with US 40. The countryside here feels isolated, quiet, and calm.

At the junction with US 40, you can head left down toward Wolford Mountain Reservoir and the town of Kremmling (27 miles), or go right, up over Rabbit Ears Pass (Route 129, p. 274) and down into Steamboat Springs (25 miles).

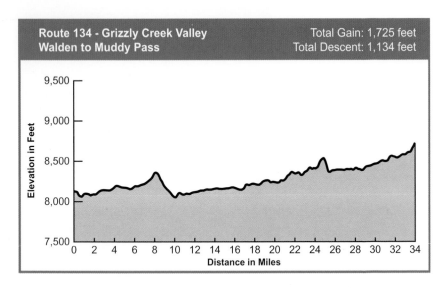

Route 134 - Grizzly Creek Valley
Walden to Muddy Pass

Total Gain: 1,725 feet
Total Descent: 1,134 feet

Route 135

WINDY GAP
US 40: GRANBY TO KREMMLING

27 Miles • Easy

In Granby you can find your basics and a bit more. There is a lot of diversity among the routes in the Granby area. Check out the map for this region (pp. 266–267), as well as the maps in the Front Range North (pp. 28–29), and Intermountain Central regions (pp. 118–119).

Named after a gap in the mountains through which the Colorado River passes a few miles west of Granby, this is a nice, moderate route on a great road. The shoulder comes and goes. You'll cruise alongside the Colorado River for a while, which you will cross just west of Granby. You may think this little trickle can't possibly be the Colorado River, but that raging torrent through

Sunrise along US 40 at Windy Gap

the Grand Canyon has to start somewhere. In this valley between Granby and Kremmling, you are not many miles from the river's origin in Rocky Mountain National Park. As it winds its way between the Rabbit Ears Range and the Williams Mountains, the Colorado is a fly fisherman's dream—and a canine's stick-fetching paradise, as my dog Ellie discovered.

The road winds and rolls moderately along. From Granby, it's 10 miles to the town of Hot Sulphur Springs, 15 miles to Parshall, and 27 miles to Kremmling. In all of these very small towns you can find the basics. And I was pleasantly surprised to find that Kremmling has espresso!

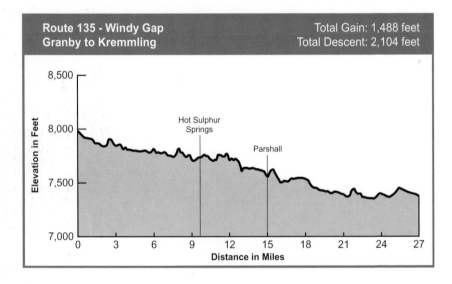

Route 128, Twenty Mile Road, typifies the quiet countryside found in northwestern Colorado

REGION 9

EASTERN PLAINS

Colorado is a land of contrasts. When most people think of the state, they immediately think of the Rocky Mountains and of skiing. But if you spend any time here, you will find a greater diversity in landscape and environment than the state's ski country suggests. Yes, you'll find vast mountain ranges, countless rivers and forests, and plenty of ski towns. However, a closer look will reveal sandstone canyons, desert climates, and small agricultural and mining towns. Add to these the large metropolitan areas like Denver and Colorado Springs that line the Front Range from Wyoming to New Mexico.

But the biggest contrast here has to be the transition from the prairie to the alpine environment. The eastern third of Colorado is the western edge of the Great Plains. As you head west from Kansas or Nebraska, the landscape changes drastically. Seemingly out of nowhere, the Rocky Mountains rise thousands of feet above the plains. To this day, it still leaves me in awe to be just east of Denver or, for that matter, anywhere east of the mountains, and see peaks as high as 14,000 feet along the western horizon. If you are touring from the east and have never seen this, your jaw will scrape the pavement as you watch this scene come into view. It must have been mind-boggling for early explorers to see this vista after a death-defying struggle across the vast prairie.

This chapter is geared mainly toward touring cyclists who are traveling across Colorado. If you are looking for short training or recreational routes east of the Front Range cities, you can find many with a good map (see below). However, in a region characterized by vast stretches of road with little or no services, I have included just general descriptions of the best major routes from east to west (except Route 139, p. 292). Alternates to these routes exist, but I would not recommend most of them. Unless you are on a long-distance tour and are self-sufficient, you might be tempting fate on those lonely stretches of highway. On the other hand, while I-70 is not lonely, I've chosen somewhat less congested and more scenic routes. Be prepared for lots of rollers on straight roads, with shoulders and pavement of varying quality.

The fact is, many areas of the prairie are more remote than the mountain regions. Temperatures can soar, and little or no water can be available. Major storm systems and even tornadoes are a real threat. In small communities with no cycling-related services, a major mechanical failure can leave you in a world of hurt. A map is critical out here, and I highly recommend the Colorado

Department of Transportation's *Colorado Bicycling Map*. This compact, water-proof map shows many options for paved roads and gives general shoulder descriptions, mileage, and traffic volume. I also recommend GTR Mapping's *Recreational Map of Colorado*, which not only presents the entire state on one fold-up, but also shows topography, major roads both paved and unpaved, and mileage between points. (See Appendix E, p. 303, for map details.)

The terrain on the Eastern Plains is fairly consistent. Having said that, I must qualify my statement. While the prairie is generally flat when compared to the mountains, looks can be deceiving. Even when the landscape seems flat, you will usually be going very gradually uphill as you head from east to west across the prairie. Roads are generally straight, but you will find occasional curves, and the rollers range from gentle and short to long and steep. In other words, a day on the plains can amount to an all-day roller-coaster ride, and the cumulative effects can be very tiring.

Some of these routes are long, and I don't necessarily intend for you to ride them in one shot. Although the routes in this region are all classified as moderate, the difficulty of these routes largely depends on your mileage. Lots of fast miles out here can make for a challenging ride. Good judgment and a fair bit of respect will keep you from bonking in the middle of nowhere. Out on the prairie, be prepared for the nearest bike shop to be 100 miles away!

ROUTES

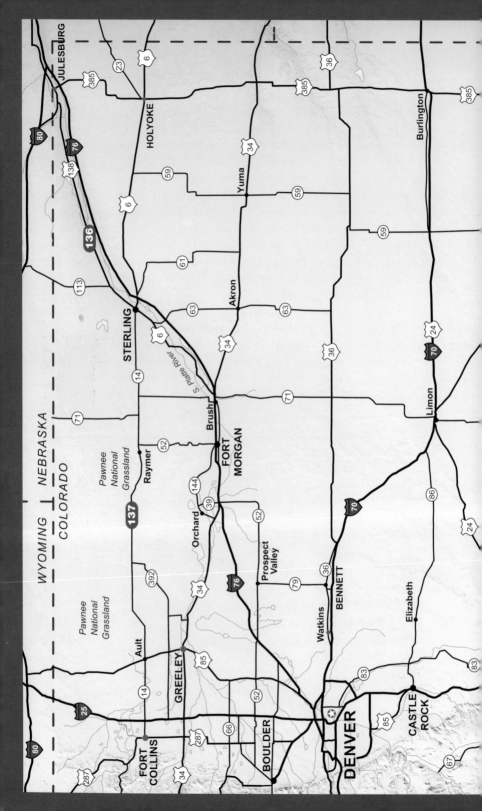

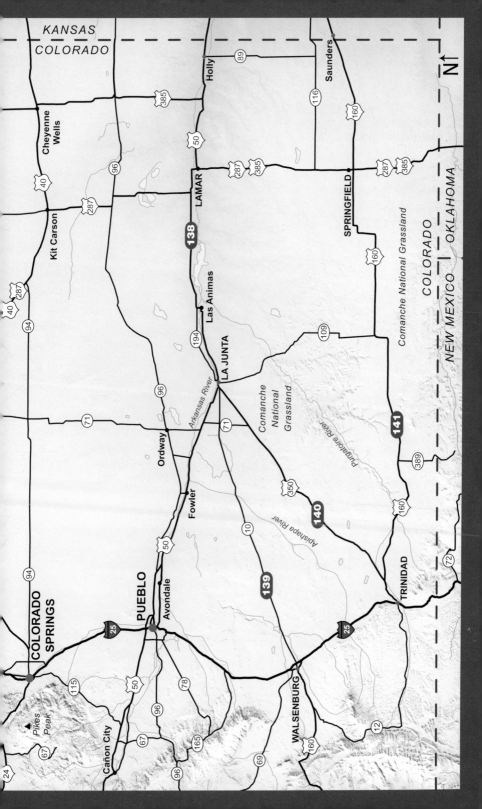

Route 136

SOUTH PLATTE RIVER BASIN
JULESBURG TO WATKINS

180 Miles • Moderate

Even though I-76 is the most direct route between Julesburg and Denver, I don't recommend it, as traffic moves very fast. An alternative out of Julesburg is US 138 to Sterling. South of Sterling, use US 6 and US 34 to Brush. From Brush, you can head west on US 34 (Platte Avenue) through Fort Morgan to its junction with I-76; here you have to get on I-76 heading west. Ride 9 miles, watching for vehicle debris, to Exit 66 and the junction with CO 39. Head south across I-76, where CO 39 becomes CO 52, continuing south then west on this highway to Prospect Valley (31 miles). From here, you can choose to continue west on CO 52 toward Denver's northern suburbs, or head south on CO 79 to Bennett, from where CO 36 will take you west to Watkins. The profile shown here gives the route via CO 79 and CO 36 to Watkins, where you can find basic services.

I-70 junctions with CO 36 just a few miles west of town at Exit 292. From here, however, you can travel on I-70 for only 3 miles before you must exit I-70 at Exit 289, which is the intersection with E-470. Bicycles are not allowed on I-70 from its junction with E-470 west into the Denver metro area. You will want to consult a good Denver bike map for recommended road routes and bike paths through the metro area. Be aware that there are minimal services out in these parts until you reach the outskirts of the congested metro area. Shoulders vary but get wider as you approach the city.

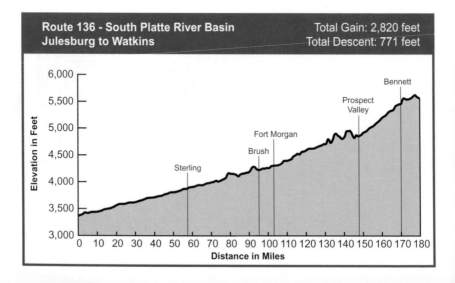

Route 137

PAWNEE GRASSLAND TRAVERSE
US 6/CO 14: HOLYOKE TO FORT COLLINS

150 Miles • Moderate

You'll find the basics in Holyoke. Take US 6 west out of town. It's 49 miles to Sterling, a bigger town where you can also take care of basic needs. From Sterling, head west on CO 14. Services from Sterling to Fort Collins will be very limited. The adventurous, however, can explore the Pawnee National Grassland on this route. Head north at Raymer and follow the signs to the remote and beautiful geological formations called the Pawnee Buttes. You will be at the southern end of the grasslands for some 65 miles of the route along CO 14.

It's about 80 miles from Sterling to Ault, where you can find the basics. You have the option here to turn left (south) onto US 85 to reach Greeley, some 12 miles away, which has everything you will need. Continue straight another 17 miles to reach Fort Collins, where all of your needs can also be met. You won't find much of a shoulder, but good roads, plenty of moderate rollers, and light traffic characterize this route.

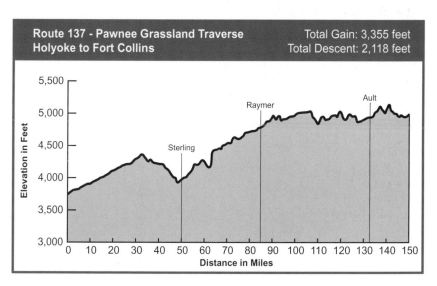

Route 137 - Pawnee Grassland Traverse
Holyoke to Fort Collins
Total Gain: 3,355 feet
Total Descent: 2,118 feet

Typical terrain on the Eastern Plains

Your biggest danger on the Eastern Plains comes in the form of thunderstorms. They can be ferocious—the clouds move east from the mountains and build into gigantic, festering, lightning-producing killers—and sometimes develop into tornadoes. This threat is not to be underestimated. If you are traveling through the plains during monsoon season from the spring to midsummer, be particularly careful. I suggest that you start your ride early and try to be in a place where shelter can be found by mid-afternoon, when the storms tend to unleash their fury. I cannot emphasize this caution enough! Be prepared, be smart, and I am sure you will have a great time.

Route 138

BENT'S OLD FORT
US 50: HOLLY TO PUEBLO

150 Miles • Moderate

A busy road all the way through Colorado, US 50 follows (from east to west) the Arkansas River, Tomichi Creek, and finally the Gunnison River to its confluence with the Colorado. Both US 50 and the Gunnison end at Grand Junction on the Western Slope. Out on the Eastern Plains you will have a bit more room than this highway usually provides in the mountains. It's about 150 miles from Holly to Pueblo, with excellent road most of the way. There are of rumble strips on this highway, but the shoulder is usually wide enough to avoid them. You'll find plenty of services along the way; Lamar and La Junta are the biggest towns along this stretch. From Holly to La Junta the road follows the Santa Fe Trail Scenic and Historic Byway, so look for plaques, statues, and museums. You can take a great side trip by heading east at La Junta on CO 194 for 8 miles to Bent's Old Fort for a taste of life on the prairie in pioneer times. You can also get there by turning right (due west) onto CO 194 about a mile before Las Animas and going about 12 miles west.

Back on US 50, expect plenty of rollers, flats, and straight road. As you approach Pueblo, look for the left turn (due west) to Avondale and Business Loop 50, just before US 50 bends northwest to cross the Arkansas River. This is a nicer route into town, with less traffic.

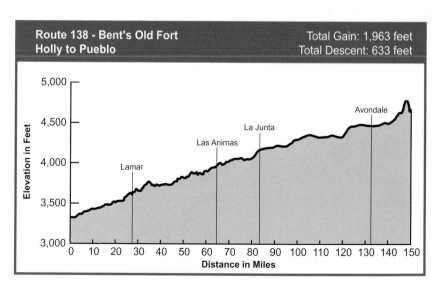

Route 138 - Bent's Old Fort
Holly to Pueblo

Total Gain: 1,963 feet
Total Descent: 633 feet

Route 139

SANTA FE TRAIL
US 350: TRINIDAD TO LA JUNTA

80 Miles • Moderate

The countryside east of Trinidad is beautiful. Rolling grasslands and scenic views of the mountains to the west await you, along with light traffic and good pavement. This route follows part of what is now the Santa Fe Trail Scenic and Historic Byway (see Route 138, p. 291). Trinidad is a quirky little town with the basics and a bit more. Situated at the eastern foot of the Culebra Range, this town is an excellent base for several routes, including US 160 to Saunders, Kansas (Route 141, p. 294), Cucharas Pass (Route 88, p. 190), and Raton Pass (Route 89, p. 192).

The signs leading you east out of town will be for US 350 and US 160, as these two highways converge for the first 7 miles. The terrain rolls slightly, and the shoulder is good, if a bit chewed up in places. As you ride along, you will notice some incredible flat-topped mountains to the right (south). That is Raton Mesa, and behind you (west) you'll get a spectacular view of 14,069-foot Culebra Peak.

At the junction where US 350 and US 160 split, you will stay left and continue northeast on US 350 toward La Junta. The shoulder will fade, and the road will be fairly straight with some mellow rollers. After about 45 miles you will be riding through the northern unit of the Comanche National Grassland, which US 350 traverses for some 22 miles. You'll find the basics in La Junta but no services along the way.

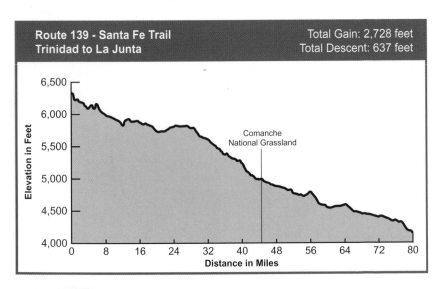

Route 140

APISHAPA CANYON
CO 10: LA JUNTA TO WALSENBURG

73 Miles • Moderate

A typical prairie town, La Junta is small, friendly, and agriculture-oriented. You'll find your basics here. I spotted a bike shop the last time I was here (a rare find on the plains), and I hope it's still around.

Head west out of town on US 50, which will lead you to CO 10 (take a left). You will weave through the outskirts of town on a good road with no shoulder to speak of. Traffic should be fairly light, but watch for the occasional farm vehicle. The road will roll along gently with some gradual hills that can add up to a bit of work. At about 26 miles in you'll cross the Apishapa River. Canyons lie to the south (left) for the next 20 miles or so. There are no services along this route. The landscape is a bit sparse, but as you get closer to Walsenburg the mountains begin to come into view. It's an absolutely spectacular backdrop, and the terrain will get more hilly as you go.

In a beautiful setting, Walsenburg offers a bit more than basic services. Other excellent routes in the area include North La Veta Pass (Route 86, p. 187), Cucharas Pass (Route 88, p. 190), and Wet Mountain Valley (Route 51, p. 114).

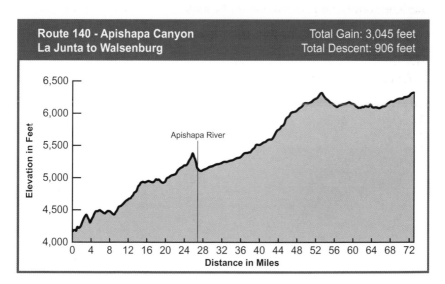

Route 140 - Apishapa Canyon
La Junta to Walsenburg
Total Gain: 3,045 feet
Total Descent: 906 feet

Route 141

COMANCHE GRASSLAND TRAVERSE
US 160: SAUNDERS, KS, TO TRINIDAD

155 Miles • Moderate

This southeastern stretch of US 160, a highway that traverses the southern reaches of the state all the way to the Four Corners, is a superb choice. There is not much traffic or much shoulder, and the road is in great shape. You'll have plenty of rollers and straight stretches of road, but there are few services of any note.

Start on the Kansas state line. After about 20 miles you will begin to cross the northern side of the southern unit of Comanche National Grassland. You will traverse these remote grasslands for the next 70 miles. The biggest town en route is Springfield, 2 miles north on US 287/US 385 from its intersection with US 160, about 35 miles from Saunders.

US 160 junctions with US 350 for the last 7 miles into Trinidad, where you will find basic services and a bit more. You will be treated to incredible views of the mountains as you approach the Front Range.

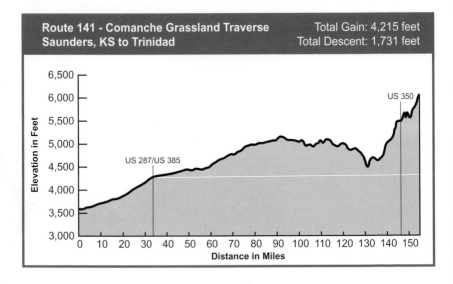

*B*eing a lover of mountains, canyons, and forests, I did not to expect to feel the way I did when I documented Colorado's Great Plains. My response to what I saw further confirmed my opinion that it's all beautiful—just different. I found tremendous scenery everywhere I went.

One of the first things I noticed was a feeling of immensity—a sense of vastness you can't get in the mountains unless you stand atop one of the higher peaks. Much of the Colorado prairie is not cornfields; it's open range in a landscape that is anything but flat. In the winter, it's as windswept and harsh a place as any. In the spring, it's a vast, rolling carpet of fluorescent green. In the summer, it can be blisteringly hot and dry.

Although I found no "wilderness," I often had a feeling of being away from all civilization—a feeling of endless possibilities. And the night sky! More stars than you can imagine. To camp down a backroad in the middle of eastern Colorado is to be more alone than in many of the mountainous areas of the west. If you are touring across the prairie, I hope you will find it an experience as worthy as cycling through the mountains.

You'll find lots of beautiful, rolling hills throughout Colorado's prairie

Appendix A

HIGHLY RECOMMENDED ROUTES

While you will certainly enjoy any of the routes in this guidebook, there are a few that stand out as extraordinary.

Appendix B

ROUTES BY DIFFICULTY

The following routes are arranged according to their difficulty. Remember, these ratings are subjective. Your personal rating of each ride depends on your fitness level and cycling experience.

EASY ROUTES

FRONT RANGE NORTH
6. Bear Lake Road, Rocky Mountain National Park
20. Fraser River Valley

FRONT RANGE SOUTH
27. US 85
28. Chatfield Reservoir
38. Guffey Road
43. South Park Highway
47. Florence Traverse

INTERMOUNTAIN CENTRAL
55. Montezuma Road
57. Dillon Reservoir
66A. Snowmass Creek Road
66B. Woody Creek Backroads

INTERMOUNTAIN SOUTH
76. Wagon Wheel Gap
77. East River Valley
83. Mount Princeton Hot Springs Loop

SOUTHERN COLORADO
85. Great Sand Dunes National Park

SOUTHWESTERN COLORADO
94A. Navajo Reservoir
94D. Buck Highway
94G. West Animas
94H. East Animas Road
104. CO 140
106. Four Corners
107. Devil's Highway
108. Naturita Canyon

WESTERN SLOPE
112. Gunnison River Valley
113. Ridgway Reservoir
118. Grand Hogback
119. Rulison–Parachute Road
120A. Sunlight Mountain
120B. Harvey Gap Reservoir
120C. Long Ridge Mine
120D. Roan Creek Valley
120E. De Beque Canyon Bypass
121. Rifle Falls
123. Flat Top Road

NORTHWESTERN COLORADO
125. Yampa River Valley
131. Stagecoach Reservoir
132. Flat Tops Vista
135. Windy Gap

Appendix B continued

MODERATE ROUTES

FRONT RANGE NORTH

1. US 287
2. Red Feather Lakes Road
3. Cameron Pass
4. Willow Creek Pass
7. Devils Gulch Road
8. Rist Canyon Road
9. Stove Prairie Road
10. Horsetooth Reservoir
11. Big Thompson Canyon

12. Pole Hill Road
13. Carter Lake
14. US 36
15. Golden Gate Canyon Road
16A. CO 119
16B. Wondervu
16C. Wind River Pass
17. Lefthand Canyon Drive/Lee Hill Drive
24. Bear Creek Road

FRONT RANGE SOUTH

26A. Parmalee Gulch Road/
      Myers Gulch Road
26B. The Evergreen Expressway
26C. Shadow Mountain Drive/
      South Brook Forest Road
26D. High Drive/Little Cub Creek Road
26E. North Turkey Creek Road
26F. South Turkey Creek Road
26G. Deer Creek Canyon Road
26H. Pleasant Park Road/
      South Deer Creek Road
29. Jarre Canyon Road
30. Perry Park Road
31. Wolfensberger Road
32. Franktown Road
33. I-25 Bypass

35. Ute Pass–Wilkerson Pass Combo
36. Gold Belt Tour Scenic
    and Historic Byway
37. Cripple Creek–Florissant Road
39. South Road/High Park Road
40. Tarryall Reservoir
41. Elevenmile Canyon Reservoir
42. Kenosha Pass
44. Currant Creek Pass
45. Arkansas River Canyon
46. Salt Canyon/Deadman Canyon
48. Frontier Pathways Scenic Byway
49. Greenhorn Highway
50. Northern Avenue
51. Wet Mountain Valley

INTERMOUNTAIN CENTRAL

52. I-70 Corridor
53. Blue River Valley
56. Swan Mountain Road
59. Fremont Pass
60. Vail Pass
61. Eagle River Valley
63. State Bridge

64. McClure Pass
67A. Brush Creek Road
67B. Owl Creek Road
67D. Maroon Creek Road
67E. Castle Creek Road
70. Turquoise Lake Road Loop

INTERMOUNTAIN SOUTH

71. Cerro Summit
72. South Rim Drive, Black Canyon
    of the Gunnison National Park
75. Slumgullion Pass–Spring Creek Pass
    Combo

79. North Pass
80. Quartz Creek
82. Poncha Pass
84. Trout Creek Pass

MODERATE ROUTES

SOUTHERN COLORADO

86. North La Veta Pass
87. Walsenburg Backroads
89. Raton Pass
90. Cumbres Pass–La Manga Pass Combo
91. Navajo River

SOUTHWESTERN COLORADO

93. Yellowjacket Pass
94B. Oxford Connection
94C. Bondad
94E. Vallecito Road
94F. Florida Road
98. Dallas Divide
100. McPhee Reservoir
101. Dominguez-Escalante
    Memorial Highway
102. Hesperus Hill
103. Wildcat Canyon Road
109. Gypsum Gap

WESTERN SLOPE

114. Douglas Pass
116. Grand Mesa Scenic Byway
117. Vega Reservoir
122. Ninemile Gap

NORTHWESTERN COLORADO

124. Harper's Corner Scenic Drive,
    Dinosaur National Monument
126. Elk River Road
127. Grassy Gap
128. Twenty Mile Road
130. Oak Creek Valley
133. Gore Pass
134. Grizzly Creek Valley

EASTERN PLAINS

136. South Platte River Basin
137. Pawnee Grassland Traverse
138. Bent's Old Fort
139. Santa Fe Trail
140. Apishapa Canyon
141. Comanche Grassland Traverse

Appendix B continued

DIFFICULT ROUTES

FRONT RANGE NORTH
16. Peak to Peak Scenic and
    Historic Byway
18. Flagstaff Mountain Road
19. Berthoud Pass
21. Guanella Pass
23. Squaw Pass
25. Lookout Mountain Road

FRONT RANGE SOUTH
34. South Deckers Road

INTERMOUNTAIN CENTRAL
54. Loveland Pass
58. Hoosier Pass
62. Tennessee Pass
65. Frying Pan Road
67c. Wood Road
68. Independence Pass
69. Arkansas Headwaters

INTERMOUNTAIN SOUTH
73. Hermit's Rest
74. The Gate
78. Cottonwood Pass
81. Monarch Pass

SOUTHERN COLORADO
88. Cucharas Pass   92. Wolf Creek Pass

SOUTHWESTERN COLORADO
96. Coal Bank Pass–Molas Pass Combo
97. Red Mountain Pass
99. Lizard Head Pass
105. Ruins Road, Mesa Verde
     National Park

WESTERN SLOPE
110. Paradox Valley
111. Unaweep Canyon
115. Rim Rock Drive, Colorado
     National Monument

NORTHWESTERN COLORADO
129. Rabbit Ears Pass–Muddy Pass Combo

VERY DIFFICULT ROUTES

FRONT RANGE NORTH
5. Trail Ridge Road, Rocky Mountain
   National Park
22. Mount Evans

SOUTHWESTERN COLORADO
95. Death Ride Loop (Routes 96–102 Combo)

Appendix C

CYCLING CLUBS AND ASSOCIATIONS

There are numerous cycling clubs in Colorado. Instead of attempting to list every local club, I encourage you to contact Bicycle Colorado for free literature on the Colorado cycling community. They will provide you with the official *Colorado Bicycling Manual,* a Colorado bicycling map, and a copy of *The Bulletin,* which includes contact information for local clubs and events. Below are some of the major cycling organizations.

BICYCLE COLORADO
Union Station
1701 Wynkoop St., Suite 236
Denver, CO 80202
(303) 417-1544
www.bicyclecolo.org

USA CYCLING
United States Cycling Federation (USCF)
National Off-Road Bicycle Association (NORBA)
One Olympic Plaza
Colorado Springs, CO 80909
(719) 866-4581
www.usacycling.org

ROCKY MOUNTAIN CYCLING CLUB
P.O. Box 201
Wheat Ridge, CO 80034
www.rmccrides.com

AMERICAN CYCLING ASSOCIATION (ACA)
(formerly Bicycle Racing Association of Colorado)
P.O. Box 7129
Denver, CO 80204
(303) 458-5538
www.americancycling.org

Appendix D

ANNUAL MULTI-DAY TOURS

The following is a listing of some of the major summer road-cycling events in Colorado. Bicycle Colorado, the Colorado state website (www.colorado.gov), and the Boulder Community Network (http://bcn.boulder.co.us/) provide links to other events and contacts. For racing info, contact the United States Cycling Federation (Appendix C, p. 301).

BICYCLE TOUR OF COLORADO
3500 S. Wadsworth Blvd. #201
Lakewood, CO 80235
(303) 985-1180
www.bicycletourcolo.com

COURAGE CLASSIC
(303) 456-9704
rideinfo@couragetours.com
www.couragetours.com

PEDAL THE PEAKS
P.O. Box 485
Cannon Falls, MN 55009
(800) 795-0898
(507) 263-2665
www.cycleamerica.com

RIDE THE ROCKIES
(303) 820-1338
rtr@denverpost.com
www.ridetherockies.com

TOUR THE PEAKS
ADVENTURES BY BICYCLE
1372 Anglers Drive
Steamboat Springs, CO 80487
(970) 879-9070
www.tourthepeaks.com

Appendix E

MAP INFORMATION

COLORADO ATLAS & GAZETTEER
DeLorme Mapping
P.O. Box 298
Yarmouth, ME 04096
(800) 561-5105
www.delorme.com

RECREATIONAL MAP OF COLORADO
(topographic)
GTR Mapping
P.O. Box 1984
Cañon City, CO 81215
(800) 268-8920
www.gtrmapping.com

LATITUDE 40°
P.O. Box 189
Nederland, CO 80466
(303) 258-7909
www.latitude40maps.com

COLORADO BICYCLING MAP
Colorado Department of Transportation
(CDOT) Bicycle/Pedestrian Program
4201 E. Arkansas Ave.
Denver, CO 80222
(303) 757-9982
www.dot.state.co.us/bikeped/

GREATER METRO DENVER BIKE TRAILS & STREET GUIDE
Swagman Publishing
P.O. Box 519
Castle Rock, CO 80104
(800) 660-5107
www.4wdbooks.com

Appendix F

GLOSSARY

bomb craters: large potholes

bonk: physical and or emotional breakdown experienced when a cyclist loses the will or ability to pedal his or her bike any longer

downhill rollers: rollers with a general downhill trend

hairpin: see *switchback*

mashin'; mash: pedaling in a very high gear; e.g., mashin' a big gear

out-and-back: a cycling route in which the rider must return the same way he or she came

pass-bagging: completing a bike ride over a mountain pass

rippin': fast and fun; e.g., a rippin' descent

rollers; rolls; rolling: hilly terrain varying in length and grade; most are short or moderate in distance, but some can be very steep at times

SAG support: a support vehicle that accompanies the cyclist, usually on longer trips; stands for "support and gear" or "support and grub"

spin; spin development: the pedaling motion; a spin with an even pressure throughout the revolution of the pedal stroke is efficient and provides a consistent transfer of physical effort into the bicycle's drive train

touring: self-sufficient bike travel; refers to multi-day cycling trips without vehicle support

switchback: a sharp corner, usually found on steep, mountainous terrain

uphill rollers: rollers with a general uphill trend

INDEX

Note: citations followed by the letter "m" denote maps.

About the Author

MICHAEL SEEBERG

Since 1980, Michael Seeberg has enjoyed biking throughout Colorado. His rides have ranged from one-day training trips to weeklong, car-supported journeys, and he has participated in numerous competitive biking events. Along with road biking, Michael avidly enjoys rock climbing, mountaineering, and distance running.